34

D0142947

Ethical Issues in
the Psychotherapies

Ethical Issues in the Psychotherapies

Martin Lakin

New York   Oxford
OXFORD UNIVERSITY PRESS
1988

Oxford University Press

Oxford   New York   Toronto
Delhi   Bombay   Calcutta   Madras   Karachi
Petaling Jaya   Singapore   Hong Kong   Tokyo
Nairobi   Dar es Salaam   Cape Town
Melbourne   Auckland

and associated companies in
Beirut   Berlin   Ibadan   Nicosia

Library of Congress Cataloging-in-Publication Data

Lakin, Martin.
Ethical issues in the psychotherapies.

Includes bibliographies and index.
1. Psychotherapy ethics. I. Title. [DNLM: 1. Ethics,
Professional. 2. Professional-Patient Relations.
3. Psychotherapy. WM 420 L192e]
RC455.2.E8L35   1987   174'.2   87-7663
ISBN 0-19-504446-0

2 4 6 8 9 7 5 3 1

Printed in the United States of America
on acid-free paper

For N'eema and Ernie,
Michael and Harriet,
Susannah and Amanda

Preface

Millions of people in this country are currently being treated by psychotherapists and the range of their problems is vast and diffuse, including intolerable anxiety, phobias, obsessions, depression, sexual maladjustment, marital disharmony, interpersonal difficulties, vocational maladjustment, and existential complaints of boredom, emptiness, a sense of meaninglessness, and other symptoms of psychological distress. Patients and clients frequently complain of an inability to love or to feel loved. In work settings frustration and unhappiness often lead to excessively competitive relationships with coworkers, counterproductive antagonisms between supervisory and subordinate personnel, and ultimately underproductivity.

There is currently widespread evidence of public mistrust of all health providers and psychotherapists and allied professionals have not escaped consumers' increasingly critical attitudes. Even without the evidence of such distrust and wariness, a psychotherapeutic relationship is by its very nature an especially sensitive one, always vulnerable to possible exploitation and abuse. It is understandable that patients and clients should be concerned about the ethics of the psychotherapist—they have every right to demand better quality control. I have written this book in the belief that therapists can improve the quality of their services by trying to arouse interest in and concern for the ethical issues and dilemmas that confront them in their day-by-day, session-by-session work. For this reason I have included descriptive case materials as well as numerous comments from practitioners about the kinds of ethical issues they encounter.

The ideas this book is concerned with developed during the course of a year-long sabbatical project sponsored by the National Science Foundation and the National Foundation for the Humanities. As a fellow in their joint program for the study of Ethics and Values in Science and Technology, I had the opportunity to examine ethical issues that emerged in group forms of psychotherapy. At that time I was completing a book entitled *The Helping Group*, in which I examined various types of group therapies. As I studied the values that seemed implicit in the guiding conceptions of psychopathology and mental health used by group therapists and leaders, I began to consider in broader and more comparative terms ethical issues involved in therapists' interventions. I concluded that ethical issues in all mainstream therapies could be considered both in terms of their conceptions—their ideologies—of causes and cures of mental dysfunction and in terms of their techniques or procedures. Ideologies and techniques, it seemed, pose parallel ethical issues in all the systems and treatments in which therapies are provided. Thus, each therapy's conception of psychological deviance and its remedies is inextricably interwoven with values, which in turn relate to the system's standards of appropriateness and moral conduct. Because each therapy's ideology is closely associated with influence techniques aimed at changing attitudes, beliefs, and behaviors, its conceptions and procedures are ethically significant.

This book is intended to serve as a personal reference, a text to stimulate the consideration of ethical issues that confront psychiatrists, clinical psychologists, psychiatric social workers, counselors, and consultants. It is my hope that it may be used in preprofessional training programs and as a sourcebook for continuing education for mental health professionals.

Each of the professions charged with responsibility for training therapists has developed guidelines for professional practice and codes of ethics in an attempt to govern the practices of their graduates. Unfortunately, they are—probably unavoidably—general and leave much room for individual judgment and decision. But any code concerning standards and ethics can be meaningful and effective only to the degree that one can relate to it on the basis of personal experience and personal reflection. I urge readers to consider their own experiences and examine their own ethical stances to better understand and apply the proscriptions as well as the prescriptions of their own profession's code. Above all, I hope that understanding of the points raised here may translate into more ethically responsible as well as caring treatment.

As I began to integrate the materials for this book, I gained a new and deeper appreciation for the complexity of the psychotherapist's work and the difficulties in articulating all the considerations behind the strategies of trying to provide effective and ethical psychological help. To responsibly render such help, one inevitably becomes deeply involved in the inner lives of patients and clients, but at the same time one must respect the inviolability of those lives. A therapist tries to maintain an image of the welfare of the individual, group, family, or organization as a goal, but that image is often unclear, and any definition of what is good for them is rarely unequivocal. Above all, one must try to understand the nature and the sources of their needs and frustrations, as well as one's own.

I believe that my interest in fostering greater awareness of ethical issues in the psychotherapies is shared by the majority of practitioners. Mental health workers are by and large honest and dedicated people who endeavor to conduct their therapeutic activities for the good of their clients and to behave toward them in ethically responsible ways. As a practitioner and a teacher of practitioners, I have tried to develop the materials in this book not as an exposé but rather in ways that may be useful to therapists-in-training and to those already in the field.

I am grateful for the support of the joint program for the study of Ethics and Values in Science and Technology, sponsored by the National Science Foundation and the National Endowment for the Humanities. During that fellowship year I had the help of Martin Golding of Duke University's philosophy department. He brought philosophic sources to my attention and discussed some of my ideas with me.

I greatly benefited from stimulating conversations about various ethical issues with my wife and colleague, Musia Lakin, who drew on her own clinical experience to add to my understanding. Other colleagues in my own department—Irving Alexander, Lloyd Borstelmann, Robert Carson, Harold Schiffman, and Lisa Wallach—were gracious and helpful not only in their willingness to consult with me about how to pursue topics of ethics in useful ways but also in discussing case materials. Morton Lieberman, at the University of California, San Francisco, helped by arranging interviews with practitioners on the West Coast, and Jacob Lomranz of Tel-Aviv University enthusiastically shared his thoughts with me. I would also like to thank David Werman of Duke University's psychiatry department for his encouragement and cogent comments.

Fortunate is the teacher who can learn from his own students! A number of graduate students in my department were consistently and enthusiastically responsive to the issues I discussed, both in seminars and personal conversations. Several took the time from their busy schedules to comment on and critique initial formulations and early drafts. In particular, I would like to mention with deep appreciation the help of the late Melissa (Molly) Hunter, Leslie Lebowitz, David Lisak, and Peter Fraenkel.

The secretarial support staff, directed by Patrice LeClerc, was courteous in coping with several drafts and I appreciate the efforts of Verbal Roberts, Edna Bissette, Hazel Carpenter, Carletta Hinton, and Marge Williams. The editorial aid of Carol Thompson was invaluable in rendering my often turgid style into readable prose. I am also thankful to Shelly Reinhardt and Rosemary Wellner of Oxford University Press for their editorial assistance.

My deepest appreciation and thanks are extended to the many anonymous psychotherapists of various orientations and specialties who were willing to confide in me and provide case illustrations from their own experiences. All names are pseudonymous. These examples are not merely reflections of abstract principles in professional codes of ethics. I was deeply impressed by the internal struggles about how to act ethically as reflected in my interviewees' comments, just as I was moved by their efforts to overcome their own misgivings about being as forthright and candid as possible with me. Since anonymity was a condition of their participation, I want to express my thanks to them collectively. Without their courageous participation, this book could not have been written.

Durham, N.C.   M.L.
July 1987

Contents

Ethical Issues in
the Psychotherapies

Introduction

Helping relationships are fraught with ethical challenges. This book focuses on those that emerge in the psychological treatments offered by different therapies: individual, marital and family, group, and organizational. Each involves exerting influence for the benefit of participants, but each, by its nature, also entails potentially exploitative procedures. To illustrate the ethical problems that have developed, I interviewed about 100 practitioners who specialize in one or another treatment. These interviews, lasting on average more than one hour, were as delicate as any therapy session because the questions and answers were unavoidably personal. They elicited considerable discomfort when respondents struggled with what is and is not ethical practice, particularly when they revealed aspects of behavior that were ethically equivocal or when they touched on how therapists had been victimized by ethically problematic interventions.

How representative is this sample of practitioners? It is not, in any sense, statistically balanced. It is largely local (Southeast U.S.) although a number of practitioners from the West Coast and the Northeast are included. It comprises both beginning practitioners and some with thirty or more years of experience in the various disciplines that provide mental health services. It includes male and female therapists. And in subsequent discussions with other practitioners not included in the interview sample I heard echoes of the same concerns described by the interviewees.

Format of the Interview

I designed the following questions with the aid of several colleagues and graduate students who were interested in ethical issues in the therapies. The questions explore four broad topics: general areas of ethical concern; colleagues' practices; recollections of personal equivocal conduct or experiences of unethical practices; and ideas and recommendations for preventative measures.

1. What is your criterion for whether a certain intervention or intervention style or technique is ethical or unethical?

2. You may have heard of unethical or ethically ambiguous behavior of therapists. Describe the behavior and tell why you consider it ethically problematic.
3. What kinds of ethical dilemmas arise for you in the type of therapy you practice and are most familiar with?
4. What kinds of ethical dilemmas arise in the therapies you yourself do not practice, but have knowledge of? Do you think that certain therapies are more likely than others to give rise to ethical problems?
5. Can you describe circumstances under which you would modify your own ethical standards of practice, or have done so?
6. What are your views about physical contact or touching in psychotherapy?
7. What are your views about the extent and kinds of confrontation of patients?
8. Reviewing your practice history, describe any intervention or action on your part that raised ethical questions in your mind.
9. As a patient or client, were you ever dealt with in a manner that was ethically ambiguous or unethical? Describe the circumstances.
10. Was a relative or friend in psychotherapy ever dealt with in a manner you (or he/she) regarded as unethical or ethically ambiguous? Describe the circumstances.
11. As a trainee, were you ever treated in a way you believe to have been unethical or ethically ambiguous? Describe the circumstances.
12. What sort of preventive or educational measures would you suggest to improve the ethics of psychotherapy practice?

How frank were the practitioners I interviewed? I tried to conduct the interviews as nonthreateningly as possible, assuring the interviewees anonymity and confidentiality with respect to identifying data. I encouraged them to elaborate as much or as little as they wished or to reject any questions they preferred not to answer. It would be naive not to expect some defensiveness in a person who is asked to reveal ethical concerns to another professional. We must also take into account the ubiquitous human need to look good. Nevertheless, I am confident that these practitioners tried to be as honest and forthcoming as they could be. Indeed, they agreed to be interviewed because they are concerned, as I am, about reports of increasingly frequent unethical actions by psychotherapists.

As I analyzed the responses to my questions, certain themes occurred with striking regularity. Although virtually all the therapists described egregiously unethical behavior and flagrant violations of professional codes of conduct by a few other practitioners, most concerns involved "garden variety" ethical problems encountered in daily practice. These common dilemmas challenge even the most well-intentioned psychotherapist and may exist in subtle ways. The order in which I discuss these "popular" themes does not indicate their importance to therapist or client or their frequency of mention because these factors depended in part on the kind of therapy being discussed. For instance, questions involving whose agent the therapist is are often more complex issues for family or group therapists than for individual therapists. Money matters are more salient for private practitioners than for those who work in public agencies. Confidentiality is typically more problematic in group therapies than in individual treatment.

The following themes emerged in the course of the interviews and will be the subject of Chapter 1:

1. Appropriateness of the therapy and competence of the therapist.
2. Therapist as personal advocate: whose agent is the therapist?

3. The limits of confidentiality: the interests and rights of spouses, parents, and other "third parties."
4. Persuasion and confrontation vs. coercion and bullying.
5. Countertransference: the intrusion of the therapist's personal interests and conflicts and sexual involvements with clients.
6. Financial arrangements with clients and insurors.
7. The imposition of the therapist's social or moral values on the client.
8. Therapists' recollection of their own ethical misconduct.
9. Personal experiences of victimization by ethically equivocal interventions.
10. Recommendations for the prevention of unethical conduct in psychotherapies.

These themes identify some of the most frequently encountered issues and dilemmas practitioners face in daily practice. They include actions that directly affect the welfare of patients and clients and may be more significant for therapy outcome than therapists' theoretical predilictions. In the following chapters we will see how they emerge in each of the currently popular types of treatment, and how ethical therapists may try to resolve them.

1

Ethical Dilemmas in Everyday Practice

Conscientious therapists must ask themselves whether they are appropriate helpers and whether the treatments they offer have a reasonable change of alleviating the problems for which help is sought. Although people who seek psychological help experience similar tensions and anxieties, differences in their specific problems would seem to invite a variety of interventions. Thus, individual treatments aim to explore a person's feeling states and personal history and to examine the strategies available to achieve greater satisfaction in living. An individual may be referred to a group therapy to develop or enhance interpersonal skills. By comparison, the problems of individuals in a marital or similar relationship may be deemed to lie in their mutually aversive interactions, which must be altered to achieve greater harmony.

If the psychological problems of a family are "systemic," interactional rather than due to a specific member, then treatment explores the interactions among family members rather than exclusively focusing on the designated "sick" individual. Interventions in organizations to influence individuals or entire units are usually launched because internal communication has deteriorated, interpersonal relationships have become marked by excessive competitiveness, the cooperation essential to sustained productivity has declined. Although basic ethical concerns such as informed consent, confidentiality, coercion, and the autonomy of participants are issues in any therapy, they may be more complex in multiperson therapies, especially when a participant has not voluntarily sought the therapist's or consultant's help.

Which, if any, therapy is appropriate for a given individual, group, family, or organizational unit? What kinds of problems lie within the competence of the helper? How does a therapist evaluate his or her capacity to help a client? What constitutes good treatment for the problem the therapist is confronted with?

John Apter,* a practicing psychoanalyst, acknowledges that what is good treatment in the eyes of one set of practitioners may not be viewed as such by those with different orientations. Consider his description of a case involving the possibility of self-destructive acts by a patient.

*Throughout, all therapist and client names are pseudonyms.

I think that our different views of the mind could create a real ethical question. For example, an analyst tends to treat a suicidal patient more neutrally than another type of therapist would. [*What do you mean?*] I don't think the analyst would be as likely to push for hospitalization or to give medications, or to set a "contract." It's perhaps putting the patient's life in danger for the moment, but you hope it will resolve the deeper problem in the long run. I think that it is a sound principle, but only if the patient is not biologically depressed.

Apter recognizes that in the case of a suicidal patient, his treatment approach, versus that of other therapists, can lead to serious, perhaps fatal, differences in outcome. However, in the end, therapists make judgments about their own competence to treat specific problems independently of their theories of therapy. Here is an example of a therapist, Dr. Agamla, who thoughtfully examines her own fitness to treat someone:

My first problem is whether to see the individual after the initial session or not. It's not easy to refer them on, but I am troubled by the question: Is this person someone I can hope to help? Am I a good match for the person? I think every therapist must consider whether the demands of a particular case are within his competence. I am conscious of my own limitations, and I really think everyone who chooses therapy is entitled to the best he or she can get. There's lots of ambiguity there. I think the therapist needs to be able to consult with others even about doubtful acceptance cases. After all, the client really is not in a position to decide all on his own. Your attitude of encouraging him to feel that he has come to the right place is determining for most people. So I think competence issues and ethical issues overlap for me.

Clearly, clients would not remain in treatment with therapists who protested their inability to help rather than appear, as most do, calmly competent. "Successful" therapists must learn to mask a lack of confidence and maintain a good aura of quiet expertise until they gain sufficient experience of success to own it. But therapists who are honest with themselves are often beset by doubts about their own wisdom and strategies for handling particular cases. They may question their abilities to help because of the severity or types of problems the client confronts them with or because of some difficulty in their own lives. Philip Hershel expresses his concerns about his role as psychotherapist in terms of values, competency, and his ability to fulfill his therapeutic responsibilities to the client.

I feel that I am being invited into the person's life because of the promissory note of being able to do something for him. You see, I think that this ethical business is in direct proportion to how much you get inside the patient's life. To feel that you can move this person you've got to use some power—and you can hurt or humiliate people more easily than you can help them. You are always in danger of interfering with the person's values. I really believe, too, that many of us therapists are not all that pure in our motives. We are not Mother Theresas! Sometimes I feel more like an accomplice rather than a healer for the patient.

By contrast, John Herblock's concerns are focused on the effects of his own psychological state on the clients he treats.

I think that one of the big ethical issues to me is what I communicate to the patient about my own state of being. If something in my life affects me strongly, there's no way that the patient is not going to sense it, because I don't think that you maintain yourself as a blank screen. I think that is a false position in the interdependent situation that is psychotherapy. Where is the responsibility? I think the therapist must be watchfully aware of his or her own inner state and how it bears on the moment. But can I say to the person, "Look, I can't work with you because of those things?" What is my responsibility and what are my own limitations? That is my dilemma.

Issues of competence, judgment, and appropriate therapeutic procedures may become involved with one another, as the following statement by Clarence Roberts attests.

> I really misjudged this situation and it turned into a case of unethical behavior. This woman had a big transference thing toward me and I couldn't move her to anything good for her. So I referred her to this female student of mine and I supervised the case. So guess what! It turned out this student was homosexual, and she got the woman to go to bed with her, with disastrous results for the client. I had all the while been getting cock and bull stories about work in therapy that had never occurred. The woman wouldn't complain to the ethics board though I tried to get her to do it.

Although such egregiously unethical behavior does not usually result from inappropriate methods of treatment or poor judgment, the consequences of incompetence can be ethically significant.

Competence is based in part on education in the sources and amelioration of disorders. Typically, much of this training does not explicitly address techniques of treatment. (This is particularly true of multiperson treatments and consultation.) As a result, few graduates of professional training institutes are fully prepared to engage in individual psychotherapy, much less marital and family, group, or organizational interventions. Usually only in the course of practice are these skills sharpened and honed. Moreover, continuing education in the fast-changing field of psychological interventions challenges new and experienced practitioners alike. A major share of postgraduate training takes place in fellowships or workshops. Although brief workshops have become especially popular, such short courses afford little discussion of common ethical dilemmas such as evaluating one's competence and the appropriateness of one's therapy for a given patient.

Part of the problem in assessing the appropriateness of a therapy is that a diversity of views has always characterized the psychotherapies. Furthermore, the ethical dilemmas associated with each approach have not been clarified. One concern that most practitioners acknowledge is that of "quality control"—both in the selection of those to be trained and in the practice of psychotherapy. Some of the interviewees attribute it to poor preparation for the role, that is, inadequate backgrounds in theories of psychopathology and personality, or the inculcation of fuzzy conceptions of the techniques and purposes of treatment. Some put blame at the doors of poor supervision and lack of experience, while others say that the personal problems of therapists interfere with effective treatment. These individuals explain the problem in terms of the therapists' "faulty repressions" or personal needs for treatment or, alternatively, in old-fashioned terminology, as "bad characters" or "bad eggs." Whichever terms these practitioners used, they agreed that there were too many such therapists who felt free to intervene in ways that were destructive to their patients.

Whose Agent Is the Therapist?

The clearest picture of agency would seem to be a therapy in which a single therapist treats a mentally competent adult. However, even then the question of agency arises, because it is a rare case where others—spouse, children, colleagues, and friends—are unaffected by what happens to the client. The therapist is, of course, mainly responsive to the needs of the client or group of clients seeking help, but effects on others involved, such as a divorce or a job change, can be profoundly negative.

The problem of agency is most dramatically manifested in family treatments or in counseling couples. As many family therapists point out, a decision to see one of two spouses, or both together, may initiate a course of events leading either to divorce or to reconciliation. Too, dealing with a family is rarely a neutral experience. Therapists find themselves siding with one or the other spouse or with one of the children; moreover, they may become enmeshed in the family's conflicts. Even the most fair-minded and objective therapists must weigh decisions about whether and how impartial to appear on a moment-to-moment basis. The psychiatrist Larry Gerson acknowledges, for example, that therapy with married couples is especially taxing and ethically complex because of the participants' conflicting goals.

> For me, the most common problem has to do with seeing a patient who is going through a separation. And one of them wants to separate, the other doesn't. What's best for your patient may not be good for the couple. This woman is getting physically abused, but this was her fourth husband who was doing this to her. So I began to push her about this crazy pattern. I asked, "Why are you staying with this guy?" But then the husband began to call me on the phone. It turns out he was very dependent on her despite the physical abuse. So I had the two of them in together. And we began to do some joint work which has the two of them back together. Now I could have referred him to someone else, but I thought, no, that other therapist wouldn't have all the pieces of the puzzle.

Dr. Gerson believes that he should anticipate the conflicts in a marriage that are likely to ensue when a married individual seeks his help. He outlines his attitude as follows.

> I'll forecast it to the patient if I think that things are likely to go in a direction that will affect the marriage. Maybe they don't want to go that way. This woman had pretty much let her husband dominate her, and she wanted to be more assertive. I told her that it might be very good for her to do that, but if she went into therapy without her husband, she'd probably end up getting a divorce. After we talked about it for a while, she decided that her marriage was more important than the change and she got out of therapy.

Another therapist, Carol Jessup, who specializes in sex therapy and in couple counseling, describes one result of a "successful" treatment program.

> According to this guy's story, she was cold and asexual. They had been married for twenty-some years. Now I warned them that there was only a low probability for a good outcome because of their long-standing pattern of mutual avoidance, but I would do it if they wanted. Well, the situation became just awful. She became much more sensuous, but he couldn't stand it. He not only became bored with sex; he would say awful things to her about her body. Now they really fight all the time and I don't know that they can stay together.

Do therapists have an obligation to be concerned about the effects of treatment on intimates of the treated person? Is the therapist supposed to maintain neutrality in the conflicts among the clients? As we see, the problem is especially visible when dealing with couples or families. In the following instance, Carol Singer worries about a natural tendency of the participants to side with one or another.

I invariably do like one member of a family better than another. I've found that I have to be especially careful that I don't undercut the woman by being sort of flirtatious with the man. I usually do feel more of a kinship with the guy. Maybe it's their sense of humor or something like that. You know, to try to be balanced and available to both of them—or in families, to all of them—it's a hell of a job!

Issues of agency and confidentiality become intermixed in multiperson therapies. Irving Ratner, an experienced practitioner, has had to face the ethical dilemmas involved in dealing with couples many times. A typical problem is exemplified in the following case.

Even when I am seeing one patient, there are others involved, and I often wonder what my responsibilities are to those people. Of course, I try to keep it limited to the patient. But when I see couples it's really unclear. It often happens that one of them is having an affair. It's just as clear as can be, but the other one doesn't realize it. So what do I do? I figure it's a "no-no" to disclose the facts. Sometimes I am asked, "Well, is she? . . . Is he?" So I say something like, "I don't feel licensed to discuss these things with you." I guess I see my role as a sort of interpreter to each about the other, to try to make each one sort of more sympathetic to the other.

The therapist who deals primarily with children often faces the problem of how to balance needs for confidentiality and trust in the relationship with the child in treatment against the legitimate concerns of the parents. Helen Eland describes how she approaches this situation.

The big issue is how much to open up with the parents when it is a child or adolescent. I mean when you have to be clinically effective and not transgress on the relationship which you are trying to build with the patient. If I know that the child has had an abortion and doesn't want me to share the information with the parent, I would try to bring the situation—I mean the child—to the point where the information could be shared. To simply tell the parents would be to ruin the therapeutic trust. So I always have a dilemma about keeping everybody's needs in mind.

What kinds of conflicts of agency arise regarding the conduct of group therapies? In the interest of effective and responsible care, group therapists would wish to be equally accessible to all participants and to facilitate positive outcomes for each. However, therapists who conduct groups may experience likes and dislikes, countertransferential attitudes toward specific individuals that may "leak out," just as in other forms of therapy. There is also another reason for the emergence of "favorites" in group treatments—group therapists are naturally inclined to enlist the aid of other members in addressing a particular individual's problem. Although group therapy certainly is not a classroom situation, its members may be favored or disfavored in ways reminiscent of early school experiences, with similar consequences.

Social comparison is inescapably as much a part of group therapy experience as of earlier groups, and so comparative self-esteem is a perennial issue. Using members to amplify one's message inevitably affects the self-esteem of those targeted by that message. Who may become the voice of the group and who will be its target become clear only as a group develops, but the constant question for members is: "How do they (he/she) choose to talk about me? How do I stand in comparison to them?" The ethical challenge for the therapist is to be aware of the likelihood of such tendencies and avoid cultivating favorites.

Ethical problems also arise in connection with the widespread practice of treating individual patients in groups led by the therapist. No doubt, most therapists who use this method do so in the belief that they are providing an important therapeutic supplement to individual treatment; familiarity and convenience are also advantages, as are financial considerations. However, one must decide what consequences may ensue from being treated by one's therapist privately and then in a group together with other patients of the same therapist. Are not jealousies and sibling rivalries unnecessarily stimulated? Since proprietary feelings are intrinsic to any therapy (e.g., *my* therapist, *my* session, *our* group), doesn't the question of whose agent become confusing or even burdensome when the group's leader is also the individual therapist for its members?

The problem of agency is especially ambiguous in organization consulting and in the interventions launched to resolve interpersonal problems in the organization. It is generally recognized that the workplace can become an arena of abrasive and demoralizing interactions. Resultant symptoms may be excessive competitiveness, debilitating anxiety, inner conflicts, apathy, and diminished self-esteem.

Walton and Warwick (1973) pointed out a number of ethical issues raised by psychological interventions in organizations; chief among them was that the personal interests of targets of the intervention may not be identical with those of the employers who pay for the consultant's services. As a consequence, such interventions are often profoundly distrusted by workers who feel that the consultant is management's agent, not theirs. An example of this problem is shown in the attitude of the organization consultant, Aaron Todd.

> Who is my client? The director will hire me and say, "I'd like you to do some team building with such and such a group," but then he'll add, "Incidentally, that manager of the division has some shortcomings, so look it over." So what's the message? I think that he doesn't like this guy, but he wants me to check him out through this team-building business. I have a really tough decision. Who needs my help and what am I going to do about it? I don't want to do the director's dirty work.

Who pays the piper calls the tune is an old maxim that would seem to apply in such cases. This consultant is faced with a difficult situation, yet his stance is probably not a common one in the corporate world. Awareness of ethical issues may be increasing among managers just as it is among therapists. Is it possible that greater latitude can be allowed organization consultants in determining the needs of their client systems? An optimistic view is reflected in the statement by Albert Grobart.

> I feel I can open the door for any employee to set his agenda or his problem on somebody's agenda, I mean somebody who can really do something about it for him. I act as a facilitator around here. I can get guarantees against the possibility of reprisals so that anybody can go and complain about anything or anybody he needs or wants to.

Managers may dictate the kinds and the limits of permissible interventions, regardless of the consultant's diagnosis of the problems, as in the following experience of Timothy Jeffries.

> I was consulting in the outfit and they asked me to work with this unit that had had the trauma of their section head drinking himself to death. This group was really upset because they had all been very involved with him. Nobody felt good and they were all beating themselves up about it. After I had worked with them five days, they felt they needed to continue, and so did I. But the CEO wouldn't permit it, and he was paying the bill.

Confidentiality

The secrecy in which therapy is conducted is one of the most sensitive issues in any psychotherapy. Clients are of course concerned that their disclosures should not become public, nor revealed to their detriment or shame. Confidentiality is at risk, however, especially in group therapies.

Another important aspect involves the protective environment almost all psychotherapies foster. A half century of public education and promotion of the idea that mental illness is like any other and that personal growth and emotional development could be positive outgrowths of therapy has not really altered the popular conception that being in therapy is a sign of fundamental weakness or moral infirmity. It's as if there were still something to be ashamed of. Consider the problem facing the counseling psychologist Roger Rycroft.

> Lots of the information, if it gets out, could be damaging to the student's future. Sometimes they ask you to send out documentation about them, apparently not mindful of what they're asking for in terms of its possible consequences for them. I just don't know what to do when that occurs. One kid is now a high official and I guess he needed the documentation, so he asked for it, and I had no choice. Maybe I could have alerted him by asking, "You want to specify what you want released and what you want kept back?"

The debate within the mental health professions about the range and the limitations of confidentiality has become increasingly complicated. Should assurances of confidentiality cover minor children with respect to their parents or guardians? What about instances where self-destructive acts are reported or when the individual seems likely to harm others? Some state rulings (e.g., Tarasoff, 1976) have made therapists quite uneasy about their own liability if a patient commits a crime. Martin Thomas, the therapist who provided the following material, works in a student mental health center. He describes his concerns about the confidentiality of records, the release of information and "judgment calls" about what is in the patient's best interest.

> I guess for me this issue of confidentiality and the release of information is about the most troubling question and one that arises frequently. Now it is fairly easy if you get a consent form, but what about parents who have legitimate concerns with how their son or daughter is doing? I mean you have to maintain some kind of alliance with parents when you treat the kid. You have hospitalization or other problems and you'll surely want their cooperation [*How do you resolve it?*] Well, with difficulty! [*Laugh.*] I respond to parents to try to reassure them, but avoiding giving them details of what the kid has said.

Children and adolescents in psychotherapy pose delicate problems in maintaining or breaching confidentiality. Those who work with children and their families have reason to be concerned about conflicts of interests and whose agent they try to be but also about what to tell parents or guardians. The following child-family therapist (David Bently) discusses historical sources of the ethical dilemmas involved and the viewpoint he now adopts.

> For over thirty years I have been working mostly with children and their families. I've got to say that the question of strict confidentiality that many others consider to be a big ethical issue, I don't. I think it's a misconstrual of an original psychoanalytic premise with adults, that the material of the therapeutic hour is private property for the client, and

under no circumstances should it be shared with others. Sure, I think it's important with children and adolescents that what they say and deal with is their private, personal thing, but it will be shared with others—family and parents—when that seems clearly needed. What I say to them is something like, "Whatever we talk about here is mostly just between the two of us. Now if anything comes up that seems to me as though it ought to be talked about with your folks, then I will raise it with you and we will decide together how to do that."

When working in a public agency one faces a different set of problems regarding confidentiality. The psychiatrist Ted Engle explains why such problems are more complex in his work for a mental health center than in his own private practice.

Over there, you are put in a situation of representing the agency. I can't really promise confidentiality because the administrators may change the policy about what goes in records. But if I get a call about one of my private patients where they want to review my notes about his treatment, I say, "I'll give you a summary." The other day I got such a request about a guy I had treated for homosexuality who's got a top-notch job as a government scientist. Apparently, he wanted to do "top secret" stuff. So I get the call from Captain So-and-So who wants to come down and see the records. Well, I was evasive and I told the captain that I would agree only to reading him my summary based on old notes; that is, if I ever could decipher them. But I was polite and of course I was telling half-truths through my teeth.

Confidentiality is difficult, if not impossible to maintain in group therapy. As suggested by Lillian Townsend, the problem is exacerbated when patients are seen by the same therapist in both group and individual therapy.

Sometimes people tell me things in individual therapy they don't want discussed in the group. My way of handling it is to go along with the contract. But my colleague who works with me says to the patient, "Look, nothing you tell me individually is sacrosanct; anything goes in the group." For me it is a struggle, you might say a dilemma, because I see beneficial aspects of both positions. If they tell me something and then work it through to a point where they can eventually bring it to the group, that is useful. But what if they tell me something, say they are having sex with another member (which is against our group guidelines by the way), and that would be cause for kicking them both out of the group? It would also necessitate an intervention to help the other person involved. Now I have the issue of needing to help the other person involved as well as this person. So I have that kind of difficulty.

Persuasion and Confrontation Versus
Coerciveness and Bullying

Although promoting faster rather than slower-paced movement or change may reflect an activist posture in the therapist, it raises the question of whose needs are being served. My respondents believe that the distinction is rarely an easy one in difficult treatment situations. Active and aggressive interviewing may be based on egotistical wishes to prove one's effectiveness. One colleague calls it bullying when a therapist tries repeatedly to get a patient to acknowledge a behavior or impulse or ambivalent feelings that he or she is reluctant to disclose or discuss. Even though the injunction "Do for the patient's welfare and interest, not for or in your own" is mandatory in all professional codes of conduct, it is difficult to follow consistently, especially when patients appear to be particularly defensive, recalcitrant, or dissembling. In such cases, frustration with the client's behavior and attitude can provoke aggressive, even assaultive interventions.

The problem of excessive pressure is to some extent more hidden—and thus more difficult to deal with or to eliminate—in group therapies. In situations where therapists employ other members to serve as mouthpieces for their message to particular individuals, the emotional processes natural to groups, families, and organizations (such as social comparison and the infectious expression of feelings) serve to amplify and intensify those messages. The ethical problem is that such group processes are likely to obscure the instrumental role of the therapist in generating or promoting verbal assaults. Of course the ethical issue becomes even more serious if the targeted person is unable to withstand or integrate the confrontational remarks of the others. Often, the other participants—family members, the spouse, other group members, or even fellow employees—may seize on the confrontation as an opportunity to settle old scores. When "feedback" occurs in this fashion, the motives of those who give it may well be sadistic rather than helpful. In any event, the therapist has set up the individual and bears the responsibility for what ensues.

Widely differing conceptions of how active one should be are characteristic of practitioners, even among those who espouse similar understandings of psychopathology. Sometimes an ethical problem will arise from the therapist's personality and temperament rather than ideology. The psychotherapy context—whatever its type—is an asymmetrical power and influence situation and, if facilitation of change is (at least transiently) abandoned in favor of pushing for change, it is difficult to establish that such pushing is for the patient's benefit. The following examples of take charge behaviors are from therapists who believed, rightly or wrongly, that they were acting in the best interests of their patients. One practitioner, Robert Casper, a self-proclaimed activist, describes his approach.

> Because my style is to be very active there is always the risk, or the question, what *degree* of risk do I take. I take the position, what kinds of corners could be cut, what risk to an individual if I move him along as rapidly as I would like? This involves a fair degree of confrontation. I used to worry a lot more about driving people crazy. Over the course of time I developed the notion that people were not all that fragile. But in the back of my mind, I still have that worry that maybe I will injure somebody with what I say. I'll give an example. This young man declares himself to be gay. He announces this in the opening session and I ask him why. He's had maybe a total of two sexual experiences in his whole life. I challenged him, "So that's what makes you gay, why I've had more of that kind of sexual experience than you and I don't consider myself to be gay. If anything I think you are asexual." Later on I said to him, "Well, when you come right down to it, I suspect your real problem is that you're afraid of pussy." Well, I think strong medicine is called for, even in the first session. Now there's a risk with "strong medicine." But at least I am wide open about it, not like some of these more insidious long-term therapists.

Here is another therapist's (Eric Murray's) interpretation of his own activist, if less flamboyant, intervention style.

> Theoretically, I am very opposed to taking over, but somehow, especially if I have been seeing a person for a substantial period, I either do it in a way the person feels good about, or else they just don't object to it. Recently this woman was about to reinvolve herself in a pretty destructive relationship with a married guy who was just using her. I guess she felt quite desperately lonely and was about to do it again. I just said, "Are you nuts?" I said, "You've got to be kidding! From everything you told me about him and

you in the past, he just wants to bed down with you whenever he wants. You want his wife calling you on the phone and screaming at you like she did before?'' I felt that I had to intervene strongly and give my opinion of what I considered to be crazy and self-destructive.

Although training texts in the field all stress acceptance and respect for clients and emphasize that one should take care not to injure a client's self-esteem, aggressively confrontational practices are common. Do they result from genuine strategic considerations and a careful weighing of possible adverse consequences? Or are they impulsive expressions of frustration and irritation on the part of therapists? The following case suggests that frustration and irritation are too often channeled into the denigration of clients. It is a personal experience that Alice Howell recalls from her residency training.

> I had become involved in a therapeutic group composed of other psychiatric residents. I recall that the group leader used the technique of fishbowl observation and commentary. [*This procedure typically involves splitting the group temporarily into observers and observed interactants.*] The leader elicited comment from the observers about each of the participants in the fishbowl. I was uneasy about the critical tone of the remarks made by the leader about those being observed. Finally, the leader exploded, calling one of the group members "just a hopeless case anyway!" So I immediately withdrew from the group and sought an appointment with the director of residency training to complain about the ethics of the group leader, but nothing changed. So I quit.

Such abrasive intervention might be defended as necessary and useful "shock therapy" to force the targeted individual to realize something or engender movement away from a stuck position in the therapy, but if a therapist's affect is a determinant of such an intervention, it is likely to be unethical.   *influence*

Countertransference: The Intrusions of Therapists' Interests

Psychotherapists are enjoined by their professional codes of conduct not to exploit the therapy situation for their own gratifications, apart from the satisfactions of helping clients progress toward mutually acknowledged goals. Simply stated, the task of therapy is to improve client welfare and well-being. It is humanly impossible to like every patient to the same degree, or to have the same response to the problems and personality styles of different patients. A patient may arouse feelings of affection, empathy, or sympathy, but also of revulsion or fear. Similarly, a patient's narrative may stimulate not only a helpful, but also an angry or punitive response.

Most therapists have experienced the frustration of unmoving or unchanging patients whose failure to benefit from therapy is in itself a mark of personal failure for the therapist. Therapists must thus deal with their own anger and irritation, and not allow it to provoke unwarranted confrontation or competitive interventions. The urge to show off and demonstrate one's superior knowledge and wisdom must be contained. Ted Nadler acknowledges that his own competitiveness in the therapy situation may play a destructive role, and that he strives to temper it in the interest of his client's welfare.

> This guy and his wife came for couple therapy. He's a competitive successful male. This fellow is really locked into left-brain stuff, so I talked right-brain for a while. Each time I tell a story he has a better story. So I had to have an even better story. Fortunately, his wife was there and she helped me to come to my senses. So I let him end with the better

story. I was on the verge of really trying to humiliate him—you know the way a father humiliates his son on the basketball court. It is supposed to be for the good of the patient, but I know different. I make ethical errors when I buy my own stories and then promote them from a position of power, because I really have a position of power. I try to catch myself and say to the client, "You know what? I got carried away!"

Nicholas Wiggins, an analyst, considers the therapy situation susceptible to abuses the therapist must be wary of.

I think there are a number of things that could occur that I call infringements on the patient. There are financial infringements, when you're exploiting the patient for your own purposes and income, or just hold on to the patient longer for financial reasons. Then there are what I call narcissistic infringements. I mean by that you could be angry with the patients and consciously or unconsciously express it in ways that he/she cannot handle. Countertransference is more than being erotically aroused or angry. It is stuff that really is your own and it is not enhancing the therapeutic process.

How does a therapist cope with feelings of frustration and irritation when working with a client who is very resistant or may be threatening to the therapist? The following comments of Dr. Wiggins are revealing.

There have been times when I've really been pissed with patients and have taken a sarcastic attitude toward them. I should have maintained enough distance from what they were making me feel so that I could handle it. Afterward I usually recognized that they were right when they said I'd been sarcastic. Maybe it was because they got to me or because of some pain or some upheaval in my own life. In any case, that's something I've got to watch.

Philosophical concern with the elements of a therapeutic relationship is evidenced in the following comments by a counseling psychologist Gregory Frankel.

I've always been conscious of the vulnerable position of the patient or client, and the susceptibility of that person to influence, positively or negatively. I guess what concerns me most is the possible exploitation of that vulnerability, and the abuse of the influence position that the therapist has. It could, I guess, range from something fairly blatant, like sexual exploitation, you know, like sexual acting out, to things that are more subtle, like the therapist getting his rocks off by the kinds of questions he puts to the patient. [*You mean what?*] Like exploring an area not because it is so relevant to what the patient is experiencing as a problem, but because of his curiosity, because it is exciting or something like that. It is sort of manipulating the patient's emotions in a way.

Virtually all the therapists cited sexual involvement as a clear ethical breach of the therapy relationship. Although such involvements can occur in any therapy, most legal actions have resulted from sexual involvements of therapists with client/patients in dyadic or group psychotherapies. We will consider specific circumstances in later chapters, but the possibility of such involvement and of negative consequences for the therapy, not to mention its life effects on the client, is an ever-present concern of those I interviewed. This concern persists despite a general awareness among professional therapists that it is only a minority of therapists who act out sexually with their patients (Holyroyd & Brodsky, 1977; Gartrell et al., 1986).

What is there about the therapy situation that elicits sexual responses from therapists? The surroundings—the privacy and coziness of most therapy settings, the contents of therapy—often intimate details about one's sexual feelings and frustrations, and the transference potential of an emotional dependence on the therapist's responsiveness—combine to exert a powerful erotic influence on the therapy relationship. Rare is the therapist—perhaps even insensitive and ineffective—who has never felt sexually stimulated by any client. It may occur in response to the client's attractiveness or because of the client's narrative with its implicit emotional appeal for a tender and caring, even loving responsiveness in return.

Younger therapists interviewed felt more vulnerable and susceptible to their clients' sexual attractions and worried about how they could avoid getting sexually involved. Several mentioned that they had sought consultation or tried to make referrals to other therapists when the prospect loomed. The difficulty is partly that one would not wish to discourage the client's exploring his or her sexual feelings with the aid of the therapist. Professional therapists are, of course, aware of ethics codes injunctions about sexual acting out in psychotherapies. Nevertheless, the problem persists and seems to be increasing (Holyroyd & Brodsky, 1977; Gartrell et al., 1986). The following comment by James Knoerr suggests why it is difficult for therapists and requires sustained attention and monitoring.

> I have a couple of young women in therapy who are really beautiful. When I am with either one of them my mind wanders. I keep thinking how pretty she is, not really listening to what she is saying. Now, one flirts with me but the other doesn't. The one who flirts reassures herself that she is worthwhile by flirting. I respond to it by acknowledging my attraction openly, but saying this is a good chance for her to learn to have a deep nonsexual relationship with a man. I think that is really where the therapy payoff is for that woman. For the other one I just have to pull myself back to seeing her as a person in need of help, not as someone for me to admire.

Walter Irving acknowledges the sexual temptations of practice and tells how he deals with them.

> When I had this very attractive female patient I would hear myself point out stuff that had sexual elements in it. It would come out of me so quickly I didn't realize it until after I had said it. But I can't see violating sexual ethics. So I switched topics as soon as I realized what I was up to.

Maurice Martel notes the concerns that are common even among ethically impeccable practitioners.

> When I hear a patient tell me of her sexually tinged or sexual encounter with a previous therapist I have to watch out for my knee-jerk condemnation. I say to myself: "There but for the grace of God go you." Part of all of us is probably some rigid puritanical defense against this. It is a mark of our struggle with it. I am aware of my potential to do the same thing.

Finally, Jack Josephs describes those circumstances in which sexual involvements are most likely, namely, when one's own love or marriage relationship has become problematic.

> I had been a therapist on this inpatient psychiatric unit. I was attracted to this patient—she was not my own therapy case—and she and I became good friends. We were both about the same age. Later that year my marriage broke up and I called her and asked her out. In hindsight I see that was an unethical thing to do. I didn't consider it to be at the time.

All therapies have the potential of becoming vehicles for self-gratification of therapists beyond the legitimate one of promoting patient welfare. The ethical danger is that the feelings of power over another person generate temptations to get certain kinds of responses. Consider a seemingly innocuous wish, the desire for the client's esteem. The problem emerges when the need to be liked is so strong that the therapist is driven by it rather than by considerations of what really is in the patient's best interests. We will see several illustrations of ways in which this need obstructs therapy or causes it to miscarry— particularly in the failure to set appropriate limits on time, fees, and in the crucial area of availability outside regular structured hours. The needs of therapists for positive emotional regard from their clients are reflected in the following comment from Jim Laurence, a psychiatric social worker.

> The first thing I think of is whose needs are being met—mine or my patient's. It is something I have to watch out for. All of us get into this work because we have something to work out. My own needs to be liked can get in my way of understanding what is going on with the patient. I might not be able to see when the person is angry with me. I may sort of unconsciously let the patient know that I don't want any anger directed my way.

Naturally, narcissistic needs are not limited just to the wish for positive responses. Some therapists get caught up in the need to demonstrate how potent and effective they are by making demands on their clients. Even such issues as the frequency of sessions may be influenced by the therapist's rather than the patient's needs, as seen in Henry Carry's account of his experiences as a psychiatric resident.

> When I was a resident I tried to get my patients to come twice a week regardless of how often they wanted to come or how much they could pay. You see, it wasn't for the money. I wasn't getting it anyhow. It was because I had the time and wanted to have good cases; good cases meant coming *two* times each week. It certainly wasn't clear that they wanted to or needed it. I just insisted on it. You know you can influence this because of your own needs, financial or intellectual or whatever. The fact that I want so much to be seen as a good doctor by my patients gets to be a problem for me and for my patient.

The following two illustrations involve ''benign'' interest of therapists when they become too involved in the lives and professional activities of their patients. They show how a therapist can easily lose the thread of what is really important to the individual being treated. Philip Dodd tells about both instances.

> This therapist became fascinated with the fact that his patient was a jazz musician. He came to watch the patient perform, enjoyed discussing jazz with him, and seemed to be as much involved with the patient's performing life as with helping the patient understand himself. Finally the patient called the therapist's attention to this overinvolvement. The therapist recognized it and therapy was terminated. But the patient continued to wonder how much of the therapeutic interpretations had been motivated by the therapist's fascination with his career rather than by what the patient felt to be his life problems.

The second case is similar.

> The patient was a world-class sports figure whose playing days seem to have been terminated by a variety of physical and psychological factors, but he fantasized about a return to the big time. The therapist was an enthusiastic sports fan and got involved with

discussing the past glories of the patient. He joined in the fantasies about the patient's returning to a role in the sports world. The patient became aware that therapist's involvement was personal and felt vaguely exploited. However, since he also appreci- ated the therapist's interest in him, he was loathe to complain. Finally, he commented to a psychologist friend that it was doing him no good for the therapist to be so involved in his career.

Money Matters: Fees, Third-Party Payment, and Financial Arrangements

The issue of money was raised repeatedly in my interviews. Obviously those in private practice would be expected to be more concerned with such issues as collections, third-party payments, and holding on to clients beyond the point where therapy is effective. But I also sensed a difference in emphasis based on the professional backgrounds of my respondents. For instance, social workers—whether in private practice or institutional assignments—were invariably more sensitive to the hardships worked on individuals and their families from the expense of psychotherapy. Such concern may, of course, change as increasing numbers of social workers find themselves in private work. This is illustrated by the response of Cynthia Logan.

> The issue of money is quite complicated. There are many cases where the people need the help and they obviously can't afford it. At least they can't afford the kinds of help they need. I think about my own financial situation and ask myself, "Should I really see this person for almost nothing?" I used to think when I first started out in this business that my real commitment should be to help people whether they could afford it or not. It sure complicates things for me about what to charge when I know for sure the person just doesn't have the money to spare. Of course I get mad if I give more than I feel I should, and that surely is no good for the treatment situation. But I really feel it's not just my own "neurotic problem." For me, at least, it is a real ethical dilemma.

Psychotherapists defend their fees because of a legitimate desire to be paid, but also because in the tradition of Freud's declaration a free therapy is devalued by the patient as being worthless. Over the years therapists have increased their fees (currently anywhere from $40 to $125 or more per therapeutic hour—typically 45 to 50 minutes), and these fees are steadily rising along with other health costs. Yet this increase has not prevented help-seekers from turning to professional therapists—as well as others—to alleviate all kinds of psychological distresses. Several decades ago, a disparaging critic referred to psychotherapy as the purchase of friendship. In fact, many novice therapists do have ambivalent feelings about being paid, either because they doubt their own professional capacities and believe their patients are actually educating them for the role and practice of being therapists, or because they share the notion that one should not be paid for the kindness extended in trying to help another human being. In any case, rapidly enough— too rapidly, critics of psychotherapy would say—the therapist who depends on his or her practice for a living must begin to feel that the therapy service provided justifies the professional fee. I cannot argue with those who claim fees are too high and that privately practiced psychotherapy is now well out of reach of any but middle- and upper-class persons. (It is, of course, also a matter of social concern that public mental health clinics and agencies are badly understaffed.)

The ethical issues of money begin with the problem of poorer patients who cannot afford payment, or who, having begun therapies, find themselves unable to continue to pay for the services they require. Although many psychotherapies—and clinics—offer sliding scale payments or even deferred payments, many do not. Is it ethical to remove aid when patients can least afford it emotionally, namely, when they lose their jobs? Should therapists allow patients to develop significant indebtedness to them? How flexible should therapists be about deferred or unpaid bills? How much consideration is the therapist ethically bound to provide in terms of reducing or deferring fees? Should therapists lend money to their patients—even when motivated by systematic concern for the patient's economic difficulties? Bernice Swanson describes the problem that often arises in connection with fees.

> My friend was in therapy with this woman who charged more than others did, and then kept upping the fees despite the fact that my friend became unemployed during this time. She was having tremendous difficulty financially, and she tried to discuss it with the therapist. But her therapist said it was all just "resistance" or some such nonsense.

In several instances, practitioners stated that they had allowed their patients to develop large debts that then obstructed therapy because the patients felt considerable guilt at "exploiting" their therapist. Two cases came to my attention where therapists had actually loaned their patients substantial sums of money which were never repaid. In both cases the therapists ruefully reported that more damage than good came of this intended beneficence in terms of the therapy itself. The patients simply terminated abruptly rather than deal with their guilt about not repaying the loans. One of the therapists, Susan Rothberg, describes the circumstances.

> I felt bad about the woman's not being able to pay, so I let her build up a huge bill over two years time. I even lent her money. She was ashamed and rather than face me she quit, paying neither the fee nor the debt. I guess it wasn't unethical, just plain dumb!

Money is an especially sensitive issue with private practitioners, depending as they do on patient fees for their incomes. The following response comes from the psychiatrist Bob Shanley.

> I charge for missed sessions. Now the question arises, do you charge for missed sessions on the bill, knowing that it will go to the insurance company? Or do you say to the patient, "Look this is your responsibility; you handle it." Sometimes I simply charge, without indicating that there were missed sessions, and that involves me with a feeling of having gypped the insurance company. Now I have sort of resolved the issue by deciding in my mind whether it was an action the patient could have really helped or not. If not, I put it on the reimbursement bill. But if the patient could have prevented it, then I submit the bill to the patient. But I am not happy about the whole thing.

Daryl Robinson is a private practitioner with over thirty years of experience, and he has a large and diverse psychiatric practice. Among a number of ethical problems that confront him daily, he describes the following concern which appears to combine questions of agency and confidentiality with financial considerations.

> Well, my colleagues and I face the issue of disclosures to third-party payers. What do you say to authorities who are paying part of the bill and tell us "You owe it to us to tell us what is going on with the patient." I often say "mixed emotional features with an adjustment reaction" or some such. But sometimes the carrier wants more specific information. So I may write, "tension state and anxiety." But with CHAMPUS and school teachers you've got to write a specific problem because they've got this peer

review set up. You could get caught, but luckily for me, I know some of the people who do the peer review.

Many therapists are concerned about the ethical implications of deceiving third-party (health insurance) payers, even though they seem to believe that it is apparently common practice. Howard Clark complains:

> This is an ethical problem created for us by insurance companies. They won't pay for marital therapy. So what happens? What do therapists do? They are forcing people to lie; you either lie or else you refuse to go along with it. I refuse to lie about it because I feel I have a responsibility to the insurance companies too. It means I don't get some people I would get otherwise. Hell, what kind of example of honesty do you set when you collude with the patients to make those kind of deals? It's for sure not modeling good behavior! That's a dilemma that anybody in private practice has to deal with.

A related problem arises with diagnosis. The therapist must designate a reimbursable mental state or condition or else the patient or therapist will not be paid for treatment expenses. Many therapists are troubled by such requirements but most rationalize their "shading" of diagnosis as being in the interest of the patient, and blame the insurance companies for forcing the deception. Besides the fraudulence of this practice, no matter how defensible, there is also the conveyance of a curiously amoral attitude to the patient. Is not therapy crucially concerned with uncovering the multiple self-deceptions and dissemblings patients practice on themselves and others? Therefore, doesn't this undermine the basic authenticity of the therapy relationship itself?

Holding on to patients for economic reasons is another source of ethical concern. It may occur most frequently in the practices of therapists just beginning to establish themselves, but sometimes patients also do not want to let go. The problem is rarely simple, as George Morel recounts in the following example.

> I think there is a temptation to keep going with patients longer than one should. Actually, in the case that comes to my mind, I'm not sure who is holding on to whom. I've been seeing this fellow for better than seven years. But I've been feeling maybe he could function very well without this. I think he uses therapy as a kind of insurance. (Incidentally, he also has pretty good coverage that allows him to continue with me.) I have actually raised the issue of termination a number of times, but each time he counters with pretty convincing evidence of how he makes use of therapy. It is a murky issue. I myself could make the case that therapy is potentially life-long, so when is the stopping point?

As we have seen, cases exist where the therapists' own narcissism prevents them from accepting that the individuals are not really progressing in their care and should be referred to other therapists or agencies. Therapists must be aware of their motives if they find themselves with such patients or with those who persist in therapy for long periods. When a client is kept in therapy for financial or narcissistic reasons, it is no less ethically problematic than other forms of patient exploitation.

The Imposition of Values: Therapists as Moral Arbiters and Agents of Social Change

The few studies that have explored the question of the role of psychotherapists' values in their practices have found that therapists consciously or unwittingly communicate their own values to their clients (Murray, 1956; Parloff, Goldstein, & Iflund, 1960; Parloff,

Iflund, & Goldstein, 1957; Truax, 1966; Wolfe, 1977). London (1986) points out that an extreme form of such value communication occurs when a therapist threatens sanctions against a client, such as warning that therapy may be terminated if the client does not comply with the therapist's advice. The therapist Hans Hobart recalls when he was confronted by his own therapist's heavy-handed proscription of his behavior; it is clearly a case of value imposition.

> I went to see this therapist because I had had anxiety attacks. I had the feeling, even back then, that I was really bisexual and I told him so in an early session. He waited until I was really hooked and quite dependent on him. Then he tells me that if I ever had sex with a man, he would refuse to see me for six months! There was no exploration of my problem, no explanation, nothing! He was in this power position because at the time I really needed his help. Even back in those days it was an unethical thing to do.

Such values, whether related to one's activities or one's relationships, can be decisive in the lives of the clients. If a therapist approves of the individual's behavior, it is reinforced; if the therapist disapproves, it may be changed. Therapists' probes, comments, and interpretations are frequently concerned with value questions involving attitudes about relationships, social obligations, work, and the whole range of human activity. If a client experiences guilt, for instance, the therapist must inquire into the infractions or impulses that cause the guilt. Inevitably the question of standards of conduct—the therapist's as well as the client's—become focal issues in their interactions. Value-neutral therapy has been critiqued by Bergin (1985) who says that contemporary therapists have not been sufficiently cognizant of the role of traditional values in fostering and maintaining mental health. He emphasizes values inherent in traditional family life, such as monogamy and fidelity. Vitz (1985) similarly stresses traditional values, particularly religious affiliation and feelings, and charges therapists with ignoring their importance. But, as we will see, many therapists argue the contrary, believing that most therapists are too traditional because they impose the sexist and role-restrictive standards of conduct they have absorbed on the individuals and families they treat.

In this section, we confront the fact that therapists are often in the position of acting as moral guides for their patients, and that ethical dilemmas will result from such a stance. The first ethical responsibility of therapists, regardless of what values they espouse, is to be fully aware of what they communicate to their clients. Equally important is to be respectful toward the clients' values and not to impose their own on them.

The accusation of value imposition has assumed increased significance with the emergence of the women's movement. Female patients have legitimate grounds for objecting to the patronizing manner in which their problems are viewed in some therapies and for the ways in which they have been treated by some male therapists. The therapies themselves may be informed by stereotypical notions of sex roles that are obstacles to equal treatment; charges of sexism leveled at certain forms of therapy have not been without foundation.

Psychotherapists are sometimes criticized for psychoengineering, that is, manipulating clients not for their own welfare but for what is thought to be good role adjustment. Family therapists are usually singled out in particular for such manipulation. A case of how a depressed woman was dealt with that appears in texts of abnormal psychology is described by Liberman and Raskin (1971).

> Whenever mother did the expected household jobs of cooking, cleaning, and so forth, without complaint, the children and the father were instructed to applaud and comment

proudly. But when she acted depressed, she was to be ignored. [After inducing changes] as an experiment, they were instructed to go back to noting and responding to her depressed state, with the consequence that she rapidly returned to being depressed. Then the therapeutic reversal was once more—this time permanently—engineered.

Focusing as they do on many aspects of marital and family relationships, family therapists have increasingly come to reflect the divisions along value lines about gender roles and relationships between the sexes. Although many espouse the values of society as a whole, there are those who would use their positions as therapists to push for changes in line with a different ideal. Thus, Hare-Mustin (1978) advocated a more feminist approach to family therapy, claiming that such therapy provides unique and unparalleled opportunities for facilitating desired changes in male-female relations. Margolin (1982) similarly suggests utilizing family therapies to change the "oppressive consequences" of stereotyped roles and expectations in the family (pp. 798–99) and both these authors warn male therapists against imposing sexist values on their clients.

Not all family therapists agree with this position, and Wendorf and Wendorf (1985) challenge it. Although they accept Margolin's right to object to the imposition of sexist (wrong) values, they question the ethicality of trying to influence clients to accept their own nonsexist (right) values. Even though Hare-Mustin and Margolin recognize harmful effects of value imposition, they don't seem to question pushing their own. Wendorf and Wendorf (1985) wonder, "Are we beginning to see ourselves as the moral judges of our society with answers for every question? Are we too sure of ourselves and becoming rigid, dogmatic, or arrogant?"

Behavioral and dynamic family therapists disagree about the ways therapies should be carried out; both systems are characterized by "school" values as well as the values of the particular therapist. As behaviorists O'Leary and Turkewitz (1978) acknowledge, "While we strive not to have our values unduly influence our clients, it seems clear that we do influence them by the questions we ask . . . and by the therapeutic targets we help establish . . . [This can lead to a] bias left unsaid which may result in a more subtle or insidious influence process which can be counterproductive." Gurman, Knudson, and Kniskern (1978) suggest that the prescriptive "pleases" and "displeases" to be reinforced per instruction by behavior therapists are equated by patients with "goodness" and "badness." But behavior therapists counter that all models of family therapy must state a conception of a "good" successful marriage. If one cannot define a successful marriage, how can one judge the outcome of a marital therapy? The rejoinder by Gurman et al. is that they object to the quid pro quo contacting by behavioral family therapists as furthering the practice of mutual controlling by the spouses.

What are the values influencing the typical family therapeutic encounter? Most therapists who work with families are committed to ideals of benign family interactions and to autonomy for each member, within reasonable limits, so that family members can develop and live as independently as possible. But a family therapist may come into conflict with more traditional, perhaps even authoritarian values with which he disagrees, as in the following case reported by Arthur Jackson.

> I had been after her to give her two boys a little living space. She really rides hard on them. Her husband split and she's had no word from him. She's trying to bring them up right and works eight to ten hours a day outside the house. Maybe she is right when she bawls me out. She gives me a look and wades right in: "What the hell do you know about raising teenage boys? They don't have a father to keep them in line. It's all up to me! I'll bet you're not even married!" I had no comeback at all.

Values concerning extramarital sex, modes of child-rearing, candor in interpersonal relations, and levels of emotional expressiveness differ according to one's own background and beliefs. They also differ for psychotherapists. But these are not the only, or necessarily the most ethically significant values in therapies. Several therapies are based on certain moral principles. Mowrer's, which we will examine in Chapter 3, is actively concerned with "sin" in the sense of moral wrongdoing and its expiation through confession followed by redemptive good works and social involvement. There are also psychopolitical therapies such as Dr. Huber's psychotherapy group, "The Socialists' Patients Collective" in Heidelberg, Germany, which spawned a considerable amount of terrorist activity on the premise that society, not the participants, was sick (Baeyer-Katte, 1982). A recent example of politically oriented therapies is that of the consciousness-raising groups so popular in our own society.

Lately there has been a revived interest in meeting the needs of religiously inclined patients. However, it has also happened that born-again therapists have tried to influence their secular patients to accept a religious answer to their problems, as illustrated in the following example given by John Summer.

> My patient tells me that she was altogether shocked and disbelieving when this guy says, "Well, I'm sure that if we pray together, it's going to be helpful for you" and then he gets on his knees and expects her to do the same! Of course, she didn't know what to do or where to turn. Her best friend suggested she come to see me.

A more benign approach is typical of therapists who want religiously inclined persons to feel they may avail themselves of therapy services without compromising their religious faith or beliefs. The following example by Abraham Lorber, describes one therapist's strategy to get around the biblical injunction "Honor thy father and thy mother."

> You know of course, that a great deal is said about parents in therapy. Often one cries about them and complains, but one also curses them for the miseries they brought on your head. The problem for Orthodox Jews is in that commandment. How can you be obeying it if you are yelling about how horrible, how awful they were? But you see, there is another commandment—Pikuach Nefesh—which means, figuratively, that when a person is ill, he or she can do almost anything necessary—break just about every commandment—to get well. So I tell them that this gives them God's own permission to be mad with their folks, or at least to talk about them.

In the wake of various kinds of social militancy—ethnic, racial, and gender—some therapists are beginning to question how they can help those of different cultural backgrounds, gender, or social class. Psychotherapy is administered mainly by white middle-class professionals whose knowledge and experience of other subcultures is often limited. It is also true that a number of therapy or therapy-like procedures have been designated as alternatives to mainstream treatments. Thus, consciousness-raising for women's groups has given way to therapies intended to foster feminist pride and self-esteem. Gay therapists are turned to by homosexuals who feel they will not be understood by "straight" therapists. Ethnotherapies have been proposed for members of oppressed or discriminated ethnic groups as a way of replacing their debilitating self-contempt with ethnic pride. Veterans of the unpopular Vietnam War suffering from Post Traumatic Stress Disorder have been treated in rap groups composed of similarly troubled individuals that are frequently led by someone with experience of that war.

Therapists are also becoming aware of their own ethnocentric proclivities as a result of the surge of ethnic and minority issues. Sometimes the problem is reflective of the civil rights issues in the streets and schools and businesses. Often it involves unfamiliarity with the cultural and socioeconomic background of the client, as suggested in the case provided by Larry Phillips.

> When I began therapy with Angela and Tim, I could smell trouble because they were so different. He was "el Waspo," passive, quiet, not a drop of revealed feelings, and she was a real Italian girl, yelling and screaming. She described her family as warm and expressive, and of course very vocal. But as we worked, I began to sympathize with Tim. She even yelled at *me*. So I tried to tone her down. She got just livid and said to me, "You are just like him, you hate Italians and so does he!"

Although black individuals and families have been successfully treated in psychotherapy, their relative number is small. A great part of their reluctance to enter therapy is a shared perception of its social class values. Jerome Costner illustrates the problem as he describes his (and their) frustration in trying to establish a workable therapeutic relationship.

> You see, they often don't come at the appointed times, and when I try to remonstrate with them, it's like I'm insulting them. They give me this look . . . "Well, OK Mr. Whitey. . . ." So I feel like I'm walking on eggs through a different world. When I tried to get them to turn off the TV when the kids were supposed to be doing homework, they say they do, but it turns out that they don't. I think maybe a black therapist wouldn't be quite so tender about it as I feel I am being.

Practitioners' Recollections of Their Own Ethical Misconduct

Some practitioners specialize in more than one type of therapy. They may view themselves primarily as individual therapists, but also do a good deal of group work or couple and family treatment. The following comments suggest their concern about the different ways in which they find themselves responding. Specifically, they may find that the treatment itself may dictate what they do more than the needs of the patient they are treating. Dorothy Rogers describes her own unease about this issue.

> I often wonder about the self-disclosure I find myself doing in group situations. I know that it's one of the most powerful things I can do there, and the patients always respond to it, but sometimes I realize it's just self-indulgence. It's as though I'm saying to them, "Look at me; I've got problems too. See you're not the only ones with problems" or I feel, "Look at how wonderful I am; pay attention to *me!*" I've felt very guilty on reflection. It's just me and my needs. It's got nothing to do with the welfare of the people.

The group atmosphere of family therapies also seems to elicit different responses from those in individual treatment. It appears to act as an excitant, eliciting excessive activity on the part of the therapist, as evidenced in the statement of Daniel Puzzo.

> You know, I really am much quieter when I see an individual, more of a good listener. I am even more reserved. But when I am seeing a family, I get much more talky and lots more opinionated. I'm likely to shoot from the hip. Things start getting out of hand and going off in different directions. It's a different stage. I also talk lots more about myself in family therapy. I worry about all this activity—is it for them or is it for me?

Psychotherapists are, for the most part, sensitive to the dangers of unwarranted infringements on their clients' lives. What concerns did these practitioners acknowledge about their own practices? Did they question their own behaviors with their clients? How aware are they of distinctions between what is in the client's interest and what they themselves get out of doing therapy? What doubts do they have about the wisdom of their strategies?

Interviewees who acknowledge ethical infractions moderate their admissions by stating that their inappropriate interventions were cases of faulty judgment. My own inclination is to believe that poor judgments or inexperience or inadequate supervision could all be faulted. Few therapists set out to behave unethically or cause harm to their clients. Judgment especially plays a key role even for the most ethically impeccable therapist. The following statement deals with a perennial problem for therapists in the light of the intimacy generated in a sustained therapeutic relationship. Loren Terry tells us of her experience.

> Can you be friends with patients? It is something I've always been taught was an absolute no-no, but I resisted the idea. It happened that one young woman I treated, well, we were on the same wave length. She asked me to have lunch with her. I did lots of soul-searching and said that I would. Over the years I've done the same thing with two others. The truth is that it did set up some kind of dependency thing that continues to this day. It's never really been an equal friendship, and it can't possibly be. I should have known better. I really believe I am an ethical person; it's these nuances that really get to me.

The following incident does not describe misconduct, yet it touches on what is a matter of increasing concern to therapists as well as all other health professionals: the threat of lawsuits. Gregory Archer tells of the anxious time he experienced.

> This teenage girl patient of mine went to this group home at my recommendation, and she got pregnant there. Her folks started talking lawsuits against me. I was really scared because she continued to be my therapy case while all this was going on. You know, you've got to take care of yourself in this business. I know my report was there in the file saying she should be in the place, so I was tempted to do away with it. Later, a colleague offered the idea of telling them I would say everything in court that they wouldn't have wanted to have come out. Believe me, I was ready to! I just got out of that case and said we just couldn't treat her anymore. I was really scared.

The codes of ethics of all mainstream professional associations discourage any but the most conventional kinds of physical contacts with clients. As a general rule, physical punishment or abuse of any kind is explicitly forbidden. But we have seen that irritation and frustration in the therapist may result in untoward verbal responses to clients. Here is a case reported by Phillip James where the child-patient so frustrates the therapist that the wish—or fantasy—of doing harm emerges.

> There was this little primitive girl who used to enrage me. She was so full of anger herself. She had been physically abused for years and she used to sort of incite me to try to get me mad. Finally, one session, I must have gotten fed up and I just grabbed her by the arm and squeezed and squeezed until she cried. She was yelling that I was hurting her and I sure was! To tell the truth, I *was* getting more out of doing that to her than I should have been.

Humor has a place in psychotherapy, but not caustic humor. Earl Entman rues the day when he spoke to a couple in the following way.

> You see, I've got this tendency to be teasing and sarcastic. Like I teased this couple after they had just come back from a trip away: "Well have you guys finally been able to make love?" Now, it turns out that the wife had had a long-time incestuous relationship with her brother, and I had had an inkling of that before. Making love with her husband or anybody was terribly anxious for her. She was absolutely furious with me. She left therapy and stayed away. She was right to be angry. I was dead wrong.

When the Shoe Is on the Other Foot: Experiencing Unethical or Ethically Equivocal Conduct

All training in the mental health professions emphasizes the importance of a helping attitude; the ingredients include an absence of pathology and a genuine interest in alleviating the suffering of others. A hard-to-define but essential element is what can only be termed good character, which is, most likely, the product of good rearing and wholesome development. But these are virtually impossible ingredients to guarantee for those seeking to enter the therapeutic professions. Indeed, the folklore is that many individuals embark on careers in these professions as self cures. And this is regarded as no drawback, provided one's problems are either resolved to a significant degree, or that they do not interfere with one's task of offering therapy to others. Both personal therapy for the therapist and continuing education in ethical sensitivity are important preventives against ethical misconduct.

Another preventive is learning from the effects of a therapist's misconduct or ethically equivocal conduct on oneself or on the life of someone close. In the course of conducting interviews, I was impressed not only by the number of instances in which these practitioners had at some time encountered therapists whose interventions troubled them, but by the affect with which they recalled such incidents. The emotional tone of the interviews changed markedly when they related how they themselves or someone they cared for had been treated badly in various therapy contexts. It became clear to me that these experiences had had great impact and that they had learned from them. They would not wish to treat others as they themselves had been treated in such instances. An example is the following account by the analyst Sally Turner.

> I am still wondering what to do—how to respond—in the most personally painful thing I ever experienced as a therapist. You see, a number of years ago, I asked this colleague who was a good friend to treat my son. After about six months or so, my boy asks this fellow for feedback. He tells my son, "You are just an asshole!" Well, the boy is doing fine now, but he kept that for ten years! I have a real dilemma; should I confront this guy, or should I go straight to the local society's ethics committee?

Obviously Dr. Turner will never repeat her colleague's action. When one has a bad experience with one's own therapist, one is unlikely to model oneself on that person—at least not on those hated tactics. The following statement by another analyst (Jeffrey Gregory) attests to this.

> I had this unfortunate experience in my own analysis. This person was considered to be an excellent analyst, very well trained, but he kept on pushing his framework, no matter

what I said. He never really listened to what I was telling him, but waited only to fit it in to his idea. Even though I am in the same profession and share some points of view with him, it was a traumatic experience. I still think so after a good number of years. It's no way to conduct an analysis.

As we noted earlier, different treatments may pose specific kinds of ethical problems. Alex Finston, who now practices in group therapies as well as in individual work, recalls the pressures put on him in a group.

This group just wasn't working out for me and I decided to quit it. But when I said this in a session, the cotherapist got on me and got the others all worked up about it too. They all began to pressure me to stay. I know from my own work in groups that there is a fine line about somebody's quitting the group. You can interpret it, but you can also put lots of heat on the person to stay. There can be too much confrontation. Maybe I should have stayed, but I felt those moves on me were really wrong.

Exploitation of patients, whether sexual or financial, is specifically forbidden in the codes of all the mental health professions. Adam Lester related what his therapist did to him.

I was in real financial difficulty and I was having trouble paying the fees for my therapy, so I told my therapist we'd have to cut back or else he would have to reduce the fee. So he proposed that I should work for him as his research assistant. I did, and it was totally miserable. I felt, and I still feel, that this guy couldn't deal with my feelings in the raw, so this was his way of exerting control over me. While working for him, I felt humiliated and belittled. So much of my problems had to do with authority and competition.

The "power position" of the therapist is, of course, essential to effective cures or amelioration, but it clearly can be abused. Ira Dodson describes a situation where the asymmetrical relationship, and the dependency it generates, can create expectations in an ethically equivocal way.

I had been seeing this woman therapist for over two years on a twice-weekly basis. It turned out that she was moving away—out of the area. I had been quite satisfied with the work we had been doing, but I was totally unprepared for the suggestion she came up with. She said that I should also move to the town she was going to so that we could continue therapy. I still—to this day—don't know what to make of it. I had a lot of trust in her, so it bothered me that she would make that kind of suggestion. What was she telling me about herself or about myself? I'm still not sure. Whenever I mention it to a colleague, they'll raise an eyebrow like, "What did the lady have in mind?" I didn't think it was romantic, but how can you be sure? How could I trust her after that?

As we have seen, it is especially painful when one's child is mistreated, but when dear friends are subjected to unethical conduct by their therapists, it is also disturbing, especially if one feels helpless to intervene. The following statement by Geraldine Santos reflects the problem.

My close friend described to me how her therapist was feeding her from baby bottles. That relationship was destructive and rapidly regressing. I felt that I couldn't just call this therapist and complain for her, so I told her to get another opinion—I mean a consultant. So she did, and the consultant agreed that this was altogether terrible for her. She did quit, but the "afterburn" lasted several years. It all sounded very exploitative to me. Supposedly it was "regression in service of the ego" or some damn thing, but it sure belonged in inpatient work if it belonged anywhere at all.

A similar dilemma confronts Joyce Stein, who watched the deterioration in her friend's marriage, which she attributes to the wife's therapist.

> He's seeing a woman therapist who sounds OK, but she's seeing this fellow who has the reputation of being not only narcissistic, but also sadistic. Anyway, when this couple threw a party at their house for a friend of theirs, this therapist of hers turns up uninvited. When she tells him he shouldn't have come, the guy says, "What's the matter; you uptight about it? You got a problem with it?" Now, I see her frequently and I just can see all this sadistic and ascerbic manner rubbing off on her. She stays with him. I know the guy's a jerk, but he's got a hold on her. It's doing her no good at all, but what can I say or do?

Irving Gordon recalls an incident in his wife's therapy that almost destroyed their marriage. It illustrates the importance of clearly defined boundaries and limits in therapist-client relationships.

> My wife had been in therapy with this fellow for a number of years. Now I don't know exactly what went on there, but I do know that she had come to regard him as sort of a friend, even though it was a treatment relationship. The boundaries must not have been very clear to either one of them. Then after treatment ended, this guy invites her to go out with him. She didn't, as it happens, and she didn't have very strong feelings about his asking her out, either, but I did. I still do till this very day. That was no way to end therapy.

I will reserve for the final chapter discussion of the interviewees' recommendations for preventive educational steps and other measures to assure greater quality control and ethically responsible conduct. Having sampled psychotherapists' own perspectives on the ethical issues they confront in their daily work, we have set the stage for a more thorough examination in the following chapters of the background of these problems and how they arise in the various contexts of practice.

2

Ethics and Negative Effects of Psychotherapies

Psychotherapy, in the words of Strupp, Hadley, and Gomes-Schwartz (1977), can be for better or for worse. In analyzing the ''for worse'' outcomes, different investigators have employed various terms: deterioration effects, casualties, and simply negative effects on outcomes. These labels imply impairment of functioning in comparison with the patient's initial status, feelings of hopelessness and depression sometimes resulting in hospitalization or suicide attempts, transient or enduring psychotic decompensation, lowered self-esteem, and various other decrements. Such outcomes may be forecast by a worsening of symptoms during treatment or the development of quite different signs of disturbance during or after therapy. Deterioration effects, casualties, and negative effects may take the form of any or all of the following, according to Strupp and his associates:

1. Decompensation or breakdown in which the patient's sense of reality is transiently or permanently impaired.
2. Exacerbation of depression, possibly with suicidal or other self-destructive features; loss of hope about future prospects of recovery.
3. Lowered self-esteem; feelings of humiliation and shame.
4. Decrease in self-control and acting out of sexual or aggressive impulses.
5. Prolonged dependency on the therapy and therapist and abdication of responsibility and self-direction.
6. Confused and impulsive actions involving family, work, or other significant obligations and commitments.

Causes of Harm or Injury

Melitta Schmideberg, a well-known analyst, described a case of a single woman in her thirties who entered therapy in the hope that it would help her get married. The therapist, attempting to cure her inhibitions, encouraged the patient to act out her assertive impulses. As a result, quarreling increased in her home, and she lost the job she held for over ten years, a job that had stabilized her and given her social standing. The attempts to remove her sexual inhibitions led to promiscuity. According to Dr. Schmideberg, the patient became progressively more aggressive, then depressed and anxious, and was finally hospitalized by her therapist who was unable to cope with her (Schmideberg, 1963).

Critics have long recognized that despite its avowed purposes of amelioration, therapy may also exacerbate the difficulties of the patient; sometimes it can literally drive one crazy (Robitscher, 1980). Substantial evidence of harms and injuries was compiled by Lambert, Bergin, and Collins (1977); and Bergin (1971) coined the term deterioration effect. Their survey of outcome in various therapies led them to conclude that the treatment processes themselves could precipitate anxieties, depressions, psychophysiologic (psychosomatic) and even psychotic reactions. Although approximately 10 percent of patients experience deterioration effects, it is not possible to distinguish what proportion of these cases could have been caused by the clients and what part by the therapists. Lambert, Bergin, and Collins believed that some patients who were already deteriorating might have been helped by more competent therapists and more appropriate interventions. In such cases, the activity of the therapists was indirectly harmful because the patients did not seek alternative, possibly more effective, treatments. However, and more significantly from the vantage point of our consideration of unethical practices, the investigators also identified deterioration effects that they claimed were directly caused by the interventions of therapists in which patients' equilibrium was upset by therapists' attitudes or actions, precipitating "a new cycle of deeper deterioration."

Even though noxious effects have been documented from pharmacological and somatic therapies with the psychologically distressed, Bergin and his associates' attempt was the first to systematically examine those stemming from purely verbal outpatient therapies. It is also significant that deterioration effects were not limited to particular orientations or systems of therapy—similar results were apparent for individuals exposed to various therapeutic techniques. The method employed by Bergin and his associates have been criticized for various shortcomings (see Strupp, Hadley, & Gomes-Schwartz, 1977); however, these methods are similar to those of most therapy outcome studies, and critics do not dispute the contention that therapists' interventions, well intentioned or ethically flawed, play a major role in a significant number of deterioration effects.

Although, as Furrow (1980) points out, considerable similarity exists among the practices of widely differing orientations and systems and even though different therapeutic approaches or techniques do not explain patient improvement, ideological commitments of therapists make a difference in how they approach treating specific problems. Preexisting client factors, such as initial ego strength, depth of disturbance, motivation for change, or even pressures of third parties, may be insurmountable obstacles to successful treatment, but a range of therapist deficiencies may have a malignant rather than a therapeutic effect. The conclusion reached by many researchers and practitioners (e.g., Dahlberg, 1970; Davidson, 1977; Langs, 1985; Redlich & Mollica, 1976; Stone, 1984) is that although client factors frequently obstruct or defeat therapeutic goals, deterioration in the client's condition is linked primarily to three therapist-controlled variables: a mismatch of treatment method wherein the therapist misjudges the appropriateness of intervention methods or persists in inappropriate ones, the use of techniques that worsen the client's condition, and personal character traits or countertransference attitudes of the therapist that exercise a negative effect on the client.

To examine the issue of negative effects from a different perspective, Strupp, Hadley, and Gomes-Schwartz surveyed the opinions of a large number of experienced practitioners, many of them leaders in the field. Most respondents were clearly psychodynamically oriented, but the range of opinions about damages to clients in or following psychotherapy was not particularly parochial. Some respondents attributed a significant portion of the blame to fringe therapies, and several who were themselves dyadic therapists, alluded to fewer controls on group and family therapies where, in their view, therapists exercised less direct control of treatment procedures. However, for the most part, they seemed to concur that a significant source of negative outcomes could be traced to therapists' inappropriate and countertherapeutic attitudes toward their patients.

Although the therapist's skills are undeniably important—inadequate understanding or empathy can reinforce pathology rather than remedy it—pathogenic therapists (those who consciously or unconsciously use dependent clients to satisfy their own personal needs) are more noxious and less effective than therapists who put the needs of the patient before their own. If therapeutic progress may vary as a function of the therapist's personality—warmth, empathy, and adequacy of the therapist's personal adjustment are significant factors—a therapist also may improperly handle the transference feelings that the patient develops, causing the individual to come to hope and believe that all possible gratification now comes from the therapist. The intensity of such a belief might then frighten off the therapist and the patient then feels rejected and abandoned. Suicidal depression may be the result (Stone, 1971).

On the other hand, therapists may improperly handle their own countertransference feelings, thereby also reinforcing the patient's pathology or introducing new problems. A therapist who reacts with hostility to a patient will most likely appear rejecting; a therapist who becomes emotionally or sexually involved loses any claim to objectivity. Strong sexual feelings toward a client may also block understanding of the individual's condition or reinforce an unwarranted dependency with the associated expectation that the therapist is the source of love. An obviously damaging consequence of such a relationship may be a rupture in the patient's real-life love or family relationships.

What Constitutes Damage or Injury? Ambiguities in Therapy Outcomes

Help-seekers come to therapy with a bewildering variety of problems. Moreover, they arrive in a state of profound emotional distress. One must sympathize not only with the help-seeker, but also with the well-intentioned therapist who wonders how to help and what kind of treatment to offer. Alan Wheelis (1973) poignantly described the familiar dilemma of psychotherapists.

> An anguished woman enters our office, sits down, weeps, begins to talk, and we listen.
> We are supposed to know what's up here, what the problem really is, and what to do
> about it. But the theories with which we have mapped the soul don't help, the life she
> relates is unlike any other. We may nevertheless cling to our map, telling ourselves that
> we know where we are and that all is well, but if we look into the jungle of her misery
> we know that we are lost. And what have we to go on? What to cling to? That people
> may change, that one person can help another. That's all. Maybe that's enough (p. 18).

The therapist's task involves helping people in such distressed states to clarify their confusions and make basic life choices. The therapist is the one the patient turns to for solace, but also for support and clarity in viewing problems and making reasonably good decisions. The therapy is the only place where help-seekers can consider their feelings and make choices in light of those feelings. The potential damage is considerable because of the client's vulnerability. Consider, for example, an individual who feels she repeatedly fails to assert herself. Assuming successful treatment, she begins to assert herself at home, in her job, and with friends. The individual's increasing assertiveness could be viewed by both client and therapist as desirable, and its achievement marks the successful outcome of treatment. But is it a success if her assertiveness results in a destroyed marriage, the loss of her job, the disruption of treasured friendships? Questions whether a marriage should be salavaged or if its breakup would be a good outcome of therapy; whether a vocational shift or locale change is a positive or negative step; whether the individual should be more or less aggressive, more or less accommodating; whether authority in a family should be strengthened or diluted; whether lessening of inhibition about engaging in extramarital sexual affairs is a poor or a good outcome for treatment—all illustrate the ambiguity of the therapist's task. No mapping of the soul provides clear answers, but the ethical injunction not to do harm obligates therapists to ponder the likely consequences of their intervention strategies.

Harms and injuries, damage that arises from unethical practices by psychotherapists, are difficult to prove because they are the result of procedures taking place in the privacy of the therapist's office. According to past legal decisions, a client's complaint about therapist activities is not always regarded as credible because the individual's condition as a psychotherapy patient is often seen as prima facie evidence of psychic instability. In many locales the evidence of unethical practices resulting in alleged damage to the individual remains at the level of hearsay, even though similar complaints have repeatedly been made to subsequent therapists about the behavior of specific individual practitioners. The following comment by one of the interviewees (Don Johnson) illustrates the problem.

> So I just don't know what to do about it. My client is only one of three who have complained about this guy who had his patients crawling around the floor and actually involved them in group sex. She claims her husband was so messed up by this guy that he wanted to make her have an "open marriage" or else give him a divorce. The other two were actually in therapy themselves with the guy, but got out, as they said, before he ruined their marriages. The trouble is, they won't make a formal complaint. I'm getting cynical about the whole thing, because everybody around here has heard of this guy's doings, but nobody can blow the whistle.

In Chapter 8 we will consider the legal actions brought against therapists for malpractice and the obstacles to such actions; however, for the present, let us simply accept that it is difficult (although decreasingly so in recent years) to get abused clients to present their claims to ethics committees of professional therapists' associations because of fears of public humiliation. Perhaps that is why complaints are so frequently communicated in private to subsequent psychotherapists. There is also an understandable reluctance of practitioners to forward a complaint of damaging behavior because of the possibility of countersuits for libelous charges. William L. Webb, Jr., chair of the American Psychiatric Association's Ethics Committee, states that any fear of being sued for reporting an unethical practice should be lessened by the knowledge that no lawsuits have been brought against psychiatrist complainants in APA ethics procedures [September 1986]. Nevertheless, in small communities, and to a lesser extent even in large metropolitan areas, reputations for unethical conduct are established, and referring therapists accordingly try to avoid sending their patients to such people. The situation may be changing drastically as a result of greater willingness to resort to litigation by those who feel they have been damaged or injured by their therapies.

Appropriate Therapies and Appropriately Trained Therapists

It is generally understood that psychotherapies differ in their approaches to the problems presented to them by help-seekers. Their orientations provide the maps of the soul that guide therapists' interventions for good and for ill. Despite recent increasing ecumenism, there is still a tendency to stick to one's orientation and methods regardless of the differences among the problems presented by various clients. Such professional stubbornness can lead to bad outcomes for clients, claims Paul Meehl (cited in Strupp et al., 1977), an experienced research-practitioner. He asserts that some psychodynamic therapists may become so enamored of their discoveries as to lose sight of the real-life consequences of treatment for the individual. The values influencing and sometimes guiding a therapist's interventions are not always discernible to the client; they are often blends of ideological perspectives and personal preferences that dictate an attitude about what the client should be doing or what the therapy should be focused on. An ethical problem occurs when these values become so influential that they obscure or override what the client feels he or she needs from the therapy. When a therapist fails to take into account client needs, countertherapeutic consequences may result. In a poignant example provided by one of the interviewees, Caroline Grant described such a miscarriage of treatment purposes.

> She was my dearest friend. She had been in analysis with this same man for more than seven years, and she suffered from this deteriorating disease that was going to kill her eventually. He kept working her over this oedipal business, even though she was dying. It was ridiculous. He wouldn't get off it. In her last year she had a chance to buy a little time through having an amputation, and wanted to talk with him about it, but he wouldn't. Instead, he called me and tried to get me to talk her into it! He just insisted on the oedipal stuff, as if that mattered. She was too dependent, too sick to do anything about it. So finally she died. He never could bring himself to deal with her about her illness.

Ellis (cited in Strupp et al., 1977) attacks classical psychoanalysts for causing iatrogenic disorders in their patients. In his view, they are as guilty of unethical behavior and of creating deterioration in their patients as those who exploit their patients for countertransference reasons. But many therapists of different orientations persist in viewing each other's practices with jaundiced eyes. Even those practicing within similar frameworks or systems frequently (and privately) express a lack of confidence in one another's intervention strategies.

The problems of providing knowledgeable and ethically responsible therapeutic services are compounded because psychotherapy has become such a household word in modern America, to be sought for an infinite number of problems in human adaptation. Because so many of these problems are outside the boundaries of traditional indicators of psychological disorder—the symptoms of neuroses and psychoses—the training and standards of practice for therapists remain heterogeneous, unsystematic, and insufficient. Training for competence in the various mental health professions is facilitated only to a very limited extent by the professions' ethical standards. Only very vague general guides exist as to what should and what may not be done in specific cases.

One cannot condemn all pressures on clients as unethical. Several therapeutic techniques may involve pressure on recalcitrant or reluctant patients for their own good—addictions, impulsive actions, and antisocial acting out are examples of behaviors that may require more forceful interdiction by therapists—but bullying or demeaning an individual, especially by the use of psychiatric or psychological terminology, is acknowledged by almost all professional practitioners as unethical and likely to be damaging. A therapist who uses demeaning or abrasive verbal techniques or appears condescending is acting unethically, just as one who pushes unsought values on the patient or demands inappropriately personal gratifications.

Because of the inherently asymmetrical balance of power and influence in the therapeutic relationship, the therapist has the responsibility to act in ways that will avoid harm to patients. In the light of this responsibility, careful thought and consideration must be given to the individual's capacity to absorb and use the therapist's probes, comments, interpretations, and advice. Therapists must exercise special care in employing high risk interventions such as confrontive characterizations of clients' motives and personality structure.

Damage as the Consequence of Mistakes or Countertransference

In the first chapter we saw that for practitioners few hard-and-fast distinctions exist between mistaken and unethical behavior. Reading the various excerpts, one could infer that many interventions regretted by the interviewed practitioners resulted from inexperience, poor judgment, inadequate supervision, or just plain bad advice. In some instances, the patients prove too fragile, too dependent, too lacking in ego strength, or simply too vulnerable to other pressures in their lives to be able to benefit from the specific procedures offered. Every therapist has made errors of judgment and has experienced failures in treatment, despite well-intentioned efforts to help.

The solutions to "mistakes" would appear to lie in greater understanding, better supervision and consultation, and the readiness to rethink one's preferred strategies. Although ineptitude and good-faith errors in judgment are certainly responsible for many bad outcomes, many experienced practitioners believe that countertransference reactions in therapists are even more likely to result in damaging consequences for patients because of the irresponsible interventions they generate.

The term countertransference originated in psychoanalysis and applies to the self-motivated reactions of therapists and consultants in all therapeutic interventions. The potentially damaging consequences of unmonitored countertransference reactions of therapists is not a new discovery. The founder of psychoanalysis warned that therapists could produce adverse effects on patients by reacting to them on the basis of unexamined conflicts of their own needs.

> We have become aware of the countertransference which arises in the therapist as a result of the patient's influence on his unconscious feelings, and we are almost inclined to insist that the therapist shall recognize his countertransference in himself and overcome it. No analyst goes further than his own complexes permit and we consequently require that he shall begin his activity with self-analysis and carry it deeper while he is making his observations on his patients. Anyone who fails to produce results in a self-analysis of this kind may at once give up any idea of being able to treat patients by analysis (Freud, 1910).

A fairly common occurrence is that a therapist's narcissism or pecuniary interest may lead the therapist to encourage a patient to remain in a prolonged dependent relationship. Difficult to prove, but widely acknowledged by practitioners, is the tendency to hold on to clients despite the lack of evidence that appreciable progress is being made, even when it becomes clear (to the therapist, at least) that the methods employed are not likely to yield such progress. Such a therapist is reluctant to admit incompetence or to acknowledge the method's inappropriateness. An opposite narcissistic motive is the need for progress, where clients are pushed toward change, regardless of their needs to proceed at their own pace. Or a pathogenic therapist may aggressively persist in probing into sensitive areas without a redeeming concern for the individual's vulnerabilities; that therapist may pursue unacknowledged voyeuristic satisfactions in demanding repeated recounting of delicate details of the individual's life—sexual experiences is an example—without working toward resolution of the person's difficulties in that area.

Therapists whose interventions are overly determined by their own needs, their countertransference attitudes, are dangerous because they are characteristically insensitive to their patient's reactions and especially because they do not recognize the danger signals implicit in such reactions. They may defend themselves by dismissing the patient's resentful or angry behavior as signs of defensiveness or resistance to be overcome "for the sake of the treatment." The individual frequently remains despondent, immersed in seemingly endless therapy, may become acutely suicidal in the conviction that he or she is truly a hopeless case, or runs away from the therapy in confusion or with a sense of defeat, only to seek other sources of help or remain mired in despair.

One of Strupp et al.'s respondents, Roback (1977), suggests that it is not necessarily aloof, coldly obsessive therapists who represent the greatest danger in terms of damage to clients, but rather those who, having established a close and warm relationship, either "come on too strong" (i.e., use their "charismatic" influence with the individual to push for certain behaviors or attitudes) or who threaten the continuation of the therapeutic relationship because they disapprove of something the client wishes. Although warmth, caring, and a supportive attitude have been almost universally acknowledged as crucial for therapeutic success, it appears that these same attributes can become factors in insidious manipulation of clients' feelings and behaviors. Given the emotional vulnerability of help-seekers, a combination of seductive and sadistic responses from therapists can have profoundly unsettling effects on them.

Few practitioners have documented the destructive effects of unrestrained counter-transference reactions in therapists. One who did is Robert Langs, a psychiatrist, who in interviews with a sample of ex-patients examined numerous misapplications of therapy with damaging consequences. Not only did the therapists in these cases behave irresponsibly and unethically, they also frequently precipitated out-of-control behaviors in their patients outside the therapy setting (Langs, 1985). Harmful life choices had been actively encouraged in some cases, and sexual exploitation was reported by a number of the interviewees. That Langs found several patients who went from one destructive therapeutic relationship to another led him to conclude that patients may actively collude with their therapists in legitimizing inappropriate acting out under the guise of psycho-logical treatment. The "psychonoxious" therapists dominated their patients through their own pathological needs and desires. They behaved inconsistently, but frequently allowed their own needs to determine their interventions, seeking personal gratification at the patients' expense. Patients responded to the inconsistency by joining in bending or breaking the rules of ethical conduct required of the intimate atmosphere of therapy. The sense of security, of being "well-held," as Langs put it (1985, p. 10), was damaged.

Langs also formulated the yet-to-be-tested hypothesis that these individuals share their therapists' pathologies; indeed, they reflect them even in subsequent treatment with other therapists. An alternative explanation may be the consequence of the power and influence differential between therapist and patient, with patient succumbing to therapist. In either case, it becomes obvious that a conclusion about whether an intervention has been ethical, however negative its consequences, cannot be based solely on client satisfaction. As Langs asserted, and as we will see from other egregiously unethical misapplications of therapy, many people who undergo flawed treatment express little regret or dissatisfaction; some who complain of abusive treatments even continue to view their former therapists with appreciation, respect, and gratitude.

We do not know what accounts for the diminished capacities for ethical judgments and decisions among these therapists, many of whom were experienced and presumably well trained. Nor can we explain the collusive tendencies of the patients, who, at least in retrospect, identified certain damaging consequences. These problems demand serious and systematic research that is only now being undertaken (most prominently in sexual exploitation: Gartrell et al., 1986; Holyroyd & Brodsky, 1977). Many other ethically abusive practices should be examined as well. Some evidence suggests that occasional therapists, made more vulnerable and needy because of changes in their personal lives, are inclined to use their patients to try to obtain the gratifications denied them elsewhere or to reaffirm fading feelings of potency. But among my practioner-interviewees, there were those who believed that some "bad eggs" had succeeded in becoming professional therapists, enjoying the feelings of power and the emotional manipulation of others often associated with the role. The question of what kinds of individuals lend themselves to such exploitation also goes beyond the scope of this book; it is an enigma that reappears in every therapy context.

When Damage Comes to Light: The Case of The Center for Feeling Therapy

If exposing patient damage is difficult because of the mainly seclusive settings in which therapy is practiced, fears of obloquy and shame resulting from sexual relations with one's therapist, for example, are also powerful. Multiperson therapies are, of course, much less secretive arrangements than traditional dyadic psychotherapies. We therefore turn to an instance in which group as well as individual therapy practices led to claims of significant damage that resulted in widespread publicity.

The case involves what traditionalists would term a fringe therapy, insofar as the conceptions of causes and remediation of psychological disturbance of this "school" are not identical with those of mainstream dynamic, behavior, client-centered, or cognitive orientations. On the other hand, it was evident that the therapists involved had received legitimate preprofessional training, were recognized practitioners, had published theoretical and clinical books and papers about their work, and were, in short, legitimate psychotherapists (forewords to their books had included commendatory remarks by leaders in the field).

The Center for Feeling Therapy began when leaders broke away from the Primal Therapy Institute, directed by Arthur Janov and also located in California. Publications describing their ideology and the rationale for their techniques were widely distributed. Books published by the group's leaders (Joseph Hart, Richard Corriere, and Jerry Binder) are *Going Sane* (1975) and *The Dream Makers* (1977). The ideology that guided their work was based on the conviction that many psychological help-seekers have lost an innate capacity for contact with their inner, deeper feelings, and that the only way to recover this vital connection is to pass through and beyond "craziness to genuineness and authenticity," and then to higher levels of sanity. According to their publications, their methods were intended to teach patients to recognize and experience such inner feelings, no matter how painful, sexual, or aggressive, and to respond to others in terms of their true emotional states. The damages to their patients became public knowledge through a suit brought against the staff members of the Center. Although the abusive behaviors in the treatment would be regarded as unethical according to the codes of all the therapy professions, they are behaviors that may occur in other therapy systems and contexts as well.

The nineteen plaintiffs were all former patients of the Center, and their suit charged public humiliation, physical abuse, and fraud. The brief was made available to me by their attorney (Marantz, personal communication, 1986), but the press account of their suit was published in the *Los Angeles Times* (July 16, 1981).

The following descriptions and comments are excerpted from the legal brief submitted on behalf of the plaintiffs.

> Initiation into the Center's program began with a three-week sequence of group and individual sessions where, in the words of one plaintiff, "First, they tear you apart, every shred of identity you have, and you get convinced you are really crazy. Next, you begin to need them to figure out who you are and what to be. Finally, you get so that you need to be like them; you begin to idolize them and to trust and depend on them completely; you begin to believe that they are really the best psychotherapists in the world."

Such aversive introductions were apparently not the experience of all the complainants. For example, some found the initiation considerably more benign. It was only later that abuses occurred, as described by one ex-patient.

> When I came in it was all about feelings—your own feelings. You were supposed to honor your own feelings above all else. If you thought you wanted to leave your wife and kids, OK—, leave your wife and kids! But [then] when my wife and I were broken up for sixteen months, they wouldn't let us [get] back together again. My wife's therapist said to her "It's him or me." When we finally did get back together again, we were severely busted for it.

Sarcasm and verbal humiliation were in some instances prologues to physical abuse, most often in group therapy settings. The ex-patients asserted that such abuses took place at the urging of the group's therapist or with his complicity.

> The members of a particular therapy group had apparently been assigned as partners to one another to help control overeating. One member worried aloud about getting into trouble with the therapists because her diet partner had repeatedly lapsed and broken her diet. She stated, "I was really upset because I was responsible for helping her to lose weight. I told her that I could strangle her." Then the therapist said, "Well, why don't you?" So I started slapping her and screaming at her, and I said, "I'll beat the crap out of you; what I'm doing to you is nothing compared to what you are doing to yourself."

Another plaintiff stated that when she objected to a therapist's encouraging her husband to date other women, the therapist threw her up against a wall, dislocating one of her fingers. Apparently, at one phase of its operation, Center therapists encouraged extramarital relationships among husband-wife pairs who were in therapy. This was part of a general tendency to intrude into the family lives of patients; in several cases, patient couples were "forbidden" to have children because, reportedly, their therapists did not believe they would be good parents. Such proscriptions and prescriptions may or may not have been countertransference-based, but they were also in line with the apparent aim of Center staff personnel to replace family feelings toward immediate relations with loyalties to the staff.

These assertions of damage exemplify egregious and, one trusts, quite rare instances of unethical conduct in therapy. Mainstream therapists will surely condemn them, but will, as I noted earlier, point out the marginal nature of the therapy. Indeed, such excesses are probably very infrequent among the over 100,000 professional practitioners offering psychotherapy services in this country. However, the potential for such damaging behaviors exists in every therapy context. This particular suit has reportedly been settled out of court, but it suggests that increasing numbers of disappointed and frustrated ex-clients will find legal ways to express their resentment at the treatment they have received.

Only nineteen former patients brought the suit, and though we cannot know how many others felt they had been injured, we are once again confronted with the fact that a very considerable number of clients, perhaps even the majority, believed they had benefited by the treatments of these therapists. As an indication of their probable "success" with other patients, it is noteworthy that only 20 percent of their patients dropped out of treatment before voluntarily terminating (only 13 percent dropped out during the intensive orientation and initiation of treatment), a rate of attrition that compares favorably with those claimed for any system or modality of psychotherapy. The plaintiffs' attorney attributes this comparatively low rate to persuasion and subsequent coercion, but this explanation cannot be verified. (Coercion in psychotherapy can vary from gross and obvious to very subtle pressures or inducements to continue in any system.) One is left with speculations about possible masochistic collusion of the kind Langs describes, but this also cannot be verified in the absence of systematic research that is difficult, perhaps impossible, to carry out.

The use of authoritarian controls by the Center reminds one of the potency of other treatment cults where those administering the techniques of helping assume that the helpers unequivocally know what is good for the others and may use whatever methods they find effective to induce change. Thus, the Synanon approach, with its assaultive methods, was greatly admired for achieving salutary changes in addicts who were deemed inaccessible to conventional treatment. It should be noted that caring methods were also employed. As treatment progressed, those being treated required fewer strictures or punishments for negative thoughts or behaviors because they began to identify with the concepts and behaviors of their helpers. Moreover, because Synanon also relied on group sessions, therapists' directives could be reinforced by other community members. Unfortunately, the organization came to an inglorious end with charges of attempted murder and revelations of numerous misdemeanors. What starts as a therapy could end up as a controlling cult. That bad consequences may ensue for the society as well as individual patients was illustrated by the otherwise unremarkable therapeutic group that spawned political terrorism in Europe some years ago. Dr. Huber of Heidelberg, a psychiatrist, led a therapeutic group to believe that the psychological disturbances of members were caused, at least partly, by injustices in society. His persuasive influence led some graduates of this therapy group to become associated with the members of the Bader-Meinhof terrorist organization that was active at the time (Baeyer-Katte, 1982).

Damage Specific to Group Therapies

The first systematic inquiry into negative effects or casualties, as they were termed, in groups designed to bring about psychological change was undertaken by Lieberman, Yalom, and Miles (1973). These investigators, themselves experienced group dynamicists and therapists, found that a significant number of participants (7 percent) became depressed or otherwise psychologically worse off following short-term group experiences, variously labeled growth and encounter or sensitivity training groups. Although such groups differ significantly from traditional, longer-term therapy groups, they have similarities in processes and leader intervention strategies. The leaders of these groups were, in fact, mainly professional mental health workers (i.e., psychiatrists or psychologists). Researchers attributed negative or deteriorative effects to the leaders' charismatic intervention styles, marked by exhortation or demanding levels of emotional expression and personal disclosures that reflected the leaders' aspiration for the group and not that of its members. Although there have been criticisms of the study's methodology and reservations about its relevance for the practices of mainstream group therapists (see Kaplan, et al., 1980; Lakin, 1979, 1985, Schutz, 1975), it has been repeatedly referred to since its publication because it identifies those dangers inherent in charismatic leadership in therapy groups. Because Lieberman, Yalom, and Miles related their observations of leadership styles, group processes, and outcomes for individuals, their study merited wide attention; its applicability for ethical conduct of change-inducing groups, whether therapeutic or quasitherapeutic, was recognized. Another criticism was that negative effects may have been discerned, but could be transient, and perhaps signified the temporary worsening before marked improvement that sometimes occurs in the wake of any therapy. The investigators' follow-up showed that "casualties," by and large, did not go on to make better life adaptations, but remained much the same as when their group experience ended.

Characterizing these psychonoxious group leaders, Lieberman, Yalom, and Miles cited not only their demanding, exhortative manner, but also their repeated forceful and invasive assaults on members' defenses, with little regard for their vulnerabilities or special needs. Interviews after the group experience yielded the following comments.

> That group hurt us. It didn't draw us together. It opened up problems, but [then] it didn't help us [to resolve them]. . . . This guy didn't bring out people's feelings; instead he would just tell you what your feelings were. . . . I was mad. . . . My leader called me a dumb shit because [he said] I didn't know how to participate.

When one researcher, concerned about members' reactions to one of the group leaders, tried to point out the effects the leader seemed to be having on some members, that leader began to blame those members for being resistant and defensive. However, paradoxically, some of these individuals did indeed blame themselves. We are left with the same enigma evidenced by Langs's ex-patients; is this a curious masochism, collusive tendency, some kind of identification with the aggressor? To analyze this question more fully goes beyond the scope of this book but it again demonstrates that judgments about an intervention's ethicality may not depend solely on participant's testimony, given their state of emotional arousal and dependency.

The similarity between these quasitherapeutic groups and conventional therapy groups exemplified the common mutual influence among the various kinds of psychological helping groups over recent decades. A therapeutic group may be consequently as likely to place a high premium on emotional expressiveness as an encounter or growth group. Pressures from other members are mobilized to encourage (to push) members in directions considered by therapist leaders to be important for them. Feedback—the focused dwelling on personal and interpersonal shortcomings of specific members—can be constructive or destructive in either group. Specified or implied standards of emotional expression become normative in all helping groups. The ethically responsible role of group leaders is not to deliberately amplify, but to moderate these group pressures in accordance with the vulnerabilities and needs of the individuals exposed to them. In this regard, charismatic leadership is motivated by countertransference. Its potential for damaging consequences must be recognized and its expressions restrained in the interest of member welfare.

The abusive initiation and mobilization of group forces are illustrated by the following occurrence in a therapy group for couples.

> A psychiatrist who offered individual, group, and family therapy organized a couples group. The therapist was apparently convinced that couples needed to explore their mutual antagonism in the group setting. So he instructed spouses to express their negative feelings toward one another; they were to "get their feelings out." In one of the couples the husband was inhibited about expressing his negative feelings, so the therapist instructed him to lie down on the floor and try to imagine the feelings he had about his wife. The husband complied and, after a time, began to moan. The others present were instructed by the leader to encourage him and they did so, voicing approval and encouragement at each moan. As this continued, the therapist commented that the husband was now really experiencing the oppression that he felt about his spouse, adding that "you married your mother." The wife became distraught and protested, but the procedure was not halted. The wife subsequently sought a private session with the therapist who informed her that there was no hope for their marriage, that her husband would eventually leave her, and that she should live thenceforth as if her husband were dead.

This incident reflects the type of injury that can occur in terms of a marriage, a family, and personal self-esteem in group therapy. In the following chapters, we will explore the ethical issues and dilemmas confronted by practitioners and consultants in various therapies. Here we see how a group context can be used as a powerful supplement to a therapist's interpretation of someone's life situation to destroy hope and self-regard. The group members collude, perhaps unconsciously, with the therapist in what must be seen as a destructive episode, regardless of its consequences for the couple involved. Glidewell (1978) wrote that group leaders have a duty to intervene, to protect a member from group pressures that constitute undue assaults on the member's defenses. In this case, the leader not only neglected to interfere but even incited the group to apply destructive pressures. Once again we confront the motives of leaders who engage in such assaultive and demeaning interventions. To what extent is this seriously misjudging what should be done, and how much is it a sign of exaggerated therapist egoism and need to show potency in producing dramatic shifts in patients? Although therapists indeed make judgments about their clients' life situations, they must distinguish between probing and inquiry on the one hand and applying pressures to follow their directives on the other. The first, sensitively applied, rarely has damaging consequences; the second usually will because it violates the principle of safeguarding the individual's autonomy.

In this chapter we have explored the sometimes damaging effects of therapeutic interventions. We have seen that deteriorative, negative-effect, casualty consequences may occur in any therapy. It has long been clear that as Strupp, Hadley, and Gomes-Schwartz (1977) held, the negative effects of psychotherapy are overwhelmingly regarded by experts in the field as a significant problem requiring the attention of practitioners and researchers alike. From their perspectives as group process researchers, Lieberman, Yalom, and Miles (1973) similarly faulted inappropriately intrusive, exhortative, and assaultive interventions by group leaders as being responsible for casualties of group participation.

Thus, in individual or group therapeutic interventions, injuries to help-seekers, to those for whom the helper has responsibility, may occur as a consequence of ineptitude or incompetence, or because the intervenor is driven by an agenda of personal need. In the next chapter we will explore the ideologies and values of systems of therapies and of therapists, and may begin to understand how therapies may be applied for good and for ill.

3

Ideologies of Psychotherapies and the Values of Psychotherapists

A major source of a therapist's legitimacy as a helper stems from an immersion in an ideology, a system of beliefs about the causes and cures of psychopathology. These beliefs, translated into interventions, are also filtered through the personalities and values of particular therapists. Concepts of therapies may thus in themselves convey moral implications. Therapists, by virtue of their unique roles and because of the special therapist-client relationship, become moral agents in their conduct of therapy.

Although psychotherapists for the most part pragmatically define their tasks as being to heal or ameliorate mental disturbance and strive for neutrality—for "nonjudgmental acceptance" or "unconditional positive regard"—they cannot help influencing the goals their clients set. Judgments of normality, maturity, and adjustment are regarded by practitioners as subject to scientifically objective analysis, yet they are, in fact, value-laden terms largely determined by considerations of what is deemed optimal or good and what is deemed bad. Such evaluations may not necessarily be personal or arbitrary for the therapist but are shaped by the culture of ideology in which the therapist has been trained.

In their *History of Medical Psychology* (1941) Zilboorg and Henry traced the development of modern treatment concepts and methods from the ages-long struggle against the prejudices, superstitions, and severe pieties attributing any form of mental illness as a kind of punishment for evil impulses or deeds. In this modern view, the medicalization of mental illness—the source of the medical model of treatment of psychological problems—was motivated as much by humane as well as by scientific considerations. If one could be understood as being sick rather than evil, rational and compassionate methods could legitimately be employed to ameliorate one's condition. This shift was accompanied by increased sensitivity to the influence of the social environment. For example, the rise of the view in eighteenth-century France that mental illness could be the result of a wrongly ordered society was revolutionary, and it contrasted with earlier religious perspectives about the dire consequences of evil thoughts or impulses. Pinel, celebrated as the great humanitarian who struck the chains from those incarcerated in asylums, was inspired by the egalitarian ideology of the French Revolution and claimed that the injustices of society had been responsible for much psychological disturbance.

43

Whatever the factors responsible for mental dysfunction, the traditions of therapy that followed the medicalization of mental illness were based on kindly but authoritarian methods of treatment. Pinel's advice was to treat the patient in a wise but firm manner. He echoed the much earlier prescription of Cicero (106–43 B.C.) that "the soul that is sick cannot rightly prescribe for itself [but] must follow the instructions of wise men."

In Pinel's historical epoch, as in our own, popular opinion has proven resistant to the idea that mental disturbance is an illness like any other. Despite successes of the mental health movement and advances in scientific understanding, an undercurrent of belief remains that the sufferer from psychological problems is morally culpable, somehow sinful or selfish. The therapist's role has been described in terms of paternal concern— one who would act as the patient's benefactor, teacher, and guide. But the psychological healer was also master of the patient, weighing evidence and passing judgment. Friendliness, gentleness, patience, and kindness were to be alternated with firm discipline. Contemporary psychotherapy has inherited much of this tradition and is often in conflict about the wisdom of permissive as opposed to authoritarian therapist attitudes.

Although modern psychotherapy has tried to distance itself from the moral considerations so prominent in primitive approaches to mental illness during the Middle Ages, the separation has never been complete. As Stone (1984) notes, psychotherapists inevitably mix moral instructions in with their treatments, often unconsciously. That they do so is unavoidable for two reasons. First, the concerns that have brought the individual, group, or family into therapy are often ethically involved in the sense that they are about disturbances in impulse, action, or relationships. Second, the therapies for such concerns are philosophical because they contain assumptions about the ways in which patients should think, feel, and conduct themselves. As we will see, the values implicit in the various systems of psychotherapy differ; one encourages maximization of socially permissible gratification, another productivity and social adaptation, a third self-control. Thomas Szasz, himself a practicing psychiatrist, is widely known for his polemics against psychotherapists as social controllers who convey unacknowledged values in their therapeutic treatments. In his many publications (1963, 1965, 1970, 1971, 1974, 1975) he has castigated the mental health professions for inculcating ethical and sociopolitical values cloaked in the terminologies of health care and medicine.

It is significant that while critics such as Szasz complain about the values therapists seem to promote, others bemoan how psychotherapy ideologies are altogether too remissive, that they sponsor a philosophy of "to understand all is to forgive all." That is, they too readily provide means of relief for ills that should be remedied through effort, personal activity, and social and political action. Psychotherapies are thus criticized for turning clients' attention inward and away from socially engendered pathology; for granting indulgences, much in the manner of the priestly confessional; for sanctioning unbridled hedonism, and for being surreptitious vehicles for the transmission of the therapist's or the therapy's values. No matter on which grounds the critics divide, they seem united in charging that while therapies may liberate clients from disabling psychological distress or disorder, they may also deprive them of their psychological autonomy, at least of many free choices associated with such autonomy, and of the burdens of bearing responsibility for what action they choose.

Depending on the orientation of the therapist, psychological disorders may be viewed from different, often sharply divergent perspectives. They may be seen as primarily biological in nature, as failures in development, as the consequence of social and economic factors over which the client has no control, or as personal moral crises. Again, depending on the therapist's orientation, remedies may correspondingly be viewed in terms of biological restoration or alleviation, enhancement of insight and self-understanding, reconditioning, social change, or moral realignment. Often these solutions are combined with few decisive distinctions between them. But whichever approach is taken by the therapist, value choices are entailed. As Mechanic (1981) stated, all therapeutic conceptions of psychological deviance and psychological cures run parallel to the society's conceptions of appropriate social behavior and its ideals of the good and decent life. In short, they are inextricably interwoven with moral conceptions. Although the ethics of practice directly involve client welfare and the therapist's actions in behalf of the client, the ethical problems encountered in psychotherapies begin with the questions of what is considered the patient's welfare and what is deemed reasonable social adjustment. Thus, therapies start with some picture of the good life and appropriate behavior.

To what extent do the values of a therapy reflect those of the culture? How much do the values of a therapy influence those of the culture? Therapies are carried out not in a vacuum, but reflect many of the culture dominant beliefs, including its norms of conduct and its standards about what is to be desired and what is to be disdained. Through the processes of interacting with the client the therapist may act as a transmitter of cultural norms and values. Several observers, notably Rieff (1966, 1978), Callahan (1973), and MacIntyre (1981), have asserted that therapists play the role of culture carriers, of inculcators of societal values. But others emphasize the influential function of therapists in shaping conduct and ideals of conduct in the society. Indeed, it has been asserted that psychotherapy constitutes a kind of folk science in American society, with its various ideologies informing us how to live as well as providing comfort and reassurance in the face of so many anxiety-arousing uncertainties.

The conflicts brought to the therapist are more often than not those of home or workplace, and the help-seekers who experience them invite direction in resolving or ameliorating them. In the typical case the patient is most troubled by difficulties in relationships with those toward whom one has multiple obligations, such as parents, spouses, children, or work associates. As Drane (1982) pointed out, people are upset by the state of these relationships or by pangs of conscience about their less acceptable impulses regarding them. These difficulties invite the therapist's intervention and open the door to the intrusion of the therapist's values.

In the first edition of his *Modes and Morals of Psychotherapy* (1964), London set the stage of considering ethical issues in the psychotherapies by examining the moral assumptions underlying psychoanalytic and behavioral conceptions of psychological disorders and their techniques for remediation and cure. His presentation focused on the implicit values in each that could affect therapeutic outcomes. The stage remained relatively empty, however, for few researchers took up the challenge of exploring ethical issues implicit in therapy ideologies. Although leaders in the fields of mental health have always been aware of the significance of ethical issues, practitioners tended to ignore the more philosophically abstract ones, such as the values fostered in a particular type of treatment. Even though Karl Menninger had pointed out years ago that "what the therapist believes, what he lives for, what he loves, what he considers to be evil, and what he considers to be good [inevitably] become known to the patient and influence him enormously," comparatively little research has been done in the process of value induction. It has been generally accepted, however, that in many treatments, successful or not, patients proceed to live out various aspects of their therapists' theories.

The studies that have examined this complex influence have confirmed that many therapists do indeed communicate their own values to their clients, often with no conscious intention or realization of having done so (Murray, 1956; Parloff, Iflund & Goldstein, 1957; Parloff, Goldstein & Iflund, 1960; Truax, 1966; Wolfe, 1977). The relatively early dates of these studies and the absence of subsequent research suggests that these findings failed to arouse great interest among practitioners.

But practitioners cannot be unaware of their own roles in sanctioning and discouraging various actions of their patients. They know that they are eagerly watched for signs of approval or disapproval. Skilled practitioners must realize that when they are seen as approving of a certain behavior, they are reinforcing it; when they disapprove, it may go underground, but is also likely to be changed. Often, even when the therapist is in fact neutral, the client tends to try to interpret that attitude in terms of approval or disapproval. The ethical challenge confronting therapists is to be aware of the value positions they take and those they communicate to their patients. Only if they accept this as their responsibility are they able to consider whether the values should be thus transmitted.

Psychotherapies as Value-Pushers: Criticisms of "The Therapeutic"

A recent work by Bellah, Madsen, Sullivan, Swidler, and Tipton (1985) suggests that most present-day therapies tend to encourage self-gratification at the expense of commitments to others and the permanent obligations of community. Questions of right and wrong are reduced to selfish considerations of "What's in it for me? Is this (relationship) going to work for me—to get me what I need or want? Am I getting from it as much as I am giving—as much as I could get elsewhere?" According to Bellah et al., clients are encouraged to think only in terms of a giving-getting model of human interaction and are reinforced in the notion that they have ultimate responsibility only for their own happiness and well-being. Moral responsibilities are reduced to such ideas as "don't get taken advantage of," and the potential richness and complexities of interpersonal relationships are lost in the contractual obligations similar to those of managers and employers to workers.

In fact, MacIntyre, the philosopher (1981), makes this charge explicit when he asserts that many therapists have come to see their function in managerial terms and to restrict their actions to realms of ends rather than means. The end is the desired "feeling better about oneself." Personal satisfactions and interpersonal effectiveness are the goals, and distinctions between manipulative and nonmanipulative relations are obliterated. Success is measured in these terms and the therapist is not concerned with ends as moral issues in themselves. They are regarded as outside the scope of therapy. Truth itself is displaced by personal and interpersonal effectiveness and positive feelings.

In this view, knowing how one feels is simply one more instrument for achieving success. As a consequence, according to Bellah and his associates, therapies, wittingly or not, encourage a zerosum game theory for their clients to employ in their relationships with others. Instead, they argue, therapies should take into account the significance of the individual's duties and obligations toward others. Using the terms of Bakan's earlier work (1966), therapies must recognize the duality of human existence. Not only must the "agentic"—the self-stricing and self-gratifying aspects of life—be acknowledged, but also the "communitarian"—concerns with belonging and mutual obligations that bind humans in common fate.

In recent years a number of behavioral scientists as well as philosophically-oriented practitioners have become concerned about the narcissism apparently sanctioned by psychotherapies as a group. Lasch (1979), Callahan (1973), and others have voiced concerns about the "remissiveness" of modern therapy practices. More recently, Wallach and Wallach (1983) also accused modern therapies of promoting basically selfish motives and ignoring social interest and altruism in a scientifically indefensible emphasis on individualism and individual gratification. These authors do not distinguish between the therapies of Freudians, neo-Freudians, and humanistic practitioners that all, they claim, are too concerned with personal autonomy and too little with self-sacrifice and commitment to public service. As they say, Freudians have been simply wrong in their overemphasis on bodily satisfactions, but Maslow and Rogers and other theoriticians have tried to shield us from external influence—authorities, the community, the society—to a degree far beyond what is good for us. The far less "popular" positions of emphasizing the importance of self-sacrifice and public service implicit in the therapeutic views of Bergin (1985) and Mowrer (1980) are noted with approval. However, as Wallach and Wallach acknowledge, there are Freudians (Menninger is an example) who also cite the need for a broader conception of the therapy enterprise than mere personal and interpersonal satisfactions.

We have examined the idea that therapists inevitably become moral agents for their clients in the sense that they are turned to for guidance in how to live. Do therapists stand apart from their culture? What is the source of the standards of conduct implicit in their stances and interventions? In *Words and Values* Rosenthal (1984) suggests that the conceptions and terms in most therapies are products of the culture and reflect its social trends. Therapists are not independent sources of values, although theories of personality development associated with the therapies, particularly psychoanalysis, have wielded a good deal of influence. In Rosenthal's view, it is not that therapists foster views of behavior that are wrong in terms of what one "ought" to do, but rather that the "oughts" have become so much more uncertain and vague. Nor is it the encouragement of "too much" individualism, as opposed to community feelings and obligations, but that code words of responsibility and mutual obligation in relationships have undergone changes in meaning. If we consider value-laden words with traditional significance such as sharing, self-fulfillment, community, or even relationship, they have increasingly come to be interpreted in narcissistic terms. For example, it is not uncommon for divorce to be interpreted as a way to improve a "relationship." One may "share" one's opinion. The media's use of the term community evidences this distorting tendency in its frequent mention of the business community or the defense community. Thus, there may not be values inherent in therapies, but the fallacies in widely shared aspirations in our own society that are reflected in the anxious search for gratification.

On the other hand, therapists are undeniably concerned with personal adjustment and happiness. If they were not sanctioned to help alleviate the frustrations and miseries of those who seek their help, they would have no legitimate function. Probably the shaman did have communal responsibilities, but the modern therapist is a secular, not a religious guide. This does not mean that no therapies are concerned with moral issues as a central concern. We will later examine some with particular moral stances and those that espouse a more communitarian philosophy of well-being. The point here is that more therapies are undeniably focused on helping individuals and family groups gain legitimate satisfactions in life. In this sense, therapies are largely individual-oriented rather than community-centered; in the terms of Carl Rogers, they are client-centered.

A perusal of the *Encyclopedia of Social Science* (1967) indicates that individualism is not only to be contrasted with the welfare of the society. The theme of self-development, as opposed to unquestioning compliance with the social order, has been a predominant one in philosophical and epistemological reflection since the Enlightenment. In its many facets, individualism represents a valuing of the intrinsic significance and uniqueness of people and their rights to freedom from undue coercion and state interference as well as the right to privacy.

The focus on self that is inevitable in a treatment context is bound to reinforce self-consciousness. But where is the evidence that such a focus necessarily leads to heedlessness of others or to enduring selfish preoccupations? In fact, it could be argued that a therapy's liberating effects could result in greater awareness and deeper sensitivity to the needs of others. The failures in life of those who seek therapy have ripple effects and create noxious conditions for those around them. Although motives and impulses spring from an individual, that person is not an isolated being, and therapy's benefits may not be restricted to the individual alone.

In their reflective response to Wallach and Wallach, Campbell and Specht (1985) point out that people's solutions to life's problems alternate between egoistic and altruistic because they are disposed to be both selfish and selfless rather than exclusively one or the other. We are polymorphous in the sense that we are equipped for generosity, but also for selfishness; for kindness, but also for cruelty; for loyalty, but also for opportunism; and for honesty, but also for cheating. Therapists, like their patients are caught up in the conflicting impulses and emotions that these polar tendencies entail. However, unlike their clients, they are presumed to be in a position of professional responsibility to help those they treat to work out viable ways of living that resolve, or at least lessen, the conflicts they experience. Therapies do offer paradigms or models of what is wrong in the individual's life and prescriptions of how to set it right. Although most psychotherapies focus on helping their clients achieve greater self-satisfaction, it is not true that they collectively foster greater hedonism.

According to Lazare (1973), implications are hidden in each system in the sense that potential clients will not ordinarily be aware of them. A biological model is usually held by medically trained practitioners who, influenced by their neuroscience backgrounds, have frequent recourse to psychoactive medication. A psychodynamic perspective believes that the individual must examine present experience in the light of earlier personal history—specifically enduring motives and accompanying feelings—to improve and recover from present dysfunction. (Therapists with Freudian, neo-Freudian, and derivative outlooks share many aspects of this view.) Behavioral and cognitive therapies eschew exploration of earlier history in favor of examining and altering presently troubling symptoms of behavior patterns. Socially oriented perspectives see the inner disturbances of the patient caused not so much by conflicting impulses as by social forces outside the individual; remedial attention to these forces will help solve the person's problems.

Each system has ethical implications because the therapist will encourage the patient's perceptions and actions that will have real-life implications outside the therapeutic contact. For instance, the central themes of psychoanalytically oriented practice will emphasize the elements of pain relief and the achievement of sexual gratification. These elements are not proclaimed, but are introduced in the course of selecting focus on aspects of the client's narrative. That is, they are implicit in the probes, comments, interpretations, and in the emphasis given to specific life experiences. As

Englehardt (1973) puts it, such therapies are forms of metaethics, suggesting ways of mediating between one's impulses and realistic constraints of one's surroundings.

According to psychodynamic systems, emotional and cognitive balance has been lost or not achieved in those who seek help. Regarding sexual gratification, one must be able to balance the urges for gratification with an enlightened calculation of costs that is the consequence of socialization and civilization. The patient must learn to choose and value satisfactions that do not separate the individual from those he or she must depend on for emotional support instead of being perpetually constrained by fears and inhibitions or constantly maneuvering to obtain surreptitious gratifications. The goal is for the person to have a better self-understanding in light of the individual's own history and thus be freed from the restrictions of parental rules and able to act with greater self-reliance.

Through techniques of recalling early experiences, free association, dream analysis, and exploration of transference feelings toward the therapist, the patient is expected to become increasingly accepting not only of his or her impulses, but also of the need to adapt realistically to the environment. In general, theories that are psychodynamic derivatives or deviations from Freudian views aim to relieve psychological distress by strengthening the person's sense of conscious, rational control so that he or she can both acknowledge and control impulsive tendencies that otherwise would lead to disruptive inner anxiety, depression, or maladaptive behaviors.

Even within these systems one can discover discrepant views about what has gone awry for the psychologically distressed individual and what must be done. Because each has prescriptive and, consequently, ethical implications for the individual's welfare, we will briefly note the following distinguishing features.

1. Differences in the degree to which people are viewed as driven by sexual and aggressive impulses and in the importance of the resolutions of conflicts associated with them. Thus, followers of Adler, Fromm, Horney, and Sullivan are likely to put greater emphasis on unmet social needs such as those in cooperative endeavor, social contacts, social interest. Although such therapists do not ignore sexual or aggressive conflicts, they have deemphasized their significance relative to social deficits.
2. Jung's followers have rejected the idea of interminable conflicts and the Freudian "dark view" of the unconscious in favor of a more optimistic view of human growth that implies reconciliation of all aspects of human conscious and unconscious experience with the historical and religious components of the patient's background. The unconscious itself is a rich repository of positive as well as negative impulse and a source of ultimate spiritual enrichment.
3. There are also dynamically trained therapists whose treatment ideologies and methods are, in their views, correctives to Freudian lack of appreciation of the psychological pain due to either social pathology—as in the cases of women with psychological problems resulting from their victimization in a sexist society—or to maladaptive actions for which the client is personally responsible—such as exploitation of others or failures to meet responsibilities or obligations to others. These therapists interpret their work as emphasizing a more comprehensive view of the human condition, rather than the hedonic goals of traditional psychodynamic therapy. In their view, the patient needs to become socially committed, cooperate with others, fight the injustices that create oppressed minorities, and so forth. Later in this chapter we will consider one of these systems, that of O. H. Mowrer, in greater detail. Less clearly delineated, but increasingly influential, is the position taken by feminist therapists who convey

explicit rather than implicit prescriptions that have consequences in families and marriages about how to think and act, and what responses to demand from spouses or children. Even mainstream dynamic therapists have begun to recognize feminist perspectives and objections to traditional modes of dealing with the problems women present in individual, group, family, and organizational therapies.

It is evident that dynamic psychotherapies vary greatly in the ideological messages they convey. When one adds to those differences the filtering through the values of the individual practitioner, one is faced with seemingly incalculable variations in what is prescribed and why. But it is possible to outline some common ethical pitfalls. One, possibly the most obvious, is the case with which the therapist can use the methods in each system to "push" a patient in terms of the therapist's perceptions of needs rather than the patient's. Countertransference impulses are widely recognized as dangerous, but they are difficult for a therapist to notice personally. Another is the question raised by Englehardt of a system's becoming an "ethical tyranny." Therapists must be aware of what values and prescriptions are implicit in the approach they espouse and, to the degree possible, that they make these understandable to the client. This is difficult, but necessary to obtain anything resembling informed consent on the part of the patient. A related issue has been raised by Callahan (1973) who asserts that modern dynamic therapies have often focused on only part of the Freudian message about the necessity of creating a viable balance between impulse and social responsibility. They overemphasize the negative role of moral authority, and, especially in their newer forms, advocate the idea of release and the fullest expression of hedonic impulses. Callahan says that the legacy of these therapies is the message "Buy, enjoy, relax, fulfill, even swing," so that even community interaction is interpreted as an opportunity not for service, but for the parallel play characteristic of children. These messages eliminate the necessary dialogue between individual gratification and social responsibility necessary for a healthy society.

A different view of the client's problems is explicit in the system developed by Carl Rogers, one that has been influential as an antidote to psychodynamic approaches. According to Rogers' views, which were widely publicized during the 1950s and 1960s, the therapist's function should be to help individuals become "congruent," that is, totally aware of and accepting of their repertoire of impulses so that they can be "fully functioning" persons, positive, creative, and more socially useful. People become psychotherapy cases because they have become alienated from their own original natures which are good; human nature in its original state is good. Problems arise because caretakers, no matter how well-intentioned, have imposed their own values on the individual; the person's development has been sidetracked, stunted. As a result, the person's natural growth pattern was disturbed. The democratic, egalitarian, facilitative atmosphere of unconditional positive regard provided by the therapist is essential to helping clients rediscover their true natures, their own impulses and values that were distorted by others' "introjected" values. The therapist's ever-accepting attitude fosters the recovery of the client's self-worth and self-direction. In this approach, needs for accurate diagnostic study and historical review are discounted along with the importance of transference and countertransference. Selective focus by the therapist on specific elements of the client's experience—sexual and aggressive, for example—is discouraged in favor of nonjudgmental positive attention, expressed in reflections to capture the client's meanings and emotional emphases.

The role created by Rogers for the therapist was that of a facilitator of experience, not its interpreter. This role contrasted with that of mentor in the Freudian model who serves not only as an interpreter of experience, but also as a model for identification and emulation. In the Rogerian portrayal, the therapist was a kind of midwife for the birth or, more accurately, the rediscovery of the true self. This reborn or rediscovered true self, congruent with individual impulses, needs no objective criteria of social adaptation or of socially approved behaviors. In its most influential period (1960s and 1970s) this system found expression not only in treatment contexts but also in broad applications to educational institutions and in administrative practices, where it was introduced to alter rigid and static structures in favor of freedom for creative experimentation in self-expression.

In the 1970s Rogers more or less abandoned individual treatment in favor of encounter groups in which he encouraged the fullest expression of emotionality. Although other aspects of Rogers's approach to individuals in treatment will be taken up later, certain features should be mentioned here. The terms used in his therapy have increasingly come under criticism for being too vague, specifically, such concepts as congruent, fully functioning, and even the various components of the self. Although his system has been undeniably effective with many highly motivated and well-educated "intropunitive" clients, its application to severely impaired patients, especially in institutional settings where Rogers tried to work with schizophrenics, has not been very successful. From its inception to the present day, client-centered theory has been criticized as naive, perhaps even superficial, although many critics have recognized the validity of some of its techniques, notably accurate reflection, and have praised Rogers for initiating research in the areas of process and outcomes in psychotherapy.

Ethical concerns are involved when client-centered therapists do not acknowledge the likelihood that they selectively focus on certain client responses to the relative exclusion of others. This problem became increasingly manifest during the years of transition in the late 1960s as therapists began to reinforce emotional expressions, whether sorrowful or joyful, and to exalt emotionality as somehow curative in its own right. This tendency found its fullest expression in the conduct of encounter groups; but, even earlier, in work with individuals, the traces of an insistence that emotionally toned utterances or displays were more authentic—hence more worthy—were already evident. The reinforcing role of the therapist who selectively rewarded such utterances with increased attention and often with personal participation and emotionality went unrecognized.

According to a behavioral therapy approach, what receives the label mental illness is more often than not a pattern of socially undesirable, deviant behaviors. Reduction of such pathological behaviors and their replacement by adaptive, healthier responses require a change in contingencies, that is, in the conditions reinforcing the maladaptive behaviors. If no payoff existed for these responses, for the disturbed and disturbing behavior that brings people to seek therapeutic help, for the neuroses and psychoses, they could be drastically reduced. Because such behaviors have been produced by either excessive punishment or other unfortunate reinforcement, they must first be extinguished through nonreward. Behavioral therapies stress providing multiple opportunities through interactions in and outside the consulting room for practicing alternative behaviors that may be rewarded.

As Skinner (1953, 1958) described the treatment, it fosters the idea of control (self-control) and may be introduced scientifically to correct problematic behaviors. The concepts of operant conditioning have been modified by successive generations of behavioral practioners, but the outlines of the system are constant.

This is not the place to consider behavioral methods in detail and the interested reader is referred to Bandura (1969), Wolpe (1973), Meichenbaum (1977), Stolz (1978), Lazarus (1981) and Spiegler (1983) who offer excellent descriptions of different behavioral approaches to a variety of problems. In recent years there have been numerous attempts at an integration of behavioral with psychodynamic approaches (Wachtel, 1977).

From the ethical point of view, several issues have been raised about some underlying assumptions of behavioral techniques as well as aspects of actual practices. Although the heyday of the relatively unmonitored use of behavioral techniques is probably behind, some questions remain as a result of the *Clockwork Orange* image of the excesses in applying such techniques. Critics worry about who will control the client. Whereas Skinner regards the imposition of controls as being in the person's own interest, another question remains: who will control the controller? Unfortunately, the powers conceded to the therapist are neither closely nor carefully defined or bounded. Who will decide what behaviors need changing and the manner in which change is to be brought about? In a famous debate before the American Psychological Association, Rogers asserted to Skinner that such decisions are not scientific but value judgments (Rogers & Skinner, 1956). Their resolution lies outside the realm of science.

Many clients do indeed suffer from various phobias, sexual dysfunctions, and a variety of other inhibitions for which behavioral methods have been found uniquely effective; the serious problems of addiction and substance abuse have often yielded to behavioral techniques. Educational applications are also considerable because the effects of reinforcement are undeniable in achieving behavioral changes with children.

However, many psychological problems are not simple ones requiring extinction and reinforcement. The scientifically respectable status of conditioning, operant conditioning, and its derivatives may not offer viable ways of correcting all the problematic behaviors of clients or the ills of the broader society. Without the keynote of meaning and value, a behavioral therapy cannot grapple with mixed or ambivalent motives, a central feature of human existence. By not attending to client motives, such therapy becomes a form of psychoengineering. Many problems presented by help-seekers demand efforts at establishing meaning in their lives; they call for self-understanding.

Intervention Styles of Practitioners

How do practitioners reflect their therapies' ideological stances in their interventions? What values are projected in their probes, comments, and interpretations? What ethical issues are implicit in their behaviors toward clients? According to Erickson (1964, 1976), a scientifically defensible position is not in itself an adequate basis for therapeutic interventions. Therapists must see the essential distinction between attempts to be scientific—recognizing that science rests on validation, on facts in the particular case—and on demonstration of the effectiveness of a particular approach and the ethics required of them as interveners in human dilemmas—realizing that ethics address the nonscientific questions of how one ought to behave, to conduct oneself. For many therapists—perhaps for the field as a whole—the lines between science and a technology of change induction have been rather vague; they have been loathe to recognize how much the practices deal with values and aims in life, with what is to be sought and what avoided. But, says Erickson, therapists may not escape the task of acknowledging that they must make value judgments about what they deem healthy and what they deem pathological. Thus, practitioners must create an ethical niche for themselves by clarifying their ideologies of healthy conduct.

It is pointless to try to infer precisely how a therapist will act in a therapeutic hour by referring to the conceptions of the orientation he or she has been trained in. As I suggested earlier, and will try to illustrate throughout, therapists' personal experiences and outlooks may be expected to shape their interventions. Temperamental factors, too, will influence the remarks or interpretations made to patients. As many a supervisor has discovered, what the therapist trainee actually does or did and what the supervisor hears on audiotapes or sees in videotapes may be discrepant.

Shostrom has produced important films designed to illustrate the activities of well-known therapists for use in teaching psychotherapy methods. The first series, *Three Approaches to Psychotherapy I* made more than thirty years ago, illustrates the interviewing techniques of Carl Rogers, the late Fritz Perls, and the founder of Rational-Emotive Psychotherapy, Albert Ellis. A brief discussion of the behaviors of these three distinguished therapists with Gloria, a divorced, attractive mother of a young girl, shows how ideological and personal stylistic approaches are blended. Each therapist either overtly prescribes or implies how Gloria should regard herself and her problems, which she defines in terms of problematic relations with men and her views of herself as a mother. Students have little difficulty in identifying the main outlines of how each therapist views human nature, the sources of pathology, and routes to health.

When Gloria tells of her shame in lying to her daughter by denying that she has had relationships with men since her divorce and complains to Rogers of her feelings of inauthenticity, he responds in terms of the ideology of client-centered therapy. She wants some advice about how to feel about deceiving her daughter and how to deal with the problem. Warmly and acceptingly, Rogers refuses to accept that responsibility. He assures her that she has within herself the means to determine an answer that is good for her. Her self-awareness and self-knowledge have become obscured because of her preoccupation with standards and values imposed by others. If only she will listen to her own inner voice, to her own impulses and needs, she will discover a solution she can live with. Were he and she able to continue beyond the single session of filming, Rogers would work to facilitate greater awareness of those wishes and needs.

By contrast, Perls, who in his lifetime became the cofounder of Gestalt Therapy, focuses on her inauthenticity, revealed in indirect and defensive behaviors. While, like Rogers, radiating warmth and good nature, Perls insists that Gloria abandon her phony little girl image and cease hiding her true wishes and impulses. The message is "stop dissembling and come clean about what you really are—a mature and sexually interested young woman—and thus assume the status that is authentically yours." His methods involve teasing and taunting her, albeit with consistent good humor. When she protests fear, and later on, shows irritation bordering on real anger, he remarks on her smile and reiterates his contention that she is a phony—"you say you are so afraid, yet you smile!" When, in seemingly genuine confusion about his attitude toward her, she asks him how he feels about her, he responds, "I feel like an artist who wants to bring out something that is hidden in you. For this reason, I reject the phony in you." Clearly, Perls's message is to be authentic. What action implications this would have for this woman and her roles as lover or mother would have to be developed in a longer-term therapy with Perls.

Albert Ellis's theory is in many ways a forerunner of contemporary cognitive approaches to psychotherapy. An individual is prevented from seeking gratifying relationships or activities only because of inhibitions based on "false constructions" of what is permissible and what is prohibited. These become translated into an assortment of personally inhibiting shoulds and shouldn'ts. Ellis's style is decidedly didactic, that is, he appears to lecture Gloria and exhort her to seek for herself those gratifications—in this case, sexual—she fears are illegitimate. As he instructs her, "You devalue yourself and beat yourself over the head just because you want to date men. You say to yourself, 'I am terrible; I am just awful,' but what is so terrible about that? Your wish for perfection is what is wrong with you. What would be so awful even if you tried and got rejected? First, you've got to depropagandize yourself. You should force yourself to open your big mouth and try." Were Ellis to continue to see Gloria, he would assign her homework tasks at regular intervals to try to seek our relationships despite the fear of rejection.

The issue of ethical implications becomes more clearly salient in Stone's (1984) discussion of another case reported by Ellis. A young woman patient of his had been complaining that she was perpetually feeling guilty about her parents. In their eyes, she never did enough for them. The father was reported as having a long history of alcoholism, and the mother had had breast cancer surgery. As a result of their demands and complaints, the young woman feels she has no life of her own. She asserts that she was brought up in a spirit of self-sacrifice, and to give of herself. Ellis's views in response to this assertion suggest something of the moral perspective he tries to inculcate in the course of treatment. According to Stone's description, Ellis responds, "We can see that your parents might have had to indoctrinate you with this kind of nonsense because that is their belief. But why do you have to believe that one should be self-sacrificing? All it's ever gotten you is guilt, and that's all it ever will get you!" The personal style, ideology, and the ethical implications of the prescription for future behaviors are vividly indicated in this vignette.

The Meanings of Human Existence as Ethical Concerns in Various Therapies

The ideologies of practitioners may be related to philosophical interpretations of the problems faced by contemporary men and women. How do people attain a degree of individual autonomy that also takes account of needs for community and mutual obligation? Goals of independence, emotional self-control, adaptability, and personal productivity may be weighed against goals of cooperativeness and commitment to the welfare of others, to the larger purposes of the community. In modern times, the moral guilt that Freud described as the content of anxiety, so influential in his formulations of mental disturbance, has been replaced for many by spiritual malaise and feelings of alienation.

In Freud's view, humankind had no choice except to seek gratifications guided only by intellect and by the knowledge developed by science. Driven by one's impulses and inhibited by the constraints necessarily imposed by civilized society, an individual can only effect compromises and experience a lessening of neurotic misery but can not escape normal unhappiness. By contrast, Alfred Adler contended that real mental health was obtained only through expressions of greater social interest—*Gemeinschaftsgefühl*—socially constructive activities with others. Consequently, followers of Adler have included prescriptions for relevant socially active behaviors for their patients. (This idea is implicit in the Adlerian interest in group therapies as opportunities for mutual aid.)

Jung's followers differed in their emphasis on rooting oneself in historic values, systems of belief, and efforts to attain inner harmony through acceptance of the disparate, often contending parts of one's self. Fromm, like Adler, emphasized bonding as curative. To be able to express the universal need to love and to be loved is the goal of healthy development. However, the need for love, as Horney's followers maintained, could in itself become an expresison of neurosis. Indeed, an excessive need for love—"I must be loved to feel secure"—becomes the predominant neurotic need of the age.

Throughout this discussion, it has been necessary to make inferences about the moral strains in the therapy systems we have considered because most therapists are reluctant to acknowledge that their approaches and methods are anything but ethically neutral. However, one therapist who has founded a system of treatment is quite frank in acknowledging the moral strain in his work. That therapist is O. H. Mowrer (1980).

Mowrer freely admits that his system conveys a moral message to his patients, that he prizes certain attitudes and behaviors and disdains others. In brief, in his view neurotic conflict results from antagonisms between self-reproach because of one's own actions or impulses and the unmet needs for restitution to those one has harmed or felt like harming. This view is diametrically opposed to the Freudian position of overdeveloped and consequently overburdened consciences. Although problems arising from sexual or aggressive drives may play a role in mental illness, they are less important than needs for openness and honesty. Because these problems result from fractured and damaged relations with others, amelioration must come from repairing the relationships. One must publicly acknowledge the ill one has done and make it good.

As London (1986) notes, the practical exigencies of this philosophy of treatment led Mowrer to shift from a dyadic therapy mode to working in groups because he found that the disclosure (confessing) and restitution (expiation) processes could be expedited by two or more patients meeting simultaneously. Currently, the Integrity Groups founded by Mowrer and his associates are virtually self-directing. The model is that of Alcoholics Anonymous. Their ideological message may be seen in Mowrer's statement: "Everyone needs support systems, membership which involves not only privileges, but also commitments . . . recovery and personal change involve the willingness to give as well as to receive, to be interdependent instead of dependent" (1980, p. 315).

Mainstream therapists are ambivalent about exploring the value implications of the systems they espouse. They are even more reluctant to acknowledge that they may, at times, exhort their patients to pursue certain actions or activities. It is widely held that only fringe therapies promote specific values yet in this chapter I have argued that this is not the case, that ideologies of "appropriate" behavior are, at least, implicit in all therapy approaches. Let us turn to several "fringe" conceptions to see how their ideologies are expressed in the treatment procedures of help-seekers.

Antze (1976) examined the ideological bases of therapeutic interventions in three therapy systems that had gained prominence as being effective for some very severe types of pathology. he studied Synanon, a treatment method for drug addiction; Alcoholics Anonymous, widely known for its successes in cases of alcohol abuse; and Recovery Incorporated, founded to deal with the seemingly intractable problems of long-term or chronic severe mental dysfunction.

In the therapeutic communities established by Synanon, aggressively assaultive and acerbic techniques were alternated with loving acceptance to shame and humiliate but also rehabilitate the addicts. These rough but "loving" methods were necessary to promote the release of pent-up feelings and to break down the patients' presumed insular defensiveness and resistances. But the routes to acceptance were clearly indicated, and such acceptance was assured, provided the individual acceded to the new role demands—the prescription—that were defined as the conditions of rehabilitation. The individual had to meet criteria of acting as a mature, well person; behaving as though fellow members of the community were family, toward whom caring responsibility had to be shown; and treating the menial jobs he or she was assigned to as though they were the most important tasks in the world. Disbelief or distrust was to be banished; the individual was to act as if believing everything he or she was told.

According to the ideology of Alcoholics Anonymous, alcoholics maintain an illusion of self-control, which clearly defeats them at every opportunity to take a drink. Its procedures are intended to destroy this illusion and make clear that there is no self-control or even the prospect of it for an alcoholic. The program is aimed at the elimination of defenses that have sustained the patterns of abuse and focuses on their replacement with socially more adaptive defensive strategies of suppression, sublimation, even reaction formation. Association with others in the same condition is intended to prevent any "successful" use of the old defenses of denial, avoidance, withdrawal, or impulsive actions. Thus, the buddy system so characteristic of AA becomes a vehicle for the expression of altruistic concern for one's comembers. Even the "good works," so prized in the ideology, may be seen as a successful defense strategy, fostered as an alternative to self-indulgent patterns that made the individual an alcoholic in the first place. In somewhat the same vein, the quasireligious ambience of its meetings serves not to promote specific religious practices, but to reduce the "big egos" thought characteristic of alcoholics in favor of reliance on the "higher power" one needs to extricate oneself from the addiction. Aspects of the treatment include increasing the person's expectations and hope that help will be given; elimination of any feeling of specialness or uniqueness through group comparison and discussions; provision of new self-definitions, that is, new norms for self-esteem in the event of positive change; support of such change through group encouragement and reinforcement. Sustained intermember support and mutual monitoring maintain the changes that occur.

Abraham Low, the psychiatrist who began Recovery Incorporated, became convinced that mental patients, even those who had been chronically distressed and hospitalized for long periods, could by dint of their own will power overcome their disabling depressions, anxieties, and thought disorders. According to Antze's analysis (1976), the followers of Low, themselves often former patients, essentially shame the patients into acting in a healthy fashion. Low told his patients to emulate his beliefs in their own capacities for improvement; paraphrasing his instructions to them, "Substitute for your fears and anxieties my belief in your ability to get well and to remain well." In his view, mentally ill individuals could overcome their afflictions through practicing behaviors they and others viewed as normal, no matter how transiently upset they felt. Low has been dead for many years, but the tradition of his treatment still lives and tape recordings of Low's lectures are used to structure sessions with the patients. A modified classroom procedure is employed, and members are routinely called on to testify or report on their uses of "practice" to stay well. A typical recital includes describing the painful or troubling episodes experienced; detailing the symptoms; "spotting" the problem (i.e., applying the concepts and techniques of Recovery Incorporated in which they had been previously instructed); and, finally, recounting the progress made since a previous occurrence of the symptoms.

It must be understood that in this perspective about psychological disturbance, the dominant thesis is that overcoming the adversity of psychological distress is, in itself, a tonic, a curative process. Many examinations of cross-cultural psychotherapy have suggested how optimistic expectations, generated by a therapist in whom patients have vested faith and confidence, provide powerful leverage for changes in mood and behavior.

The Responsibilities of Practitioners

It is undeniable that the role and function chosen as a life's work by a therapist involve profound and complex ethical challenges. The delicate balance between achieving relief and imposing values that may not be appropriate to the patient is not easily attained. Bergin (1985) has urged therapists to be cognizant of their own moral responsibility to act like good teachers and parents, instructing compassionately, but in full awareness of the values they are inculcating and, to the degree possible, explaining those values that guide their interventions and prescriptions. The therapist's position, like that of the parent or teacher, should be in the service of fostering the conditions for eventual greater autonomy—but ethical and moral autonomy—on the part of the patient. The individual should be enabled to make better, more responsible and enlightened life choices. Because of the relationship's asymmetry, care must be taken to consciously enlist the patient in the choice of goals and the articulation of values.

One obstacle to conscious evaluation of the ideological elements in the theory one espouses is the process of professionalization itself. Any reviewer of the process by which one becomes a credentialed psychotherapist can only conclude that professional socialization is for many trainees an extremely powerful influence. They must adapt by absorbing the values as well as the techniques and terminologies of the systems in which they are trained. Although therapist A and therapist B might differ considerably in terms of their personalities, life experiences, interpersonal styles, and live markedly different lives as persons, as trainees, and as psychotherapists, they will learn to similarly employ the general approach and tactics of the orientation they share. They will have been exposed to a systematic viewpoint about healthy as opposed to morbid ways of living. Will they be sensitized to distinguishing definitions of problems and procedures that are based on scientific research and those that are rooted in philosophic values about the nature and problems of human existence? Indeed, only an unusual trainee would be able to consistently make this distinction. On the other hand, as Barton (1974) points out, it would be a most unusual trainee who fails to get the message about what values to espouse as the result of successful navigation through a specific therapy training program.

For therapists A and B the ethical injunction, the standard of conduct, is that they should act to benefit their patients. As Rychlak (1973) interprets the therapist's perception of his or her mandate, "It is right and good that I . . . with my knowledge and training make decisions (for) . . . and consciously and deliberately influence my patients' behavior in ways that my research tells me are good ways, correct ways, or at the very least, conventional ways of behaving." It should be clear that exception may be taken to this attitude of authorization, not least because the system in which A and B had been trained fosters values at variance with those of the client.

This is not to suggest that therapists A and B can avoid value questions about what is good and what is desirable for humans to feel, think, or do. It is inevitable in our secular age that therapists should function in what was once the exclusive province of religious guides (London, 1964, 1986; Rieff, 1978). Although there are religiously inspired treatments (e.g., Alcoholics Anonymous and Mowrer's treatment conception), that communicate nonremissive values of seeking forgiveness and making restitution, most therapists are regarded as holding secular values. In fact, Vitz (1985) faults most contemporary conceptions of therapy for being not only nonreligious but essentially antireligious, and for holding views on family life, divorce, and abortion issues that stem from their following of Freud (see Freud's *Future of an Illusion,* 1949). It must also be recognized, however, that a theologically inspired therapy is profoundly value-laden. Every therapy may be seen as psychopolitical, not just curative.

Robitscher (1980) complains that therapists have taken over roles as moral philosophers as well as agents of social control. He asserts that they have become very important hidden decision-makers, using charismatic influence and making their own rules about what is in their patients' interests. Against the possible ethical abuses that could flow from their leadership and influence position, he proposes that therapists must become more aware not only of the values and motives behind their interventions, but also recognize the power and potential influence they wield and the need to exercise self-restraint. As an attorney, Robitscher is also attuned to the inhibitory power of legal actions that may be launched against therapists who abuse their prerogatives or default on their responsibilities. Ethically, therapists have no choice but to become more aware of the moral implications of the kinds of influence—stemming from their ideological positions or from their own values—they exert on their clients. Although therapists increasingly realize that theirs is not a value-free profession, they have not been trained to understand how their own values or those of their orientations are reflected in their interventions, or how to modulate their effects on clients.

The Therapeutic Alliance: An Ethical Partnership

To safeguard against unethical conduct therapists must exercise unceasing self-scrutiny. This can best be accomplished not only by self-observation, awareness of the values in one's theory and of those one prizes in one's personal life, but also by frequent consultation with colleagues and continuing self-education. Moreover, such self-scrutiny involves establishing a therapeutic alliance—an honest partnership—with one's clients. Despite the partnership's inherent imbalance, it is possible to try to clarify the mutual obligations of therapist and patient in ways that serve the purposes of both and fully involve the patient in the treatment program.

Levine, a dynamically oriented psychiatrist, has described his attempt to establish a therapeutic alliance with his patients in the following words.

> Look, I am not going to try to dominate you; I do not want to establish that I am better or stronger. [But] I am saying that out of my professional experience there are comments I can make to you about ways in which you are blocking yourself or others, or certain misdirected feelings and ideas that you experience, and we will have to talk about them. I will not try to punish you and I will try not to shame you. What I am saying is that I am a trained person who wants what is best for you and for those around you. In order to achieve this goal, I am going to urge you to take a look, and still another look at this or that part of yourself, at this or that part of your personality or behavior (1972, p. 126).

Although Levine was dynamically trained and carried on therapy in the psychoanalytic tradition, his ethical stance could be emulated by therapists in almost all therapy systems and traditions. He promised to work for the individual's welfare, and not to exploit the individual or to demean the person in any way. This approach is sensitive to the client's self-esteem and human dignity and makes little demand for faith in the system espoused by the therapist. Levine also argued that an ethical relationship between client and therapist is not based on unquestioning faith or trust; the client should be expected to have only very tentative trust, perhaps even benevolent skepticism. In this view, the therapist's and the theory's values may not be arbitrarily thrust on the patient. The legitimacy of mutual scrutiny by client and therapist creates an ethical basis for productive confrontation of the conflicting and contradictory forces in the client's life.

In this chapter we have explored the ethical implications of certain therapy systems viewed as ideologies and have considered how the values of those systems serve as prescriptions for behavior as well as vehicles for the expression of therapists' personal values or needs. We have seen that the therapist is inevitably confronted by moral dilemmas not only in his or her role as mental healer, but in terms of the problems presented by help-seekers. From this perspective, the best preventive against unethical conduct and the conscious or unwitting exploitation of the patient is self-conscious scrutiny of one's own as well as one's theory's values and the establishment of an honest therapeutic alliance.

4

Ethical Challenges of Individual Psychotherapy

Estimates of the number of people in this country who seek psychotherapy vary widely, and no reliable statistic is available to describe this population. However, it is generally accepted that this number is in the millions; Langs (1985) estimates that as many as seven million individuals are currently in treatment. To serve their needs over 100,000 psychotherapists practice an assortment of psychological treatments. This figure includes counselors, psychiatrists, psychologists, credentialed pastoral counselors, and psychiatric social workers who treat a range of problems from disabling depression and anxiety, symptoms of neurosis and psychosis, sexual dysfunction, addictions, difficulties in family life, to interpersonal relationship problems and uncertainties about vocational choices. The vast majority of help-seekers with these problems are given treatment in dyadic, one-to-one relationships.

Contemporary practitioners and students of psychotherapy increasingly agree that whatever the therapist's orientation, the therapeutic relationship itself is the primary source of influence on the client. Although the dimensions of this relationship are potent aspects of the therapeutic process, paradoxically, they are the most difficult to describe or forecast to the patient. Consequently, the problem of informed consent—which we will later discuss in this chapter and throughout the book—poses a difficult challenge to the therapist who sincerely wishes to appraise the person of how therapy will be conducted.

Individual psychotherapy is unique among psychological treatments because of its private and seclusive nature. It is a dialogue about patient concerns that are associated with feelings of shame, weakness, vulnerability, and anxiety. In disclosing such feelings and the events that gave rise to them, the client is necessarily bestowing faith and confidence in the therapist—even though the basis for such faith may not have been established through extensive experience. The client is thus increasingly bound to the therapist, despite a sense of vulnerability. Revealing one's worrisome or shameful secrets to another has the effect not only of relief but also of enhancing the other's power. We will repeatedly speak of transference—that carryover of emotionalized attitudes and feelings from earlier experiences with others—but not only transference feelings are elicited with disclosure. The inherent ambivalence about exposing one's secrets is also amplified.

Dyadic therapy is a very special dialogue: the narrative of one is the only legitimate topic; the therapist actively listens, receives, accepts, and understands, but also functions as interlocutor, advisor, and critic. Although some therapists (see Rogers, 1951) have insisted that psychotherapy should be viewed as an egalitarian I-Thou relationship where the therapist's expertise is placed at the client's service and where the therapist serves merely to facilitate self-exploration, this view is held by only a shrinking minority. The majority of practitioners acknowledge that therapy is not a relationship of emotional equals; the therapist does not seek the help of the client (even though many relationships with clients are indeed helpful in various ways to the therapists). The therapist sets the terms for the relationship, interprets the reality—the justification of feeling reactions— guides and advises, or selectively points out areas of apparent conflict or contradiction.

Because of this intrinsic but frequently unacknowledged imbalance, and its potential influences for ill as well as for good, legal critics such as Robitscher (1980) and Furrow (1980) have called for clarification and redefinition of the therapist's responsibility for the patient's welfare. They argue that the therapy relationship should be understood as a fiduciary one, in which therapists assume greater responsibility for therapy outcome. Otherwise, they believe, the therapist's powers are virtually unchecked.

The role and function of the contemporary psychotherapist have been variously described as healer, spiritual guide, moral arbiter, priestly confessor, ideal parent figure, and similar terms, used by some to praise and others to denigrate. In *Persuasion and Healing* Jerome Frank (1974) depicted a general function for psychotherapy of reversing the process of demoralization individuals experience after feelings of helplessness in coping with their problems. Although many life experiences can reestablish hope and build morale in the person, psychotherapy endeavors to accomplish this through procedures involving self-exploration, practice of more adaptive behaviors, and greater self-direction. Individual psychotherapists may assume different roles in the eyes of their patients in trying to achieve such goals.

Modern therapists, like their historic counterparts the shamans and physicians, are preeminently healers. In this definition the therapeutic relationship, notwithstanding certain caveats we will shortly consider, is like that between doctor and patient (and it may, of course, be a psychiatric physician–patient contact). Because the therapy exchanges between patient and therapist almost always involve impulses, behaviors, and events about which the individual feels a sense of shame or inhibition, the therapist assumes some of the functions of priestly confessor. To the extent that conflicting and contradictory values impede the individual's pursuit of adaptive and socially useful goals, the therapist may also be seen as a moral guide and spiritual mentor, especially for the secular client. Because nurturance and guidance toward adult values and responsible self-direction are part of the therapists' responses, the therapist may come to be regarded as a kind of good parent or parent substitute (even though such a relation will elicit ambivalent transference responses). We will now examine each of these perceptions in greater detail.

Therapy as Doctor-Patient Relationship

Although many people are treated by physicians, most psychological help-seekers are not. Even in nonmedical settings, concerns with the possibility of organic involvements and the spreading use of psychotropic medications to relieve anxiety frequently involve referral to or consultation with medical practitioners. However, in the absence of such considerations, the goals of psychotherapy—even the term therapy—and many of its procedures continue to be expressed in medical or quasimedical terminology. Social workers, counselors, psychologists, and other practitioners speak of mental health and mental illness. They describe symptoms and syndromes even when defining the client's problems as difficulties in living rather than illnesses. The terminology of medicine continues to be used in the training of therapists, of which a considerable amount occurs in clinics or hospitals. Psychotherapy is described as treatment, and adequate treatment is preceded by careful diagnosis.

Despite continuing criticism of mental illness as a myth and rejection of the medical model, the medicalization of psychotherapy remains one of its key identifying features—a legacy of the shift away from moralistic views of psychological disabilities. However, many psychiatrists as well as nonmedical practitioners recognize the limitations of the medical model. As London (1964) pointed out, "the therapist bandages no cuts, administers no pills, and carries no needle" (p. 3). Even the relationship between physicians who provide psychotherapy and their patients is by common agreement markedly different from those in which physical ailments are the focus. As Van Hoose and Kottler (1985) suggest, the therapist, of whatever professional background, deals with issues that cannot be seen through a microscope, cultured in a laboratory, or cured by any of the means commonly used in medical practice. Even the term cure is misleading for the results of a therapy where a diminution of psychological suffering, not the elimination of a disease, is a mark of successful treatment. Thomas Szasz's many publications on the subject (1961, 1971, 1977) contain multiple criticisms of the role and function of medically trained therapists who, he claims, exercise social control functions and impose values on their patients beneath a cloak of medical authority and seeming professional objectivity and scientific method.

Despite increasingly strident criticism, the idealized doctor-patient relation serves as a model aspired to by most therapists, probably because of its enduring image of a caring and responsible healer who accepts and copes with a patient in an ethically responsible way. The prestige and authority attributed to the role are not without their attractions for therapists of other disciplinary backgrounds. Moreover, degrees of disturbance or periods of heightened perturbation in the patient's life seem to call for the authority historically associated with the doctor's function. As Bayles (1981) indicates, the doctor-patient model may be appropriate in recognition of the impairment of an individual's judgment by profound emotional distress and the implicit need for the therapist to prescribe and structure changes to restore emotional equilibrium.

The historic affirmation of confidentiality and attention to ethical issues in the Hippocratic Oath pertains most directly to the one-to-one therapeutic contact. The healer undertakes to come for the benefit of the sick, remaining free of all intentional injustice, of all mischief, and in particular of sexual relations, all the while maintaining confidentiality. "What I may see or hear in the course of the treatment or even outside of the treatment in regard to the life of the [patient], which on no account one must spread abroad, I will keep to myself, holding such things shameful to be spoken about" (Musto, 1981, quoted in Edelstein, 1967, p. 17).

The Therapist as Moral Guide;
Dyadic Psychotherapy as Dialogue About Values

Englehardt (1973) proposes the idea of therapy as a metaethic. That is, the therapist helps the client to make rational choices even though the route to autonomy involves the anguish of recall and recital of emotional trauma. Engaging the client in such a dialogue involves the responsibility of a special type of teaching-guiding relationship. But the therapy should not push prescriptive choices on the client. In the ideal therapeutic guidance, the therapist's commitment to the principle of client autonomy restrains the therapist in proposals to the client on how he or she should choose to live. Given the determining values of candor and self-awareness, the therapist models a value echoed by Barton (1974).

> To express underlying feelings is seen as admirable and brave, as deepening one's honesty, overcoming taboos, and heroically facing the dangers of one's netherworld . . . virtue includes those things that foster honesty about motivations not ordinarily held in esteem. Vice [becomes] those that hinder openness. To speak truthfully becomes identical with speaking about those non-esteemed motives and emotions which also belong to one. Strength becomes the capacity to face those aspects of self without excessive shame, guilt, or panic (p. 79).

According to this view, dyadic psychotherapies should be essentially Socratic rather than prescriptive. They must be tailored and nuanced to fit the individual's needs and capacities and the person's life circumstances. The therapist may not grant absolution—as might the religious counselor—for the relief of guilt or shame, but rather help the patient to see the source of those feelings. In this sense, therapy becomes a learning experience in which individuals are taught to use themselves as investigators and even as experimenters. The greater the degree to which patients have the feeling of self-discovery and of personal choice regarding actions rather than being directed by the values of the therapist, the more likely they are to own the consequences of the therapy.

Frequently the emotional state of the person seems to demand directive actions by the therapist that contradict the principle of personal autonomy and self-choosing. And indeed the dyadic setting enhances the power and prestige of the therapist's directives. There can be no fail-safe preventive to value impositions on patients in individual psychotherapy. Consequently, the ethical therapist must act with as much self-awareness as possible, self-consciously reflecting on and scrutinizing self-espoused value positions as well as those adopted by the client.

Dyadic therapy, with its unhampered dialogue, is in many ways a unique opportunity for the weighing and balancing of choices in the face of ubiquitously conflicting and contradictory forces acting on the individual. With the patient and wise guidance of a therapist, one can usefully contemplate these forces and respond in a way not totally determined by simple extremes of good or bad, true or false, right or wrong (see Raths, Hamrin, & Simon, 1978).

The Therapist as Parent Substitute

Ralph Collins is a psychiatrist with over thirty years' experience. In the course of our interview he acknowledged that he was aware of criticisms that paternalism is seemingly implicit in many aspects of psychiatric and psychotherapeutic practice. But he believes that a good practitioner must have the attitude of a good parent.

> I know what lots of folks say, but it actually helps me to think of the patient as though he or she were my own son or daughter. I often find myself asking, how would my own kid feel if he were in this predicament? I even find myself saying to the person, "Now

if you were my own son or my daughter I would say to you . . ." and then I say it. It invariably means to the person that I really care about them and I'm really trying to see with them a better way for them. It really works.

Just as ideal parents are concerned with fostering growth, self-reliance, and autonomy, and just as they express nurturant caring, many therapists define their function as parentlike. The therapist's role, in this view, is to soothe the client's wounds, to help the individual establish or reestablish feelings of self-esteem despite personal adversity. The patient's inevitable dependence is viewed as a transitional necessity; support and nurturant guidance, as with one's child, are given until the individual is ready to function alone.

Undoubtedly, many therapists—perhaps even most—share Dr. Collins' sentiments. One could go even further and say that the caring and nurturance implicit in the psychological helping role inevitably elicit parental feelings from the therapist. And, of course, often patients try to evoke such feelings in their therapists. Particular feelings, usually ambivalent ones, develop toward the therapist. These are more clearly transference-based; however, the more general as well as the more particular attitudes toward a parent figure are bound to develop more quickly and more profoundly in a dyadic than in a group setting.

We are not concerned only with those cases of extremely dependent persons or with psychotherapists who perpetuate dependency needlessly, but with the nature of ordinary dyadic interactions. Most therapists will acknowledge that they have had to take strong directive and paternalistic stances with certain clients at certain times. This is reflected in the following statement by the psychologist Sylvia Miller.

> This woman was simply allowing herself to sink into self-absorbed despondency and ignoring the welfare of her kids while she was alternately playing around with these two guys. One of them literally "kept her," paying the bills, and the other was a romantic figure about whom she fantasized. I just told her that she had a responsibility to those kids and not to just lie around all the time. She had to decide how she was going to earn her own living and how she was going to look after them. I told her I wouldn't continue to see her unless she began to shape up. You know what? She shaped up! She really snapped to, and began to really take account of what she was doing.

The therapist has to make a judgment about the helpfulness of such interventions. In what specific cases are they called for and when do they foreclose the opportunity for self-exploration and self-choosing? Self-destructive patterns obviously demand some action, yet chastising and directing the patient toward therapist-endorsed patterns of behavior can negatively affect the individual's self-esteem and feelings of self-worth.

The problem becomes far more subtle and more difficult when the values of therapist and client conflict, where the client's behavior patterns and associated values are not self-destructive, but devalued, either consciously or unconsciously, by the therapist. In such cases, paternalistic intervention styles and attitudes have the effect of denigrating patients. In recent years many protests have been voiced against the condescension implicit in the attitudes of many male therapists toward their female clients, homosexuals, and others whose life-styles may be different from their own.

Problems of Caring and Loving: Psychotherapy as an Affectionate Relationship

The problems of feelings of attraction and affection are captured in the following comment by a teaching therapist, Harold Riklis.

When I train student therapists I make a point of exploring the erotic potential of the one-to-one therapy situation. If you are skillful and a good listener you'll have somebody responding to you who appreciates your attention so much that you've got to watch it. What I mean is, as I tell the students—and there's more than just a little truth to it—if you were going to put together an ideal program for somebody to become a fantastic seducer, you couldn't do better than to give them a program of psychotherapy training! It's just made to order for seduction. Regrettably, too often that's just what it turns out to be.

The same intimacy and client neediness can also tempt the therapist to respond—to express caring or affection—in ways that are appropriate not to psychotherapy, but to ordinary loving relationships.

Langs (1985) as well as others has asserted that some therapists repeatedly become involved with their patients in sexual liaisons during the course of therapy. On the basis of his interviews with a number of ex-patients, many themselves professional therapists, Langs found that most had been abused by at least one therapist; the abuses were typically sexual in nature. One therapist caustically rebuked a female for not trying to seduce him. A female therapist had conducted sessions while lying in her bed dressed in her nightgown. When another of his interviewees protested to her analyst about his having an affair with the patient's lover, the therapist declared that the patient was merely projecting oedipal fantasies. Although surveys support the contention of feminist therapists that sexual exploitation typically involves male therapists and female clients (Chessler, 1972) there are also instances of female therapists acting in sexually exploitative ways.

How widespread the sexual exploitation of patients in therapy is may be underestimated from the evidence available: surveys of practitioners willing to respond to the question; the outcomes of cases that involve litigation (many more are settled out of court and the public remains unaware of them); and cases that come to the attention of ethics committees or boards of review of the various professional therapists' associations. (Incidentally, ethics committees do not, as a rule, publish details of their findings, partly out of deference to the sensitivities of complainants, but also out of fears of suits or countersuits by those accused of unethical acts.) However, the problem is generally acknowledged by practitioners to be serious. Herbert Pritikin, an analyst, comments:

> There are just certain people who either aren't aware or just won't accept that some stuff—particularly sex with clients—just can't go on. But I'm afraid you won't knock it out of them. There are surely some fools; well OK, they're not good, but these other types—they think they can get away with anything. They're bad characters, narcissists. If you get a psychopath who is able to get through, and he practices, watch out! You won't teach them to be good people. I think it's a question of character when you get in there with the patient. We need reliable characters and these others shouldn't be permitted to practice.

In *Powers of Psychiatry* (1980), Jonas Robitscher, a legally as well as psychologically trained observer of psychotherapy practice, discusses the role of transference and countertransference feelings in generating sexual involvements between therapists and their patients. As he claims, the asymmetry of the relationship, particularly the confidence vested in the therapist and the prestige accorded by the patient, facilitates erotically tinged communications and tempts the therapist to express caring in a physical way or to use the individual's expressed needs as justification for acting on his or her own desires. Even though all the professional associations have taken firm stands against sexual involvements with patients, they continue to pose a serious problem because of their frequency and their often damaging consequences to patients. That therapist-patient sex is one of the most ubiquitous ethical problems of dyadic psychotherapy was recognized as long ago as the Freud-Ferenczi correspondence in which Freud warned his colleague of the dangers of yielding to the erotic importuning of patients or responding in terms of his own impulses.

Currently, very few therapists would defend sexual relationships with clients as being therapeutically valuable. However, several sincerely hold such a belief. Kardener et al. (1973) published one of the first systematic studies of attitudes and behaviors of therapists concerned with erotic contact with their patients, characterized as kissing, manual or oral stimulation of the individual's genitals, mutual genital stimulation, or coitus. Whereas 80 percent of the psychiatrists of the sample of 112 practitioners who responded asserted that erotic contact could not be beneficial for patients, 20 percent disagreed. They thought such contacts could improve specific sexual maladjustments, free up individuals who were sexually inhibited, and the like. Such interventions were reported to make therapy go faster and deeper.

The actual numbers of practitioners who admitted (anonymously in most cases) to having had erotic contact with their clients are relatively constant over the last decade. Other studies have also concluded that similar numbers of psychiatrists and psychologists—between 5 and 10 percent of psychiatrists and approximately 7 percent of psychologists—admitted that they had sexual contacts with their patients. (In several cases the sexual liaison was reported to have taken place at the conclusion of treatment or within three months of termination). Subsequent studies, notably those of Holyroyd and Brodsky (1977) and Gartrell et al. (1986), made similar estimates of the frequency of sexual involvements.

However, these investigators believe that their results, based as they are on admissions by practitioners, are almost surely underestimates for obvious reasons of shame or guilt or fear of punishment. Practitioners cannot fail to be aware that the vast majority of therapists condemn the practice as unwarranted exploitation. But, as Stone (1984) pointed out, licensing boards and professional associations have neither the power to subpoena nor the means to thoroughly investigate each complaint; nor do they have large legal staffs to protect the rights of those who may be wrongly accused.

Exception has been taken to the establishment viewpoint by some practitioners, among them Eugene Levitt (1977) who asserts that sex between therapists and their patients might be therapeutic, facilitating a "transference-building mechanism," promoting self-esteem for those with "inadequate or disordered gender concepts," and breaking down inhibitions and the "suppression of impulses." In response to these and earlier assertions of the therapeutic value of sexual contacts with clients, Marmor and his colleagues (1976) have noted that they might be more readily accepted if the implicated therapists had become involved with elderly or unattractive female clients, not with youthful, attractive ones.

If some have portrayed the therapist as Ulysses avoiding the Sirens, others, such as those in the women's movement, put the matter in a somewhat different light. Feminist therapists charge that it is not the purported seductiveness of female patients but the seduction by the male therapist that is the problem; in other words, therapists take advantage of the emotional states of their clients and then blame them for initiating the intimacy. They tend to agree with Robitscher's contention that victims of therapist seduction should be compared to rape victims because they are equivalently stigmatized, disbelieved, and shunned. A more appropriate analogy given the fiduciary, even the paternalistic models, may be to battered or sexually abused children who should have been properly cared for but instead have been victimized by their supposed care-takers.

As Robinson (1973) notes, it is true that troubled therapists may succumb to the temptations of sexual relations with their clients. However, according to Robitscher (1980), these transgressions continue not so much because a relatively small group of therapists oversteps bounds and exploits patients, but because the associations of therapists do not deal seriously with the problem. To clean house would require devising effective disciplinary mechanisms so that erring therapists would not be able to practice. In my own interviews there were many examples of difficulty in persuading victims of sexual exploitation to bring their complaints to the attention of ethics committees. And in the absence of such complaints, therapists are reluctant to press charges against colleagues. The situation is now changing for a reason most therapists are ambivalent about, namely, the greater readiness to bring suits for damages against psychotherapists.

Therapists often make a distinction between erotic and nonerotic physical contact. Sometimes, and with some patients, touching is seen as a way—often the only apparent way—of establishing important emotional communication. Although touching may arouse fears of invasive contact or sexual exploitation that can reach panic levels, it may also be important for calming a panic state in the person, and for many experiencing depression—for example, grieving individuals—touching is a way to express reassurance and solace. Holding, soothing, even cuddling have been responsibly used to establish contact with severely disturbed or distressed psychotic patients. For instance, children, some adolescents, and many very elderly persons may be patted or hugged. My interviewees who dealt with these age groups routinely used such methods for establishing closer or more trusting relations; the exception was adolescents who were sexually mature and likely to interpret touch as a sexual signal. In several cases, patients asked to be hugged, and in no instance had the therapist refused, even though at least two suspected that the individual was experiencing sexual feelings. Generally speaking, the interviewees were quite aware that the signals involved in nonerotic touch could easily become translated into erotic invitations for both client and therapist.

Some clients invite physical contact, even sexual contact—emotionally needy clients imply or even directly suggest it. The therapist who refuses may be perceived as cold, distant, standoffish. Supervising therapists have to instruct novices in how to respond to such requests—implied or overt—without rejecting or denigrating the individual. Weinberg (1984) tells how the therapist may express appreciation for the interest and admiration or attention, but point out that therapeutic help can be given only by avoiding any "dual" relationship. Because touching is so easily misunderstood as a sign of sexual interest, only conventional and socially acceptable touching may be used, with the exceptions noted above. The simple advice given by Weinberg is that the therapist should do nothing in the privacy of the office or consultation room that would not be done in public.

Caring and loving—though not in the erotic sense—are important elements in psychotherapy. As Weinberg suggests, a readiness to feel and full awareness of one's own emotional reactions to the patient are vital ingredients in conducting therapy. Therapists are ineffective if they ignore or cannot recognize being loved by the person, just as they must realize when they are annoyed, irritated, or feel helpless. What frees the clinician to act with clear therapeutic purpose and ethical responsibility is acceptance of, and relative comfort with, the feelings that are bound to be elicited in the intimate interactions of dyadic therapy. The therapist must endeavor to behave ideally, recognizing personal feelings must be separate from the professional responsibility of dealing with the individual who legitimately depends on his or her help.

The Therapist as Friend

It is probably not possible to really understand another fully or help that other in the absence of friendly feelings. As Hobson (1985) asserts, insofar as therapists are poor friends, inadequate lovers, or bad parents, they may have difficulties in establishing good therapeutic relationships, for such relationships partake of these fundamental human attributes. But as therapists seek to satisfy needs properly expressed in friendship, love, or parenting, they will surely distort the purposes of treatment. They will be attempting to gratify themselves, not benefit the help-seeker.

Because therapy is not an egalitarian relationship with an equality of needs and expected benefits, it cannot be a friendship in the usual sense. Expectations of treatment and the special nurturant attitudes associated with it are markedly different from those of typical friendships, and the tensions of disappointed or unmet needs remain obstacles to egalitarian relationships even after therapy is terminated.

Therapeutic Relationships and Therapy Ideologies

Through reviewing the individual's life experience in the light of current problems in living, the psychodynamic therapist may seek to render explicit and ultimately to help alter those motives that resulted in maladaptive and unsatisfactory relationships; the cognitive therapist questions those conceptualizations of self and problems that disrupt the individual's life; the behaviorist focuses on changing maladaptive patterns through appropriate reinforcements; and the client-centered therapist listens for the distorted needs of the true self. Even if therapists of other orientations would not agree with the dynamic bent of Strupp and Binder's (1984) characterization of the therapist's function, they would accept it as describing an ethically desirable stance: what is critical in the therapeutic relationship is shared understanding that results from a cultivated therapeutic alliance. The therapist asks, What actions of mine can comfort and relieve but at the same time forward this person's sense of self-worth and effectiveness in the world? The guiding principle must be: What is the most constructive thing to do for this individual, given the goal of promoting the person's greater satisfaction, personal autonomy, and fulfillment in life?

Strupp and Binder believe therapists do this by listening empathically, trying to understand the person's feelings, anxieties, inner struggles, and concerns. The individual is allowed to pursue any topic, explore any question, follow any lead, and, to the extent possible, make self-discoveries. When appropriate, the therapist inquires about gaps or seeming contradictions in the narrative, but not in an aggressive or prosecutory manner— never "Now I've caught you; you're not being truthful"—avoiding dogmatism and offering interpretations or suggestions tentatively. Assaultiveness toward the individual's defenses is also to be avoided, as are rebukes and exhortations. Like unshared insights— "Let me tell you this about yourself"—they are especially damaging to an individual's sense of esteem and dignity.

The ethical problem of treating an individual appropriately is not resolved, however, by simply behaving in a professionally responsible way. Patients are typically unaware of theoretical justifications or of the techniques likely to be used when they come for treatment, and therapists usually use the techniques they've been trained in, regardless of the problems confronting the help-seeker. Ethically concerned practitioners are increasingly sensitive to this dilemma, as suggested in the following comment by the psychologist Ted Clifford.

> One of the worst ethical offenses against patients is to try to make them fit some conception of what therapy is rather than taking their specific needs into account. I am thinking of this guy I see now who had kicked around in an analysis for over 15 years. Now, don't get me wrong. I have respect for psychoanalysis; I've had it myself. But this guy hadn't been making any move for years and had repeatedly expressed dissatisfaction. He said that his current problems—and he had lots of them—weren't being addressed. He said this guy was simply going on in the same way and he had no way to defend himself against it except to quit.

Unfortunately, although perhaps an extreme example, this perpetuation of an inappropriate treatment is by no means rare. The most ethically sensitive therapist must be plagued by such questions as: is my background of training, my knowledge, my skills, my way of doing therapy appropriate for the problems this individual presents? There are no easy answers as Gerard Gingold, a privately practicing psychiatrist, acknowledges.

> Unfortunately, we have the hardest time in making good matches between what people need and what they get. Now I'm not talking about the other stuff—you've got these people who are really working out their own problems on their patients. Then you've got a certain proportion of dunces who, no matter what you do, don't have the capacity to understand what the patient really needs. That first type—the psycho-obnoxious therapists—are menaces and should be excluded. But I really think that they are a much smaller number than your run-of-the-mill people who just figure that they have got the treatment for everybody who comes through the door. I think lots of those cases of deterioration could be the result of bad fits and inappropriate therapy. If you are open to yourself and have a decent humility, you quickly learn that there are patients you shouldn't try to work with and should refer to somebody else.

Grayson (1982) proposes training psychotherapists in more than one system as one solution to this problem. They would then have unbiased introductions to the various mainstream therapy approaches so that they could recognize when it is appropriate to refer patients elsewhere. In his view, it is unethical for a psychoanalytically trained therapist not to be aware of the potential benefits of, say, behavioral therapies for the treatment of certain sexual dysfunctions or phobias. By the same token, it is unethical for a behavioral therapist to remain unaware of the potency of transference and countertransference feelings that may emerge in individual therapy sessions.

The doctrine of informed consent offers another way to avoid inappropriate treatment. As Furrow (1980) argues, the model of informed consent is employed to assure clients of their rights to receive adequate information about what will occur in treatment. It is intended as a corrective for a possible overreaching paternalism on the part of the therapist and also functions as an equalizer for the acknowledged asymmetric power and influence relationship between therapist and client. Not to be overlooked is the implication of the possibility of litigation in the event of false promises or malpractice by a therapist.

The pressure of the demand for informed consent requires full disclosure and should lead a therapist to explain more completely the risks of a therapy as well as to carefully consider the probability of a useful outcome. The assumption is that if the therapist leaves the nature of what will transpire open-ended and undefined, the patient's expectations may move toward exaggerated wishes and fantasies, whose disappointment could be devastating and lead to the deterioration effects discussed in Chapter 2.

In dyadic as in group therapies, the idea of obtaining informed consent poses considerable difficulties. Many therapists are convinced that explaining the procedures and rationales of a therapy to a distraught help-seeker is counterproductive. Moreover, a preprogramming of procedures would seem to many practitioners to preclude the possibility of developing the spontaneity so valued in most systems of treatment. Despite these understandable caveats, informed consent is likely to be increasingly demanded from a legal perspective, if not from an ethical one. Leaving aside individuals so emotionally distressed that they are unable to understand what they would be told, the overwhelming majority of help-seekers would indeed wish to know the basis for what the therapist will do, the evidence that people in their situation (with their kinds of problems) can be helped by these methods, and the likelihood of improvement. It could also be argued that explaining what will be done and how can be reassuring, especially to very distressed patients who could gain a feeling of security that a plan is being formulated for their benefit. Periodic redefinitions of the treatment purpose as well as reviews of its progress—or lack of it—should be built into the therapy. What are we trying to accomplish? How will we achieve it? What must we do to enhance it? Shall we stop? Should we continue? Such questions are not one-time issues, and their repeated reemergence should be legitimated.

My own efforts to help therapist-trainees formulate statements to their clients about what they do, how they'll do it and why, and how to speak with clients about the importance of the therapeutic alliance have convinced me that the idea of informed consent can also stimulate useful self-scrutiny by the therapist. It forces a therapist to consider crucial question: Am I right for this person? Should I try to provide the kinds of help he or she needs? Do we have a basis of mutual understanding sufficient to proceed and a reasonable prospect of success in alleviating or ameliorating the individual's distress? Or should I refer this individual to someone who may be more likely to provide the help needed? The ethical therapist keeps the definition of competence in mind— sufficient knowledge, skills, and strength for the task of treatment.

Taking Over: Emotional Manipulation in Dyadic Therapy

The dyadic context, involving as it does the patient's narrative and the therapist's observations, tempts the therapist to assume the role of all-wise seer. This is counter to Levine's (1972) depiction of the desirable message to the patient: "We shall both make use of this knowledge in trying to understand what you feel and what you want." But the temptation can be overpowering, as the psychiatrist Frank Luchins acknowledges.

> My biggest ethical problem is in showing off. I get this terrific impulse to prove myself to be oh so clever. It happens when I see something the person hasn't observed. I can almost feel that kind of smug satisfaction I get when I can pause dramatically and say to him, "Look at what you are doing; don't you see it yourself?" I know that it's a kick for me when I have seen right through him. It's very hard to resist, although afterward I say, "What in the hell did you do that for?"

Becoming familiar with the intimate details of a patient's life emboldens some therapists to become progressively more intrusive and to demand knowledge beyond therapy communications. They do not limit themselves to the narratives voluntarily brought into therapy sessions but assume that they can be privy to anything in the person's life. The problem is illustrated by the actions of a therapist-in-training, described by his supervisor, Nancy Dainow.

> It wasn't that she wasn't making progress in therapy. That part of it was OK, but this fellow decided that she could go even faster. So he suggested she keep a journal—a kind of diary. Now that is fine with me. But he went further than that. He insisted on reading it, and it consisted of a pretty intimate account of all of her feelings and thoughts. She didn't want him to read it, but since he insisted, she felt she had to do so for the sake of her treatment. I told him to lay off. "You can't insist on her being open to you in that way. It's enough she tries to do it in the sessions." Actually, I figured we were beginning to see his needs, not hers.

The dyadic therapy context offers unparalleled opportunities for intrusiveness, for taking charge of an individual's life, for emotional manipulation. Insofar as the therapeutic activity is collaborative, it may offset the dangers of "guruism," whereby the therapist takes the attitude of being omniscient about the individual's problems or what the person should do to alleviate them. Therapists will acknowledge that they employ psychoengineering in that they may try to stimulate or modulate an individual's anxiety level or provoke certain kinds of emotional responses when they deem it useful for the client. The developing model of shorter-term psychotherapies, in particular, seems to demand manipulation of the transference feelings of clients to achieve quicker results. (See, e.g., Davanloo, 1980; Horowitz et al., 1984; Sifneos, 1972; Strupp & Binder, 1984.)

However, the ploys a therapist uses can lead to an ethically ambiguous situation where the client begins to accept the version of reality proposed by the therapist and abandons critical evaluation in favor of unquestioning faith. In a widely circulated article (1974), Gillis proposed that therapists are entitled to be devious in the interest of therapeutic movement and change. They should "take power over the patient, push ahead with solving the problem, then convince the patient that he or she is better even if it means being devious. . . . [the therapist] can develop ploys beyond the wildest dreams of a used-car salesman." There are, of course, a multitude of ways to stage manage the dyadic interaction so that one's comments and interpretations will be accepted as true. The view expressed here, probably shared by many practitioners, is that since therapy is effective because of certain common elements—expectations of benefit; belief in the healing ritual and in the healer; the position of influence of the therapist; suggestions that change is already occurring—what the therapist should be doing is enhancing those effects through various manipulations. Even flattery may be used to foster movement. Gillis concludes, "[These] kinds of tactics are justified by empirical studies in social psychology and by clinical evidence . . . [therefore] this is what therapists should be doing, and the more effectively and consciously, the better" (p. 95).

Gillis acknowledges that this approach will seem outrageously manipulative to some people. However, it is an important perspective to consider from the ethical point of view. Many experienced practitioners have come to believe that validity or "the truth" may not emerge in the course of treatment—it may not even be a relevant consideration. As Robinson (1973) points out in his critique of the ethical implications of therapies, the resolutions arrived at in psychotherapy may be plausible, but not necessarily the only possible ones, or even the correct ones about the reasons for the individual's problems or how to ameliorate them. In this view, their value is not lessened for the person seeking therapeutic aid. For practical purposes—relief, readjustment, greater satisfaction in life— the "truths" arrived at in therapy may be quite sufficient. Carotenuto (1985) addresses the same issue and concludes that the meaning of a person's life coincides neither with the truth nor with the reality of the individual's existence. The therapist's interpretations (broadly defined to include selective queries, comments, and explanations) are focused not on getting at the truth of the matter, but are instead an attempt to impart meaning into what has previously been experienced as relative chaos. The therapist helps to create a psychological field in which patient and therapist collaborate with the purpose of facing and healing the individual's psychological wounds.

This collaboration obviously occurs at different levels of awareness and skills. The therapist encourages the client not to flee before the emotional aspects of life, or to bury them in denial, but, in the words of Levine (1972), to stop and examine them, to have another look, and yet another look so that one can consider and reevaluate one's feelings in relation to one's life goals. It cannot be maintained that this idea of how therapy should proceed has nothing to do with truth. Although therapy clients, because of their psychological neediness and vulnerabilities, are certainly capable of being manipulated, should therapists regard the validity of client narratives and opinions as irrelevant?

Self-Disclosure by Therapists: For Whose Benefit?

What kinds of things, and how much, does a therapist disclose? Although it is obvious that therapy is undertaken for the benefit of the patient, it is important to realize that therapists often become personally involved in the patient's narrative. Empathic respon- siveness demands not only sensitivity to the person's problems and life-styles, but also a kind of identification with them. Moreover, the conditions of dyadic therapy foster that sensitivity and that identification. The problem, as Melvin Morris acknowledges, is to remain sufficiently detached—while being so closely involved—to retain objectivity and be able to help the person perceive and understand what he or she is experiencing.

> I realize that most, if not all of us, get involved in this field and do therapy because we have needs and problems of our own. We have "unfinished agendas," so to speak, and often these people are talking about stuff that bothers us too. I have frequently been tempted to get in there and say, "Listen, I have that problem too." But it won't do. The question for me that's always front and center is whose problem is it anyhow—whose needs have got to be met, yours or the patient's? Sometimes you can come in with experiences of your own to illustrate something for the person, or show that you made it, so they can too, but it's a judgment call. It's never crystal clear. The rule you have to go by is that the more you keep your own needs and yourself out of it, the more it's their life story and it's their therapy.

In some therapy systems, notably humanistic and client-centered approaches, sharing with the client has become acceptable and even laudable as a way of enhancing and exemplifying the egalitarian aspects of therapy. The therapist is shown to be another fallible human and the client's self-esteem is thereby expected to be bolstered. Therapists of other orientations may believe they are modeling self-disclosure when they reveal their own problems to their clients. The problem with therapist self-disclosure is well stated in the previous psychi- atrist's comment. The therapist's emotional problems could become salient in the treat- ment, thus obscuring the real purposes and goals of therapy. A therapist's disclosures, if sincerely made, may easily distract a client from personal concerns. The fragile faith that a therapist is strong enough to help—an essential element of competence—may be undermined. At the very least, such disclosures entail the risk of diminishing therapist objectivity and beclouding therapist judgment, even if only in the eyes of the client. Just because the dyadic setting seems to invite an exchange of confidences, the therapist must resist the temptation to burden the communication with personal problems. If disclosures are to be made, they should be in consideration of client, not therapist, needs.

Confidentiality and Gossip

A great deal has been written about maintaining confidentiality, perhaps more than about any other ethically sensitive issue in verbal psychotherapies. For the interested reader, excellent treatments of the problems involved are to be found in books by Edwards (1982); Rosenbaum (1982); Bloch and Chodoff (1981), and Keith-Spiegel and Koocher (1985). In addition, each of the professional therapist's associations thoroughly discusses the code of ethics including safeguarding patient or client confidentiality and circumstances in which it might be ethically breached.

The related issue of gossip is relevant for our consideration because individual therapy, like gossip, involves the illusion of mastery over another's life through the exchange of narratives about the person. As Spacks (1984) has written, gossip is essentially a turning of life experiences into stories, and we come to feel that we understand the persons who are the characters of those stories. Weinberg noted (1984) that there is an inevitable affinity between the narrative and the exchanges about it—almost always involving persons important in the patient's life—and the stuff of gossip, such that, as he says with tongue only partly in cheek, if one loves gossip one has a chance for greatness as a therapist. Thus, therapists may hear endless variations on themes of unrequited or frustrated love, thirsts for vengeance against those who have wronged the person, and fantasies of achievement in areas beyond the person's capacities. Not infrequently, the narratives are peopled by persons known to the therapist (another psychotherapist, for example) and the patient would certainly welcome the therapist's participation in discussing the characters mentioned. Such mutual involvement would seem to build feelings of trust and a conspiratorial closeness between therapist and client. However, it is precisely for this reason that it poses problems. The therapist may need to be reminded that if he or she joins in gossiping about persons outside the therapy, the client may well fear that he or she could be the next subject of gossip with a colleague, or even (it has happened) with another patient.

Because the contents and processes of individual therapy contacts are often fascinating to us therapists as human beings, it is tempting to discuss them casually with colleagues or with intimates. I believe that so powerful is the impulse, so widespread the practice, that it would be like trying to halt some natural phenomenon to get therapists to limit their communications about clients or patients to professional consultations or staff meetings. Nevertheless, those with supervisory experience or responsibilities are often made painfully aware of inadequate sensitivity to this issue, not only among trainees or novice practitioners, but also among those with many years of experience. Unguarded or casual discussion about patients or sessions is unethical and must be avoided. Censoring oneself—avoiding gossip about patients and colleagues—is one of the constraints on doing "what comes naturally" that one accepts with the professional role.

5

Ethical Issues of
Group and Dyadic Therapies:
A Comparative Approach

Although conceptions of causes and cures of mental disabilities may be similar in group and dyadic forms of treatment, the use of interaction between group members as a therapeutic medium gives rise to ethical problems different from those encountered in dyadic therapies. In groups, collective influences are mobilized and focused on individual members through consensus, conformism, and the development of norms of emotional expressiveness. Group patients, however relied on, are not professionally accountable as is a therapist faced with ethical dilemmas of initiation, facilitation, or prevention of unwarranted group pressures for change. This chapter compares therapeutic processes and the implications for ethically responsible practice of group therapy.

Most of those who seek psychological help for their problems do not approach a therapist or a clinic with understanding of the sources of their difficulties or how help will be provided. Typically, a framework of understanding is provided in the course of the therapy. Whether in group or in individual treatment, self-understanding is fostered through clarifications, interpretations, or restructuring by the therapists conducting the treatments. Group forms of treatment have been increasingly employed by mainstream systems of psychotherapy in recent decades; Freudian and neo-Freudian, cognitive, behavioral, and Rogerian systems have all developed group methods for the simultaneous treatment of from eight to twelve individuals. Although mainstream therapies have adopted group forms, mainly for the purpose of extending treatment to remedy presumed social and interpersonal deficits or disabilities, many individuals are referred to groups for economic reasons. It is cheaper for the clients, but it also is an added source of revenue for therapists. The choice of treatment, group or individual, is frequently arbitrary. Nevertheless, there are generally accepted bases for inclusion or exclusion: levels of communicative skills, degrees of emotional vulnerability, and tolerance for interaction with others. Typical contraindications for group treatment are suspiciousness to the point of paranoia or such extreme anxiety that the ability to communicate with others is impaired.

Three sources of tension characterize most helping groups: (1) the intrapsychic or inner tension that drove the individual to seek psychological help in the first place; (2) an intragroup tension—the conflicts engendered among the members by virtue of competing needs; and (3) an intergroup tension—a we/they contrast of what we are like in here contrasted with what they are like out there. In the group, participants are repeatedly reminded of their similarity in feelings. In individual therapies one's uniqueness—the specialness of one's problems—is constantly reinforced in the attention to one's symptoms from the single therapist.

Although self-help groups are probably at one end of this continuum (shared afflictions), all helping groups emphasize common experiences, whereas dyads are likely to focus on differences. A therapy group's emotional expressiveness may help some individuals correct a social deficit, but one would not argue that a group whose composition encourages an individual to maintain a maladaptive pattern is preferable to a dyadic therapy that challenges it. There are differences in how group processes are used to effect changes in symptoms and gain insights into conflict and interpersonal patterns. That is, differences exist in the meta-learning involved in the therapies: in how the client learns to understand personal difficulties; how he or she resolves conflicts; and how the person copes with anxiety. Differences in deutero-learning (learning how to learn about self) may be significant factors in the outcomes of these different treatments. Thus, the patient may be directed toward thinking about impulses or interactions with others. If interpersonally focused problems are better confronted in a group, and existential issues such as purpose and meaning in one's life more productively worked on within the dyad, referrals to the one or the other might be considered in terms of the presenting problems.

Successful group participants and successful patients in individual therapies may adopt styles of coping that reflect the processes of their therapeutic experiences; a group, by virtue of its being a group, and a dyad, by its intrinsic nature, highlight different aspects of the human experience—*inner* self and the *interpersonal* self (how others see me)—respectively. But are a particular individual's problems best dealt with in a group or a dyadic context? Ethically responsible referral to one or another treatment should be on the basis of therapeutic appropriateness rather than solely because of economy or availability.

The following comparison of the therapeutic group and the therapeutic dyad is intended to stimulate thinking about how therapists in each may take account of—or fail to consider—the ethical challenges implicit in their own practices. Whether the aim is improved self-understanding, diminution of excessive self-criticism, flexible or more adaptive behaviors, or better self-control, therapeutic influences in a group are brought to bear on patients by fellow group members as well as the therapist leader but solely by the therapist in individual therapy. Contrasting properties of group and dyad dictate their respective ethical issues.

1. In groups, members reward and support behaviors that conform to group norms of appropriate behavior, and they discourage or mete out punishment for those who violate them. In dyadic therapies only the therapist questions or censures or supports and encourages.
2. To the extent that the group qua group is the therapeutic medium, it is a system of mutual influence and interdependence. By contrast, a dyadic therapy is structurally asymmetrical; dependence on the therapist is explicit.
3. Communal feelings are important for the group's therapeutic effectiveness; members are enjoined to help each other. Individual therapy engenders a therapeutic alliance but does not produce a mutuality of helping.
4. Moods are ''caught''; feelings are transmitted from member to member and charac-

terize a group's atmosphere. The sensitive individual therapist will perceive a patient's emotional state, but his or her own is not determined by it.

5. Group members generate and reinforce a consensual version of reality (including evaluations of narratives, attitudes, and behaviors occurring in the group) that may be a basis for feedback to individual members. The task of reality testing in individual therapy, although conceptually conjoint, is actually vested in the therapist.

6. Narratives in groups are necessarily multidirectional even when ostensibly aimed at specific others (other members can and do frequently join in). By contrast, narratives in the dyad are exclusively unidirectional. The patient tells his or her story to the therapist.

7. Roles in groups are potentially exchangable; spectators may suddenly find themselves central performers. The therapeutic role is, to some extent at least, shared among group members. Roles in the dyadic form are fixed; the role of patient and of therapist are permanent for the therapy's duration.

8. Privacy and secrecy are normative for individual psychotherapy. Except in circumstances of potential danger to one's self or others, dyadic therapists are obliged to maintain the confidentiality of their clients' communications. Groups are public by their very nature, and the boundaries of privacy are permeable. There is a powerful incentive for members to gossip about what one has heard or witnessed at a group session. The responsibility for maintaining confidentiality is shared and necessarily diluted.

9. Influences of a group are brought to bear by peers who do not have either the accountability or the professional background of the therapist, even though the group's influence is tempered and guided by a professional. Dyadic treatment typically encourages more detailed narratives and recurrent analyses of conflictual elements but does not include live peer reactions; these are inferred from the patient's narratives. Although patient narrative is the recurring central event in both contexts, a greater emphasis in groups is usually placed on here-and-now behavioral manifestations because the reactions of peers are so readily available and such a vital part of the therapeutic experience.

Case Studies Involving Questionable Techniques

Ethical practice is not, of course, merely adherence to a professional code; it is based on understanding of how the treatment itself—the group mode in this case—and the techniques employed in it are likely to affect a range of participants. Occurrence of negative effects, untoward outcomes, or therapeutic casualties are certainly causes for concern. Perhaps many of these could be prevented by a greater consciousness of the value and ethical implications of the strategies employed in treatment.

Ethical problems can result from combining therapy contexts as many therapists do when they provide group therapy supplemental to individual treatments, as shown in the following illustration.

> Ronald Granger, a psychiatrist, and his cotherapist Shirley Patrick, a nurse practitioner, are troubled about the sibling rivalry that appears to result from putting his private patients in the same group together. Dr. Granger has had reservations about grouping these patients but, as he says, it is very difficult to organize a group outside his own

patients. It is clear to both that the patients all want his approval and they attack the female cotherapist, who is treated as another rival for his attention. Another ethical problem is that the therapist has information about each patient from individual sessions. He wants to hold on to the patients because of financial reasons. According to Granger, any member's departure from the group threatens the success of the whole venture. And members become demoralized when any single individual decides to withdraw. He acknowledges that in "final sessions" members who decide to leave are coaxed or cajoled to remain. Moreover, he has encouraged this pressure because of his interest in keeping members. He fears that departures could precipitate a domino effect of demoralization.

The Ethical Problem   An obvious ethical problem in this case is the pecuniary motive in wanting to keep patients. But it is by no means an easy one to resolve. Therapists who practice privately must make a living, and establishing a practice can be difficult. However, exploitation of clients for this purpose is inexcusable.

The practice of grouping one's individual patients is probably widespread, but no one really knows how general it is. In my discussion with specialists in group therapy I inferred that many did so; in fact, the practice was strongly defended as an ideal combination with considerable client benefit. The questions I am posing here did not occur to these practitioners. Indeed, they resisted the idea that an ethical issue was even involved in grouping one's patients.

In the above illustration, one of the elements that concerned the therapists was the degree of rivalry for attention that seemed to characterize their group. Such feelings are characteristic in group situations, and indeed many group therapists regard their occurrence as a sign of progress in attaining a recreation of siblinglike relationships and providing an appropriate context for examining the ambivalent feelings of each member toward his or her family of origin. The following case describes such a situation.

> Laurie had been in analysis for about two years when her analyst recommended that she join the therapy group he conducted. He was of course her personal analyst as well and continued to see her alone several times each week. She found herself becoming increasingly angry at the therapist in her individual sessions, but furious at other group members in the group sessions. Her analyst told her that these were good developments, that she needed to "rekindle her anger at her siblings and at her father." Laurie told her psychiatric social worker friend that these procedures were "tearing her apart" and that she felt more depressed and hopeless than when she began therapy, but she was afraid to quit.

The Ethical Problem   Although it may be desirable for Laurie to reexperience her ambivalent feelings about her siblings in a group context, should she be placed in a group of her analyst's other patients? Such a placement may have undermined her confidence in the therapist as well as her own self-esteem. The conjoint group and individual work increased therapist control and made the patient feel more dependent than before. Even though there may be therapeutically positive effects, it is also difficult to see how patient autonomy could possibly be enhanced through such an approach.

Relationship issues are a frequent topic in group therapies. The group is a forum for discussing one's problems with family members, friends, work associates and for sharing and comparing interpersonal experiences. Since intimacy and trust are developed among members and because intimate disclosures may generate even more feelings of bonded-ness, the question of what is appropriate and what is not assumes great importance. What limits are set on the interactions that may take place between group members? Who determines them?

An article by the psychologist-theatrical producer Jacques Levy (1971) who directed and produced the musical *Oh, Calcutta!* addresses the question of acting out generated by the atmosphere of intimacy and involvement. One of my interviewees (Avery Evans) an experienced group therapist, acknowledges this problem and describes his attitude.

> Sure, the group is a meeting place for people who are dissatisfied with what they've got. And I usually have groups of younger people who become sexually interested in one another. Some of them are married, but that doesn't stop them from making contact with other members. I do worry about it sometimes. I ask myself "Are you a procurer or what?" Maybe some of them do get hurt or they damage their relationships outside. Actually, I don't really think they come out badly in the long run, but I do worry about my role in all this.

The Ethical Problem   Groups elicit and generate powerful feelings. It would be counterproductive for a therapist to try to prevent them. Actually, the techniques of group therapy make the best use of these feelings to promote insights and develop mutual aid. However, group norms can become potent inducements as well as regulators of interpersonal behavior. Should a group therapist ban extra-session contacts? Should a group therapist try to enforce regulations of intermember conduct?

To foster group as well as individual autonomy, leaders should make as explicit as possible those rules and regulations essential to the group's conduct. Among them will usually be regular attendance, rules about payment of fees, and a ban on physical assault. Aside from these, the norms of the group should be repeatedly considered by the members. For example, the therapist's obligation is to make sure that members recognize the consequences of violations of confidentiality, of extragroup sexual contacts, indeed of anything that could affect the welfare of the individuals in the group. These matters *are* the therapist's business but not ones he or she should regulate. Naturally, the therapist must deal directly with self-destructive behavior or danger to others, and should be prepared for such likely occurrences. In the best instances, group members will also become increasingly sensitive to ethical problems and act cooperatively with the therapist to maintain a therapeutically optimal group situation.

Assaultive Techniques in Groups

Dramatic illustrations of assaultive techniques are provided in *Going Sane: An Introduction to Feeling Therapy* (Hart, Corriere, and Binder, 1975), which depicts how such techniques were routinely employed in group therapy. Members were contradicted, criticized, and castigated for "lying," for being "just dead," for saying "a lot of head stuff," or for being just "all fucked up."

The perpetrators of this type of group therapy have been sued by their patients, but the attitudes implicit in their styles of interventions are an extreme of those currently encountered among some more activist group therapists. We will examine their rationale in some detail. The authors claim to have taken as their model the Rogerian ideal of the "originally" good individual who has been "ruined by parents'" socialization through denial of real feelings and genuine impulses.

Their position is that one is real and genuine only when one is expressing real feelings; then one has transcended his or her "defensive strategies." The demand is for total congruence between feeling and expression. The therapist refuses to permit incongruence, claiming that clients cannot be allowed to perpetuate a "lying" life of falsehood (p. 34). To move a patient from nonfeeling to feeling requires identifying the feeling and demanding its expression. The therapist is the lie-detector who ferrets out any dissonance in a patient's mismatched words or actions. The patient's inauthenticity can be felt as interference in communication by the therapist. This book is characterized by an arrogant and simplistic reliance on the expression of feelings as a cure-all and it borders on therapeutic fascism.

Similarly assaultive techniques are apparent in the following example from Kopp (1977, p. 31).

> Outside the group, Peter was an unhappily married clinical psychologist. During the sessions, he usually held the voluntary appointed office of the nice-guy-who-tries-so-hard-he-always-antagonizes-everyone (cum chronic complainer). . . . His clinical experience had served to refine the excellent training which his psychotic mother had long ago provided. . . . He complained: "My head is blocked, there is a suffocating pressure in my chest, I feel that my genitals have disappeared and that my body is turning inside out, like my asshole is open and everyone can hurt me." . . . He turned pathetically to me, whining, "Shelly, won't you please help me?"
>
> I'd had it for the day. "Can it, Peter," I blasted. "I've had a headache for the past four hours. I don't need any of your shit on top of that. Now you either talk about what's going on in your life and deal, or take your ass over to St. Elizabeth's Hospital and spend the rest of your miserable days in that human warehouse, pouting with the rest of those stubborn looneys. If you want to play schizophrenia, go do it somewhere else."
>
> Peter was quiet, but suddenly seemed clearer and more alert. He began to talk about an unfinished fight with his wife, and his messed up relations on the job. The group joined in and some things got a bit straighter for him. At the end of the hour he smiled warmly at me saying, "Thanks for curing my psychosis." "That was easy." I answered, "Now if only I could cure your neurosis . . . and my headaches."

The Ethical Problem One may wonder about the kind of ideological stance behind this seemingly arrogant and brutal approach to Peter's problem. The therapist obviously felt entirely justified in making such an assaultive intervention. Nevertheless, this is surely a demeaning response to the patient, whatever else may be involved. How can independence, autonomy, self-regard, or self-esteem possibly be enhanced through such a cavalier approach? Although there are undoubtedly patients for whom verbal shocks may have salutary results, one must conclude, however, that this therapist arrogates to himself ethically dangerous prerogatives.

Games Groups Play

The emotional atmosphere created by intimate disclosures encourages a psychodramatic ambience of unusual intensity. Members may look forward to group sessions as high points in their weekly lives: an action-packed session becomes prized as much for its charged sense of involvement as for the potential it offers for personal relief or insights into problems. Group leaders are often induced by members to provide eventful sessions that leave members with the sense that exciting things have happened.

In the heyday of growth and encounter groups, a tendency developed to quickly generate such emotional atmospheres through use of exercises or games that were purported to rapidly break down barriers between people and bring them "in touch with their inner feelings," or promote therapeutic interactions among members. Such exercises and games were depicted by several writers, among them Cohen and Smith (1976) and Gunther (1968).

Cohen and Smith describe a technique called "Surrender and Support" which they claim may be used at any time during the group's life, but especially when an individual is anxious, defensive, or in need of stroking. It may also be employed to strengthen emerging group norms of trust and intimacy. In the following case, one woman has been complaining that others have repeatedly disappointed her.

> *Group Leader:* "I want to suggest something that may be helpful now. Come stand in the center. The rest of you join me in forming a circle around her." Addressing the target member, he adds, "It's important for you to keep your feet, knees, and lower legs firmly planted, but let the rest of you move wherever we move you. Close your eyes, relax the muscles in your body, and let your head fall back." The group rotates the individual until she seems comfortable and satisfied with the activity.

> *Results:* The authors assert that when a person surrenders his whole body to others and finds that they will take care of him, he must examine his feelings toward them in a new way. The advantage claimed for this nonverbal experience is this. Cooperating with others in the circle brings about a feeling of togetherness in the common task of giving pleasure to another. They claim that this experience usually dissipates any heightened sharpened anxiety or defensiveness as well as promotes the establishment of norms of group trust and intimacy.

> *Group Slap:* The recipient of the slapping bends forward from the waist, torso parallel to the ground, legs well apart and braced, arms hanging loosely down. The slappers stand facing each other across his or her back. . . . On a signal, everyone starts slapping in unison and in the same rhythm, covering all areas and trying to maintain the same slapping pressure among all slappers. This continues for about two minutes. . . . After the slapping is finished, the recipient remains bent over and feels the effect. It is often followed by a group bear hug. According to the authors, this can be a very satisfying and emotionally involving experience.

> *What is my place?* Group leader says, "Look around at someone else and try to decide where you think you belong in a line, based on whether you feel you're a more or less important person than whoever is next to you." This exercise is supposed to precipitate a discussion involving leadership, authority, and feelings of self-worth.

> *Experiencing closeness; affection blanket:* The object of this exercise is to encapsulate the group member in affection and "unconditional positive regard." Recipients of feedback are simply to receive the information from other members and to "sit with it." A nonverbal accompaniment is accomplished by members receiving feedback being in the center of the group and receiving physical "stroking" of some nature, i.e., holding, rubbing, hugging, etc. [The authors warn about pressuring the person to whom touching is very threatening.]

The Ethical Problem   The use of techniques that arouse or stimulate affective response is ethically equivocal because such approaches tend to offer standards of conduct to clients rather than encourage them to deal with their own problems. In groups these techniques are especially problematic because members may respond more in terms of what is expected or demanded of them by other members (and the group's leader) instead of from inner needs or feelings. The element of emotional coercion is implicit regardless of provisions that members are permitted to say no. The theatrical nature of such techniques can easily lead to their abuse.

Group leaders should resist any group pressures or their own impulse to artificially heighten the drama or the interactions in their groups. The troubling problems members bring are real enough and naturally occurring interactions—questions and responses, signs of support, growing levels of mutual trust, and the sharing and comparing that go on—accomplish what can be ethically done in group meetings.

Ranking of one another by "importance" or any other characteristic is another ethically equivocal activity yet well-meaning therapists may use this technique to stimulate communication. Kaplan and Sadock (1972) describe the use of a similar technique with schizoid patients.

> They are asked questions such as who in the group is ugliest? Prettiest? Least intelligent? Most intelligent? Most sexually attractive? Needless to say, most patients find such queries anxiety provoking, but they acknowledge that they are forced to express feelings that they would never verbalize under normal circumstances.

The use of a similarly evaluative technique was bitterly resented by the following individual who had been in a group therapy.

> Well, there was this group experience which was weird. The therapist insisted we begin by telling each other three things we liked and three things we disliked about one another. That could have been OK but it got out of hand. You know some things were being said that were really insults, like describing one very good person as "passive" and "dependent." Whenever a "recipient" took offense and protested, the people got annoyed. They asked "Why get so defensive? It isn't a putdown." When others came to her defense, this leader says that "You see the others come to your defense; that just proves how passive and dependent you are!" That leader was part of the gang, rather than being helpful.

Going Upstream: Ethical Issues in Group Norms

Every group ultimately develops norms of conduct for its members. Sometimes these are dictated by the conditions leaders set, but many therapists try to provide an egalitarian atmosphere by enlisting member participation in establishing the patterns of interaction and socialization within and following group sessions.

The bases for such norms are the assumptions of members and leader. Haskell (1975) described the following ones; each may be considered from the point of view of its possible ethical implications.

1. *The group is wise and offers good solutions for personal problems.* Laboratory studies have established that group problem-solving may have certain advantages over individual problem-solving under certain conditions. Multiple perspectives can result in novel views of one's psychological problems. However, the therapeutic use of this principle skips over the character of logical-rational decisions in the lab. Therapy groups could propose solutions for an individual that may not be appropriate to the individual's

problem; they may be products of group pressures. Group pressures to conform and status influences can actually interfere with rational information-based decisions.

2. *Group conceptions are valid.* The potency of majority perceptual judgments has been demonstrated in classic social psychological experiments (Asch, 1956; Sherif, Sherif, and Nebergall, 1965). These studies show that an individual's perceptions, even of physical objects, are modifiable by the judgments and opinions of others. As Cartwright (1966) asserted, the groups' influence on its members is related to the degree of attractiveness it holds for them. Therapeutic groups typically are preloaded with ideological premises. The leader and members, acting in concert, create a reality for the members who may not have previously accepted it.

3. *Group therapies are democratic.* Validity has been assumed for the pluralist position that countervailing forces within the group will keep power distributed equally in the groups and that: (a) there is harmony of interests among group members; (b) group members all have equal access to pertinent information and are equally informed about the issues the group deals with; (c) all members have equal influences in the group; (d) members will not act out of ignorance. The idea of group democracy carried to its logical conclusion is a stimulus to the periodic incidence of ritualistic revolts against the therapist. Therapists may welcome such developments as a basis for discussion of authority and other transference questions, but their relation to the basic ideology of the group is rarely examined. In fact, the characterization of benignly authoritarian is typical for most groups. This in no way denigrates the value of general participation and collective norm setting.

The assumption that members will not act out of ignorance is not warranted. Members can and often do give one another feedback based on superficial impressions. The cultivation of sufficient mutual understanding in interactions with one another takes time and nurturant guidance.

As for equality of influence, it is an ideal state not often achieved. Group consensus is often subject to power relations, in which the majority exerts pressure on the deviant member or members. The group reaction to such deviance is to try bringing the individual into conformity with group thought and feeling. Deviation from others in thinking or feeling—that is, unpredictability—is seen as potentially dangerous to group order. Perhaps the philosopher MacIntyre (1981) was describing the group problem when he suggested that the desire to be able to predict the behavior of others contrasts with the equally strong wish to remain unpredictable and inviolable oneself. Of course, this desire is especially problematic for therapy groups, in which members are ambivalent about becoming "transparent" to one another (Jourard, 1971).

Responses to Group Power Factors

The potency of curative factors in groups (Yalom, 1975; Corsini and Rosenberg, 1955) has been alluded to repeatedly in the literature of group therapies. However, what has received little attention is the possible countertherapeutic effects of some of the most significant forces developed in the group. Let us consider some group power factors and their ambivalent potential effects on participants.

Cohesiveness: The Power of Belonging   Feelings of togetherness and belonging are important for the group's success. However, the person who values membership is open not only to support, but also to damaging evaluation. Members who exercise their independence of judgment or action or question the group's position on any matter may be subject to the criticism "You are not behaving as we do," with its threat of possible ostracism. A less ethically significant, but nonetheless influential, development is that the group's wish for a cohesive atmosphere congeals into an attitude of defensive investment in preserving the group's emotional comfort ("Don't rock the boat"). Such attitudes demand conformity to the status quo.

Behaving in Conformity with Group Norms   Norms for abiding by group rules (e.g., attending regularly, being as honest with other members as possible, maintaining confidentiality about the content of group discussions, and avoiding physical violence are important. However, helping groups also demand certain levels of emotional expressiveness. Sometimes, these pressures produce attempts to meet group demands by premature disclosures, excessively emotional reactions, or even dissembling. Insofar as many groups' norms tend to be implicit, shouldn't they be openly reviewed at frequent intervals? Is it not unethical if pressures for emotionality are exerted on individuals who are unable to act in accordance with the group's demands?

Consensual Validation of Personal Perceptions   Because a majority of the group takes a position vis-à-vis a member, this does not establish that the majority is correct. Members and the leader influence what is perceived as real and what is held to be meaningful. Pressures on individuals to accept feedback should be tempered by leader-stimulated group self-reflection. Such probes as "How did we come to this conclusion about Tom?" "What bases do we have for our feelings about Joyce?" can elicit reflections that prevent a consensus from becoming a collective tyranny. Also, although transference reactions to authority may be collectively played out in the group, valid individual negative reactions to the therapist's intervention strategies can occur.

The Expression of Emotional Immediacy   Although the rapid spread of emotionality among members may aid in opening up a participant who is constricted in expressing feelings, we may question whether displays of emotionality are in themselves helpful. The release of feelings—the disinhibition of emotions—is a factor that has been recognized as a "ticket of admission" in groups. The danger is that emotionality itself may become a standard for self-expression in the group; this could be damaging to individuals who consider themselves group failures if they don't achieve it. The role of leaders in assessing group members' capacities for emotional expression is obviously ethically important.

Group Problem-Solving   Even though many heads do not necessarily generate the best solutions to specific problems, they can present alternatives to one's self-view and attitudes. Reactions such as "You can be helped; we'll help you to help yourself" are major factors in reassuring and aiding the individual. Other members can assume a consulting role that in itself may be therapeutic.

Hierarchic Flexibility   It can be therapeutic for habitually submissive members to assert themselves, whereas naturally dominant individuals can benefit from increased sensitivity to the needs of other members. Therapeutic groups generally espouse an egalitarian ethos, but there is a tendency to assume accustomed positions of influence or habitual postures of inferiority. Such tendencies are difficult to counter because some members frighten others with the intensity of their claims or stimulate fears that they will react catastrophically to confrontation.

Role Differentiation   A distinctive advantage of group treatment is the potential for flexibility in roles taken by a participant. Members may be encouraged to experiment with more socially useful and gratifying role enactments such as initiator, clarifier, and harmonizer. However, participants naturally gravitate even to such socially disparaged roles as blocker, group clown, or group foul-up. Morever, role interchange is not easily achieved, because a group tends to persevere in perceiving a given individual as being in a given role because of its predictable social characteristics. The prevention of pigeonholing a member requires leader interventions so that the member will not be victimized by such fixed perceptions.

Pressures for Intimate Disclosures   At one extreme are members who sit through session after session, clearly resistant to sharing any but the most superficial facts about themselves. At the other extreme are especially anxious members who may disclose too much too soon, before the members develop even a rudimentary understanding of one another. Personal disclosure is one of the most powerful aspects of helping groups, yet the demand for disclosures has ethical implications. When pressure for emotional expressiveness or disclosure is excessive, it is hard to know whether it is really authentic. A likely consequence is eliciting superficial and inauthentic support from other members. A more dangerous result is that of disabling depression or anxiety in the premature discloser.

The same group experience may have rewarding or punishing consequences for different individuals. A person with intense needs for belonging may respond to the cohesiveness of the group very positively, but another may feel hemmed in. With respect to conformity, one member becomes more accountable, but another uncritically adopts a majority opinion and pattern of behavior. Although achieving consensus is satisfying to the group, it may be brought about at the cost of denying real differences, and this also has ethical implications.

Here is an instance of a group's coercive pressure applied to a participant.

> Pat disclosed to the group that she had grown up painfully shy. She felt she was unattractive, a regular ugly duckling. In fact, she said, "I don't ask for attention, so I don't get any. I act like a wallflower." At a subsequent session Joe and Phyllis reminded the group of what Pat had said. They decided that she needed to assert herself, to get angry and to demand attention. When Pat did not respond to their exhortations, members began to goad her, "C'mon Pat, get mad. Show how furious we are making you!" She refused. Finally, some members began to make negative comments about her. Among other things, they accused her of wanting to stay a wallflower. "Or maybe you like being ignored. You just make yourself into a zero!" Pat tearfully pleaded with them to stop but the group's leader joined in the continuing assault. Finally Pat fled from the room and did not return.

The Ethical Problem   Although it could be argued that Pat invited members' attentions to her problem through her disclosures, the way in which they responded seems overly aggressive. Indeed their efforts were self-defeating if their aim was to help. Suppose Pat had yielded to their demands and shown how "mad" they were making her; would this have been helpful to her? Group insistence on emotional catharsis often leads to a response motivated not so much by one's own inner concerns as by a wish to appease the group or escape criticism. A related element is the fear of ostracism for failure to accede to the group's demands. Especially important in this instance is the group leader's failure to correctly assess Pat's emotional status or to deflect the group pressures that were directed at her.

> A college girl participated in a therapy group conducted at the University Counseling Center. She sought help because she was unhappy in her sophomore year. She felt homesick and inadequate in coping with the social situations in which she found herself. She worried that her academic performance was poorer than her parents had expected. Joan said that the members got on the subject of parents and demands of parents for a high level of academic achievement. As the session progressed, the leader suggested that some members really resented their parents. The discussion became more intense as several members vied with one another in saying how much they hated their parents. The leader said that each member should tell something about their parents that made them hateful. Joan objected. She said, "No, I don't hate my parents; or my brother or sister for that matter, I love them!" The group fell silent as the leader stared at Joan. Finally, one member said "You must be really crazy if you feel that way!" Joan heard murmured agreement from other members. She looked at the leader who just shrugged. She left the group and subsequently sought individual therapy. She asked her therapist, "Who was crazy—me or them?"

The Ethical Problem Ambivalent, conflicting feelings are the stuff of therapeutic interaction. Therefore, groups take up, elaborate and even magnify their resentments, especially those that are shared. It is often therapeutic for an individual to experience the sharing of resentment or even stronger negative feelings. On the other hand, groups are notorious for seeking and providing simplistic solutions for complex problems. The answer expected from Joan was that she too hated her family, particularly her parents. Therapists must be alert to the tendency to oversimplify and demand conformity to group opinion. Such a group tactic does not permit members to consider their feelings in all their complexity; it forces individuals to align their responses with those of the majority, no matter how they really feel. A group member complains that his group often goes out for drinks after each session.

> The therapist encourages it because he says that going out together makes the group more a part of real life, and that my protest about it means that I just don't want to be really engaged or involved. They are all in therapy with the group therapist and I am the only one who is not. So they could feel that it is jealousy or something like that. I began to think that this is inhibiting me because I don't feel free to say anything about the person after I have just been drinking with him. When I tried to say this in the group, it was rejected by everybody there. I felt I was going against the stream of the group's norms, especially when the leader agrees with them and he is the one who sponsored it in the first place.

The Ethical Problem We see here the unfortunate consequences of being in a group composed of the therapist's individual patients and of therapist-sponsored norms that extend to outside-the-group contacts. The member who objects to the post-therapy drinking sessions is confronted by the difficulty of overcoming an "in-group" pattern that can diminish rather than help his own self-esteem.

Although therapies almost always involve exploration of client's attitudes and feelings, the requirement that members of groups disclose on group demand is countertherapeutic for some. An individual may not be ready or able to reveal troubled feelings. The therapist's awareness of this is not always shared by group members who may excessively probe, exhort, or even goad a person. An indication of the group's excessive badgering is seen in this demand for a recitation of shortcomings.

> Shelly seemed quite reticent during the first six sessions he attended the group. Joe grew impatient with him and demanded he tell why he was silent. Joe was joined by a chorus of similarly insistent members and Shelly blocked and seemed confused. Finally he blurted out, "I feel ashamed all the time." At this, members began to murmur supportive reactions: "Oh, you'll be OK." Joe hugged him and members moved on to discuss someone else's problem.

The Ethical Problem The instance described is fairly common in therapy groups. Disclosures often have salutary effects of establishing the individual's legitimacy as a group member with needs and motives. On the other hand, the push to make a member disclose may be premature; it may constitute unwarranted pressure that could be less in the individual's interest than for the group's sense of accomplishment. The indication of a superficial transaction is that the group, satisfied that a disclosure of imperfection has been made, moves quickly on without considering the consequences. Was the disclosure useful to Shelly or did it serve simply to get the group off his back?

Group members' therapeutic interactions with one another are expressed in mutual reactiveness, ideally guided by injunctions to be helpful rather than destructive. Their interdependencies are not dissimilar from relationships in the ordinary world where others may be looked to for support and encouragement, but also as models and sources of self-comparison.

Practicing Group Therapy Ethically

Fostering Acceptance in Group and Dyad

Dyadic therapists usually provide acceptance as a sine qua non of a helping relationship. But such a response is not guaranteed in a group. In the dyad, the sanctions of the professional role offer a relatively secure environment for personal disclosures. A group leader and its members also give assurances of acceptance and nonevaluation. However, becoming known to the group carries a risk of punitive reactions by other members and a higher likelihood of breaches of confidentiality. The degree of mutual acceptance in the group is continually tested, and members often try to accommodate to the group. The ethical point is that the group participants as well as its leader should recognize what conditions they are imposing on new members, and that newcomers should be helped to know the group norms for acceptance.

The presence of an audience puts a premium on revealing events or feelings that elicit an emotional response. Expressive disclosures, sometimes described as spilling your guts, may be used to gain such attention. But a group may also pressure a member into disclosing so that they may have a drama to focus on. The anxiety of filling the time— diminishing the panic of a vacuum—although therapeutically potent for some members, elicits countertherapeutic pressures on others who are forced "onstage" regardless of their readiness to reveal troubling aspects of their lives. The therapist must monitor such pressures and their effects to determine whether a member is being helpfully or exploitatively urged to make disclosures.

Acceptance, encouragement, and the provision of hope and guidance are typically most important early on, when group members have had little experience in interacting with one another. It is important to be aware of pressures to confess personal inadequacies, express strong feelings, and accept adverse feedback reactions. The ethical consideration is that members should not be unduly coerced by comembers or by group leaders. Group leaders must consider what premium is placed on the goals of emotional release and the expression of impulse as therapy goals.

Ethical group leaders will respond to the dilemmas posed by the group context by helping their group balance belongingness needs with tolerance and respect for individual initiatives and differences; by using group arousal, but moderating its implicit demand for a standard of individual participation; by trying to develop a consensus that does not mandate unquestioning acceptance of its judgments; by striving toward a balance between expressiveness and vulnerability; by teaching the group how to usefully consult with its members; by encouraging, but *not forcing*, experimentation with status and role shifts; and by monitoring the intensity of group demands for personal disclosures as well as their effects on members.

Parsons (1951) argued that the desirability of a contractual arrangement between helper and help-seeker is opposed by a need on the parts of patients to exalt their therapists. However, according to Levine (1972), the psychotherapeutic alliance between help-seeker and therapist should be a collaborative partnership, based on stringent self-scrutiny. The therapist's stance should be the encouragement of "benevolent skepticism," *not* an effort to get the patient to agree with the therapist's position.

How could group leaders present the procedures of group therapy to a beginning group? I would suggest something along the lines of the following.

> We have considerable evidence that groups are helpful in dealing with the kinds of problems you're having. Sharing and comparing often lead to a significant improvement in mood and abilities to function. In the first few sessions, I'll say very little. That way you can work out how to talk to each other about problems, feelings, and reactions of your own. You will also begin to look to each other for help, not just to me. This can be frustrating, because each of us will be aware of aspects of other members that are likable, but also some that are not.
>
> Try to keep in mind that what happens here and what happens outside (home, job, social) affects what you say and do here. Let's see how we bring those together in our talking about ourselves. Another very important question is how honest can we be with each other? We want what goes on here to be open and genuine, but we'll not push anybody harder than he or she is willing for us to push when it comes to talking about feelings. As for me, I'll come in where I think I can be of help, but not otherwise. I leave it to you to organize because I think that's the only way the group can really be yours and the good therapy experiences of your own making.

Ethical Guidelines for Group Leaders

Various professional associations have established special committees to review ethical issues and develop ethical guidelines for groups. Such codes are typically divided into two main components: (1) responsibility for providing accurate information about the service to be offered, and (2) responsibility for offering ethical group services to participants. The following examples are drawn from the code of the American Association for Specialists in Group Work, affiliated with the American Personnel and Guidance Association.

1. Group leaders should conduct pregroup interviews with each prospective member for screening and orientation. They should select group members whose goals are compatible with the established goals of the group and whose well-being will not be jeopardized by the anticipated group experience.
2. Group leaders should fully inform members that participation is voluntary and that they may exit from the group at any time.
3. Group leaders should fully inform group members of the goals of the group, qualifications of the leader, and procedures employed.
4. Group leaders should stress personal risks involved in any group, especially those of potential life changes, and help group members explore their readiness to accept such risks.
5. Group leaders should protect members by defining clearly what confidentiality means, why it is important, and the difficulties involved in enforcement.

According to the ASGW code, responsibility for providing ethical group services is exemplified in the following guidelines.

1. Group leaders should refrain from imposing their own agendas, needs, and values on group members.
2. Group leaders should make every effort to assist members in developing their personal goals.
3. Group leaders should protect members against physical threats, intimidations, coercion, and undue peer pressure.
4. Group leaders should promote independence of members from the group in the most efficient period of time.
5. Group leaders should not attempt any technique unless thoroughly trained in its use or under supervision by an expert familiar with the technique.

Some Problems in Following Ethical Guidelines

Informing potential group members about group goals and procedures is easily prescribed, but can a leader share the techniques that will be used and the reasons for using them? Experienced group leaders know that members find it difficult to comprehend the rationale for intervention strategies, especially in screening interviews and beginning phases of a group. Leaders' attempts to give detailed explanations are often irritating and exasperating rather than informative, because beginning members are preoccupied with their emotional reactions. Moreover, one might argue that a participant should not, in fact, be prepared for the group therapeutic experience because its effects are context-dependent: telling is so vastly different from experiencing, and much of the impact of the group experience will depend on unpredictability. Participants will be less able to rationalize or defend against unanticipated reactions (whether critical or supportive) than those they have been forewarned about; and the group interaction, to be effective, should appear to be spontaneous, that is, experiences in which the participant plays an unprogrammed part. Finally, the participant is not in the same position as the leader. The member is also not familiar with research and practice literatures. Despite these considerations, it *is* ethically important for leaders to experiment with disclosing as much about their strategies as possible, just as they encourage members to try out new behaviors in facing other obstacles in their lives.

No leader can responsibly promise group confidentiality. Participants are made uneasy by a pretense of confidentiality when they know it is not honored. How frank the group can be and the degree to which group discussions occur outside the sessions is an important issue for any group. Indeed, in what situation is unequivocal and complete trust instantly achieved? The leader can help the group to develop a more authentic standard for mutual trust by initiating discussions of the relationship among disclosure, security, and confidentiality. Such discussions are important in providing a consensus for what is to be privileged: a base line by which violations may be judged and responded to. Ethical responsibility should not be restricted to group leaders, but must become part of the therapy process itself. This is true for stranger groups, but holds even more strongly for within organization groups (such as a university or a corporation). In such nonstranger groups the issues of controlling one's fate are more immediate, and irresponsible talk could have dire consequences for participants.

An increasingly frequent ethical problem arises when individual therapists group their individual patients, as many currently do. Problems of confidentiality may become intensified when therapists cannot separate what they hear in individual sessions from what transpires in a group. From the participant's point of view, the therapist may be interpreting from either or both contexts. The issue of authoritarian control also becomes more salient when the therapist fills the function of group leader as well as individual therapist. Because therapy is an influence process, there is also a danger of encouraging an attitude of unqualified faith as a consequence of being treated by the same therapist. Erikson (1976) said that the ethical position of psychotherapy can be found if therapists take a stand between the extremes of wishing it to be an objective science and an ideology of healthy conduct. If group therapists are able to more clearly perceive and understand the ethical issues posed by context and process in their psychotherapies, then they should be better able to act for the benefit of patients.

6

The Ethical Minefield of
Marital and Family Therapies

For more than three decades family therapies have constituted a distinctive group of treatments. Researchers studying family components of schizophrenia in children, the primary focus of some early work in the field, found indications that family members of many afflicted children often reinforced patterns of disturbance in those children. This impression was shared by several clinicians who became frustrated in trying to help the children. Efforts to treat the family as a group were launched in various parts of the country at about the same time. According to Guerin (1976), among the first to attempt therapy in a family context were Bateson, Jackson, Weakland, and Haley in California; Bowen in Kansas and in Washington, D.C.; Lidz in Baltimore and afterward in New Haven; Whitaker and Malone in Atlanta; and Scheflen and Birdwhistle in Philadelphia.

In 1950 Kluckhohn and Spiegel published their views about family treatment in their report for the Group for the Advancement of Psychiatry. They were a declaration of the importance of redefining treatment procedures in terms of family processes and interactions rather than in traditional psychiatric terms of the intrapsychic problems of individual family members. This effort was motivated by the need to make the idea of working with a family's behaviors, rather than with the designated patient alone, comprehensible to traditional therapists in the field.

By 1960 Ackerman had founded the Family Institute in New York to provide a center for organizing and teaching the methods of therapeutic work with families. In 1962 he and Jackson collaborated in initiating publication of the new field's journal, *Family Process*. Meanwhile, in 1957 the first public presentation and discussion of family approaches and methods took place at a panel organized for the orthopsychiatry meetings that year. The Philadelphia Family Institute was formed in 1964, and about the same time, Boszormenyi-Nagy and Framo (1965) collected reports of much of the family work being done in various parts of the country in their *Intensive Family Therapy*.

It appears that clinicians' frustration with the apparent failures of traditional methods of treatment was not limited to work with schizophrenics. Similar experiences resulted in trying to deal with delinquent children and their families. The problems of the severely delinquent children of Wiltwyck school, where Minuchin and Rabkin worked, propelled them toward using a total family approach. They, too, had concluded that it was ineffective to try to change the child outside the family context. Meanwhile, Ackerman, trained as an analyst, independently came to the conclusion during his work at the Southard School of the Menninger Clinic that conventional dynamic psychotherapy with individuals was ineffective. The family experiences were so influential in the child's pathology that they had to become the focus of therapeutic change efforts.

Contemporary family therapy practice is extremely diverse. As Gurman and Kniskern (1981) note, there is no one family therapy model. The numerous family and marital therapies have overlapping but also divergent assumptions about the nature of pathology, necessary treatment goals, and the routes to effective change. Among the family therapies are parental management training, social work with families, concurrent work with several family members, behavioral marital and family treatments, as well as dynamic systems of practice. The definition of family therapy has been broadened to include virtually any treatment in which the goal is to alter patterns of interactions among family members. As Gurman and Kniskern state, family therapies are psychotherapeutic endeavors that focus on altering the interactions between or among family members to improve the functioning of the family as a unit and thereby improve functioning of individual members.

One of the many ideological conflicts between the various "schools" of family therapists that began in the early days of the field is between those who are psychoanalytically or dynamically oriented and those who espouse a systems approach. For the first group, a major issue was their insistence on the importance of transference and unconscious processes. For the systems practitioners, the here and now interactional patterns of the families were primary. Since the death of Ackerman, however, the field as a whole has shifted toward emphasizing systems approaches and focusing on interactional patterns. One influence on this shift has been the general acceptance of the Lewinian (1951 and 1952) model of social change, which holds that change for individuals is most effectively accomplished through treating the set of relationships in which an individual is involved.

Variants of dynamic models are currently found in the work of Whitaker, Van der Veen and Levant, Satir, and Kempler who are identified as experiential, client-centered, humanistic, and Gestalt therapists, respectively. They attempt to provide growth-enhancing affective experiences for the families they treat. Their focus is not on the alleviation of symptoms, but on enhancing the quality of life of family members. Although their concepts are outgrowths of the individual therapy systems they were trained in, they avoid theoretical constructs in their work. By contrast, behavioral family therapists use traditional behavioral methods through reinforcement of positive behaviors among family members and reduction of aversive actions toward other members. This method is applied both to the treatment of whole families and the problems of married spouses.

As Johnson (1986) points out, however, family therapy does not mean that all therapists work with entire families each session; they may see only single members, although they usually see more. A 1970 monograph of The Group for the Advancement of Psychiatry, "The Treatment of Families in Conflict," attempted a classification of family therapies on the basis of their primary focus: whether they worked exclusively from a family-systems position or primarily with its individual members even though they occasionally involved the entire family unit. However, it has proven extremely difficult, because of overlapping stances, to establish firm distinctions or place specific therapists at definite points on a scale of individual-family emphasis. Guerin (1976) also tried to classify family therapists according to their conceptual systems: (1) general systems therapists; (2) structural family therapists; (3) strategic family therapists; and (4) Bowen's family systems therapists. Guerin saw a difference between the pragmatic approaches characteristic of the first three and that of Bowen's ideas of a corrective emotional experience for the family. He sought to build on what he regarded as an inherent potential for self-corrective growth and change. If family members could experience themselves in healthier, more adaptive ways during therapy, if they could reach a positive level of feeling in response to the therapist's interventions, positive changes could result. This more psychodynamic model espoused by Bowen, but also by Lidz, Fleck, Cornelison, and Wynne, among others, views the development of insight and awareness as an essential component of the treatment process.

In contrast to the Bowenian model, which could be described as moderately optimistic about human potentials for self-correction and growth, the strategic model, like the structuralist, is relatively pessimistic. To reach pragmatic goals of better intrafamily relationships, it defines reality in terms that might be solutional for the family's problems. Its practitioners do not hesitate to use paradoxical interventions or other forms of emotional manipulation to bring about what they regard as therapeutic goals.

The structuralists, like those who follow the strategic approach, try to induce changes in the social context to produce changes in individual family members. This model, adopted by Selvini-Palazzoli, Zuk, Haley, Epstein, Stanton, and others, is articulated by Minuchin who argues that when the structure of the family group is transformed, the positions of the members in that group are altered accordingly and each individual experiences changes in intrapsychic processes as well as in overt behaviors. Of particular interest to this school are "enmeshed" subsystems, where one family member has yielded autonomy to another or one member is overly involved with another; and "disengaged" subsystems where one member is underinvolved or uncaring about others in the family.

In addition to these competing approaches to family rehabilitation, there is also a partial return to the traditional view of the psychoeducational family therapists. They insist that primary therapeutic concern should be with the psychologically disturbed family member because of that person's core biological deficit which causes vulnerability to stressful stimuli from the environment. This treatment is typically used in cases of severely disturbed psychotic individuals. The therapist sees as a primary function the communication of knowledge about the nature of that individual's disorder, including appropriate use of medication and effective guidance of other family members in relating to the ill member. Other members are taught concrete problem-solving and crisis-management skills, and are coached about ways to decrease tensions and negative emotional displays in the family.

Each of these systems of family psychotherapy has a rationale for its methods. Consider the basic premise of the Jackson-Haley group, who believe that the so-called solutions the family adopts for its conflicts often become the sources of their problems. Jackson-Haley attempt to provide more functional solutions. Minuchin uses concepts such as "boundaries" and "triangulation" to describe the nonfunctional relationships within the family. Papp (1983) combines the strategic concepts of the late Milton Erickson with "paradoxical" interventions to get families to alter their pathological patterns of interaction.

There has been considerable criticism of the methods and outcomes of family therapy systems in recent reviews. Gurman and Kniskern (1981), Wells and Dezen (1978), Wendorf and Wendorf (1985), Gurman and Kniskern (1978), Walsh (1983), and Lansky (1981) have criticized practice as well as research methods of family therapists. They charge that meaningful assessment of either the biological subsystems of individual family members or the larger social and economic influences on family interactions is obscured by the focus on interpersonal transactions. As Gross and Wilson (1974) complain, there is a consequent failure among family therapists to correctly diagnose or note deficits of biological origin, and stressors of environmental origin are frequently neglected. Briar (1978), Fahs-Beck and Jones (1973), and others have identified cases of family breakdown (e.g., incidents of violence, abuse, neglect, and depression) that could be traced to unemployment but are attributed to either dynamic or interactional patterns in order to match ideologies of the therapists and their methods.

In their evaluation of outcome research, Gurman and Kniskern (1981) state that many studies were subject to serious methodological deficiencies. The few that met criteria of adequacy indicated a superior efficacy for behaviorally and educationally oriented interventions. Parent management training in behavioral principles received the most substantial support in the treatment of antisocial behavior in children, and psychoeducational approaches were found relatively effective in work with families of schizophrenics. Structural family therapy was demonstrated to be effective in psychosomatic disorders of children, and a combination of structural with strategic family therapy seemed to help in cases of substance abuse. Little ground for optimism regarding insight-oriented approaches was found.

Aside from the vexing question of how therapists decide what is an appropriate therapy for a family, or whether a family approach is warranted at all, it seems clear that research does not, at least to this point, confirm the optimism of family therapists in some of the most prominent schools. A barrage of techniques has been developed, such as paradoxical interventions, provocative exaggeration, and family sculpting, but no empirical data establish the usefulness of these techniques for a particular family or its problems. Moreover, the terms family therapists employ to describe the dynamics of family interactions are so imprecise as to mean only what the particular therapist says they do.

Gurman and Kniskern (1981) attribute much fanciful theorizing about families to a kind of professional guruism among some leaders in the family therapy field. "Despite the extravagant, even grandiose claims made at times by certain leaders in the family therapy field about the universal applicability and efficacy of their approaches, there can be little doubt . . . that such assertions are entirely unsubstantiated. . . . The convictions about the efficacy of particular methods of family therapy have been largely based on devotion to a small number of charismatic figures in the field, at times bordering on professional cultism" (pp. 748–53).

As long ago as 1966, Beels and Ferber reported that the clinical styles of intervention by family therapists were marked by highly personal predilections. For example, they described conductors whom they characterized as aggressive, forceful, highly public personalities who often intervened in a charismatic fashion. These were contrasted with reactors, viewed as less forceful personalities. Both, however, exercised a good deal of control over the participants, with conductors doing so more directly and reactors working in less direct ways (they frequently employed paradoxical interventions). Beels and Ferber concluded that the personality characteristics of the family therapists, not their theoretical positions, were the determinants of their styles of intervention. They reached these conclusions after detailed examination of films and videotapes of the therapists in action as well as observation of their work in on-site demonstrations.

It is difficult to overestimate the influence of the charismatic family therapists who have appeared at countless workshops throughout the country to demonstrate their techniques. We have earlier discussed the problems left in the wake of such workshops where a brief—and typically highly dramatic—family interview is presented to eager learners wishing to absorb new and effective techniques. I stated earlier that their brevity and highly charged atmospheres usually leave little room for attention to ethical questions. Whitaker may demonstrate problems in interaction by symbolically invading the family to take over and act out the roles of different family members. Alternatively, he may emphatically express his anger or frustration at the lack of movement in the therapy directly to the family members present. According to Guerin, Whitaker tries to engage the family in an "experiential happening" to elicit some conflict in their here and now interactions. After several years of trying to provoke such conflicts, Whitaker is reported to have shifted from attempting to elicit them to demonstrating his own emotional responses. The premise is that if he as therapist models a way of expressing emotions, particularly negative ones, the family will derive therapeutic benefit (Guerin, 1976).

Whether attained in preprofessional or postgraduate training, skills of family therapists, like those of other therapists, are supposedly applied independently of values and moral considerations, aside from that of serving clients. Family therapists, as others, are enjoined by the codes of their professional associations from making moral judgments about their client's life-styles, sexual preferences, social values, and religious or political beliefs. But this is rarely possible, for ethical themes involved in family conflicts emerge in almost every therapy session. For example, issues of role relationships, mistreatment of one family member by another, differing attitudes about sexual practices, and similarly ethically involved problems surface repeatedly. It is unrealistic to expect that judgments of right and wrong, or good and evil, will somehow be suspended by family members or by their therapist. As Wallerstein (1976) noted,

> Any interpersonal enterprise that deals with the values and the rights and the needs and sensitivities of people is liable to be, and often is, guilty of improper coercive pressures on the individual seeking help; some of the pressures are deliberate and avowed, some are unrecognized and unavowed, [indeed] unrecognizable because they are buried within the framework of the very assumptions on which the whole endeavor rests. We are ethical only when we are constantly worrying about doing what is right (pp. 371–72).

Although Wallerstein was describing ethical questions in terms of individual treatment, his words fit the dilemmas faced by family therapists.

In a special issue of the journal *Counseling and Values,* Doherty (1985) stated that leaders in the field of family therapy have only begun to examine the ethical concerns arising in their practices. Several factors have been responsible for focusing attention on ethical issues in family therapists. First, the rise of the women's movement made it impossible to ignore the ethical implications of family therapy for gender roles; publications by Hines and Hare-Mustin (1978) and by Hare-Mustin (1980) among others, had brought this issue to public attention. Second, a professional code of ethics had been developed by the American Association of Marriage and Family Therapists. Third, changing state laws concerning marriage, divorce, and parent-child relations, along with increasing regulations for marriage and family therapies, stimulated new awareness of complex ethical and legal questions such as the therapist's role in conflicts involving divorces and decisions about child custody (Kaslow & Steinberg, 1982). Fourth, the problem of harms and injuries or negative effects of therapies (see Strupp, Hadley, & Gomes-Schwartz, 1977; Lieberman, Yalom, & Miles, 1973) had become increasingly salient for practitioners. And last, a number of observers and practitioners, among them Gurman and Kniskern (1978) and Margolin (1982), had begun to discuss the difficult issues of confidentiality, therapist responsibilities to different family members when their interests clash, and children's rights regarding treatment.

The special issue that Doherty edited included contributions by Weiner and Boss who discussed the implicit sex-role stereotyping in some practices that has the effect of discriminating against certain family members. In that issue Stein (1985) described family therapy as involving an intersection of a family's and the therapist's own values, and Ryder (1985) asserted that a serious ethical problem is presented by therapists who may cloak their own values under a veil of supposed objectivity in their assessments of family difficulties, but are really neither objective nor impartial in their interventions.

Management of the Family Therapy Context

Treatment-linked ethical problems arise primarily because of the different therapist-patient relationships that are generated in different treatment contexts. Failure to appreciate the significance of such distinctions, rather than malevolent intentions, is the source of much ethically inappropriate activity by therapists in any system. Family therapists, however, seem especially vulnerable in this regard for a number of reasons. Not only must they have good intervention skills, they must also combine these with ethical sensitivity because they need to remain constantly aware of the needs of the family unit as well as of its individual members. To be sensitive to a family's social and cultural character, to be analytical without being destructive, to foster insights that the family members can absorb and use, and to be respectful not only of their potential, but also of their limitations, places a level of demand on a therapist that is perhaps the most extreme of any type of psychological treatment. Problems of fair distribution of attention, of "air time," are especially difficult in the atmosphere of accusations and counteraccusations that characterize family sessions. Thus, a background of knowledge and understanding must be blended with good professional skills, especially a sense of timing.

Within certain models of family work, therapists try to manage existing coalitions within the family, or facilitate new ones to bring about changes. For instance, a seductive alliance may be intentionally set up with the child or children to establish leverage for encouraging parents to become actively involved (Boszormenyi-Nagy & Ulrich, 1981). Some propose the relabeling of behaviors (see Barton & Alexander, 1981) when and if it is deemed to facilitate more appropriate, less contentious behavior. Such relabeling may not be accurate, but is viewed as justified to encourage a family's efforts and generate an optimistic outlook on prospects for improvement. For those who do such relabeling, the ethical question is not that of truthfulness, but whether the family members can assimilate and use concepts that make them enthusiastic participants in the therapy process. Strategic and structural family therapists, who have little confidence that most families can tolerate more candid discussions of their difficulties, use such manipulations to prevent clients from coming to conclusions so discouraging that they could not continue.

As mentioned previously, group therapists face similar ethical problems in what they think they can honestly say about their intended strategies. The problem is perhaps even more difficult with family members, some of whom are bound to be very ambivalent about participating in the first place. How candid can the therapist be? What is informed consent for family members? Should truthfulness be maintained, even at the risk of diminishing family morale and motivation to continue in treatment?

As in other therapies, an intervention that serves one individual's interests may be countertherapeutic to another's. However, in family therapies the problem is much more acute. Consider, for example, a married couple where one spouse desires, or claims to want, mutual candor and full disclosure, but the other feels unable to tolerate such complete frankness. Another conflict of interest is illustrated when family members want to have the behavior of other members changed, and define their participation in the therapy exclusively in terms of such goals. The ethical dilemma faced by the responsible family therapist is that the therapy must meet the needs of all; the potential ramifications of any change for each must be considered.

But what about the situations that have become intolerable for some members? A family therapist may be in the dark about the conflicts among family members until therapy is well along; even then family secrets may remain closely guarded, often by those who suffer most from abuse or other mistreatment. As Margolin (1982) points out, legal as well as ethical considerations mandate investigation into cases where physical or sexual abuse has occurred toward minors. Similar considerations apply to spouse abuse. The therapist cannot know the truth until the family has been seen for several sessions, but situations exist in which the therapist cannot ethically maintain the role of total system advocate because of such abuses and the intolerability of a family member's position in it. In a less severe, but nevertheless painful sense, the therapist may be helping one person extricate from the family. Examples are of adolescents whose legitimate wishes for greater autonomy are being denied by arbitrary parental injunctions and of spouses who are determined to separate from mates who refuse to accept the reality of their emotional disaffection. Clearly, such a view of the various functions of the family therapist is different from the idealized therapeutic alliance depicted by Levine (1972) or Goldberg (1977). On the other hand, therapists in most other systems do not face the complex, often conflicting ethical dilemmas that family therapists do.

The Workshop Problem;
Preparation for the Task of Family Therapy

As we have noted, there are several institutes that teach family therapy, and an increasing number of preprofessional programs train therapists in this specialty. However, as with group therapy training, a great many practitioners, without thorough training in the field, add treatments of families to their practices. A popular form of postgraduate experience for these individuals is the brief workshop, often given at the sites of institutes dedicated to family work, but also provided in appearances by itinerant "stars" for several days or for a weekend. Such one or two-day exposure to family therapy demonstrations of techniques have become increasingly popular vehicles of continuing education and often provide continuing education credits as inducements to participation. But their brevity and the inevitable element of showmanship involved do not encourage reflection about ethical issues. Rachel Ichilove, a family therapist for the last twenty-five years, described herself as shocked by the following incident during a workshop she recently attended.

> This man is a big name in the field, a man with an international reputation. The family were all sitting there and the son—a nine-year-old—hadn't said a thing. You could see that this therapist was annoyed about it. So he says he will use a paradoxical strategy. He asked for some tape, and then he proceeds to tape the kid's mouth shut. He said to the boy, "So if you won't talk, we'll just make it harder for you to say anything at all." The boy just looks completely humiliated and confused. The amazing thing to me was that this fellow had no feeling for what he was doing to him. And you know what? Nobody in that professional group said a word in protest! Afterward, I tried to speak to the therapist, but he just waved me off.

One can imagine that a novice family therapist, wishing to absorb new techniques, may imitate such an intervention style. Who knows how often such imitation may occur with negative consequences for the patients? The following example is taken from an interview with a practitioner, Norman Root, who wanted to learn about "cognitive" therapies with families and attended a workshop devoted to the subject.

> The therapist was a big, booming, expansive sort of person, and I do think he radiated a lot of warmth. He started to concentrate on this thirteen-year-old girl in the family and kept trying to get her to talk to him. Finally, she says she is shy in front of people. He booms, "Why do you think you can't speak up right now, in front of these nice people?" She is first real quiet, then whispers, "I'm afraid people will laugh at me." Then he booms again, "So what?" Well, it just went on and on, and he wouldn't let go. She looks more and more browbeaten and unhappy. Finally, she just begins to giggle uncontrollably and can't stop. She had to leave the room. I think there was a serious ethical problem here and this "expert" was completely oblivious to it.

Probably the "audience effect" noted by Triplett (1897) back at the turn of the century is more pronounced in group therapies in general; but it is surely evident in workshops. They pose an ethical danger because of the tendency of practitioners to mimic their mentors. High-risk, provocative interventions are especially dangerous because of possible enduring negative effects for family members. It seems to me that they have no place in workshop demonstrations. A novice family therapist who attends them and sees such tactics cannot, on the basis of limited experience, forecast their consequences.

As with other group therapies, there is no painless automatic progression from doing individual work, no matter how competently, to effective therapy with families. Elizabeth Darcy reflects on her own transition.

> In contrast to how I feel about my individual work, I am often confused when I deal with family issues. A good part of the time I seem to simply be a kind of traffic cop; I sort of have to direct traffic and sort out what is going on for them as well as for myself. I get caught up in my own feelings of frustration—even anger—when they abuse each other. They really do behave badly to one another. I have to keep asking myself, what do they need from me at this very moment? What can I say or do so that they can take away something positive from this? I know timing is important in every therapy session, but it seems so much more so in work with families. I've done lots of individual work and I've led a number of therapy groups, but family work is a much tougher assignment.

The decision to propose family rather than other forms of treatment is in itself crucial. Although there are no absolutely reliable criteria, clinicians should be able to make that decision by a careful assessment of the problems confronted by family members and a judgment of reasonably good prognoses for such treatment. Because family therapists face tasks markedly different from those of dyadic or "stranger" group therapists—often they involve trying to change the quality of interactions of family members toward more harmonious and cooperative behaviors—they must be especially aware of the limits of their own backgrounds and competence. Practitioners in other systems must try to secure adequate training experiences so that they can responsibly work with family units.

One of the greatest challenges facing family therapists is to understand the changes that beset contemporary families in our society. Economic and social pressures on families are important influences, if not determiners, on the mental states of members. Consider, for example, the unresolved issues about norms governing relationships between generations, those between males and females, doubts about the validity of such traditional values as fidelity. All of these become issues in a treatment aimed at ameliorating anxiety, guilt, depression, hostility, and other classic symptomatology. In trying to help a family grapple successfully with such problems, the therapist may be confronted with social or economic factors that have powerful effects on the symptoms themselves. More than other therapists, the family therapist deals with combinations of psychological and social stressors.

Participation in Family Therapy; The Issue of Informed Consent

Informed consent is difficult to implement in psychotherapies. It implies conscious decision making by patients who are presumed to be aware of and to comprehend all relevant information regarding the nature of the intended therapy procedures, the risks involved, and to some degree the probable outcomes. For family therapies, obtaining informed consent is especially problematic because its procedures are, as stated, not at all standard; the risks involved depend on such factors as the types of interventions employed by the particular therapist, and, of course, the severity of the family's disorder.

Hare-Mustin (1978, 1980) and Everstine et al. (1980) have several recommendations for ethically responsible orientations of clients to family treatment:

1. A full explanation of the procedures of the therapy and their purposes.
2. Discussion about the qualifications of the therapist and the role to be taken by the therapist in sessions.
3. Disclosure of anticipated discomforts and risks as well as benefits.
4. Exploring alternative treatments and referral sources that may be available and better suited to the needs of the client family.
5. Establishing a firm understanding that individual and family members of the whole family may discontinue treatment whenever they wish.

The requirement that a therapist should provide accurate and honest descriptions of the intended procedures presents an overwhelming, if not impossible, challenge for the strategic family therapist who will attempt to mobilize the oppositional tendencies of various family members through "paradoxical" interventions and interpretations. To forecast such intervention strategies is actually to doom the possibility of their effectiveness, in the views of practitioners. (See, in this connection, Bodin, 1981; Stanton, 1981; Watzlawick, Weakland, & Fisch, 1974.) Therapists who practice according to such principles would naturally want less conscious awareness of their strategies by clients than those who make no such use of paradox. By contrast, Patterson, Reid, Jones, and Conger

(1975) assert that they practice according to above-board principles of behavior modification and can fully inform their clients about what they will do.

Because family treatments often involve minor children, family therapists may need to be sensitive to their specially vulnerable position vis-à-vis other family members. According to Lo Cicero (1976), it is important to describe what will occur in the family sessions in a simplified way that the child can understand. He recommends reviewing what has been proposed so that it is established that the child understands at least some important aspects of the therapy.

There is a likelihood that family therapy can lead to outcomes not desired by particular family members. Rarely are all members equally enthusiastic about the prospect of treatment; some are bound to be more reluctant than others. A therapist should consider such feelings and allow the reluctant family member to take an observer role, at least temporarily, or, in the event of sustained resistance, offer treatment alternatives if they seem indicated. Other therapists may be willing to treat individual members of families instead of insisting on treating the entire unit. A related issue arises when and if one of the family members wishes to terminate treatment "prematurely." Why should this mandate the disruption of therapy for the remaining members? Fortunately, the practices of family therapists are so varied regarding total family participation that satisfactory modifications can meet most families' needs and individual wishes about inclusion.

Issues of Confidentiality in Family Therapies

How do standards of confidentiality in family therapies compare with those of conventional one-to-one therapies? Obviously, the difficulties of maintaining confidentiality are considerably greater in any group therapy. The number of different people involved and, in families, the complex relationships among them outside as well as within the treatment context, make it impossible to assure the participants of complete confidentiality regarding their disclosures. In family therapies, the therapist is often concerned with trying to get family members to share the "secrets" that might not otherwise emerge in sessions. However, some therapists recognize that such sharing poses difficult emotional problems for participants and they work with individual family members to enable them to do so at some point in the therapy without excessive and debilitating anxiety. Some therapists arrange for a separate session to explore the personal significance of the secret for the individual. But others reject this, fearing that divulging the secret to the therapist alone creates the circumstance where a secret alliance, a collusion, between the individual and the therapist develops to the detriment of confidence and trust in other family members.

One commonly encountered dilemma for therapists in marital and family therapies is the confiding by one spouse of involvement in an extramarital affair. The disclosure is often made to the therapist alone, and the client asks the therapist not to divulge it; in fact, the client often demands secrecy. Even though the therapist may believe that dealing openly with the issue of the affair could have long-term benefit for both spouses, revealing it may not be done without violating confidentiality unless the therapist has openly taken the position, as an increasing number apparently do, that he or she will not assure confidentiality regarding matters that vitally affect the family as a unit or where there is evidence of criminal behavior or intent. A therapist who does assure confidentiality is obligated to maintain it for each family member and to be consistent so as to discourage repeated attempts to reveal what was told. If the policy is "full sharing," then family members should be so informed. The exceptions of self-destructive or dangerous actions or legal violations will be discussed in Chapter 9.

Although we will consider other legal issues later, legal concerns are raised resulting from violations of confidentiality in family therapies. As Bersoff and Jain (1980) point out, where the legal doctrine of privileged communication is upheld for psychotherapists, it permits them to refuse to testify in legal proceedings deemed confidential in order to protect the privacy of a client who has not waived the right to privilege. However, the patient, not the therapist, is the holder of the privilege; thus, the patient bears responsibility for deciding if the privilege is to be waived or not. The relative clarity of that position holds only for individual treatment, but what happens in family therapy? Who holds the privilege? A Virginia judge has ruled that when a husband and a wife are in a counseling session with a psychiatrist (psychotherapist), privilege does not apply because the communication is *not* in private to a doctor but in the presence of the spouse (see Herrington, 1979). States vary in their rulings on the question of confidentiality and privilege. It appears that not only the ethical, but also the legal questions of confidentiality in family therapy receive no unequivocal resolution.

The Impact of the Therapist's Values in Family Therapy

In Chapter 1 interviewees described the ethical issues they confronted in their practices. Among those was the question of imposing their own values on the clients they treated. But this was one of the most difficult issues to conceptualize and articulate probably because it is so embedded in habitual modes of thought and action and therefore hard to deal with objectively. Values are usually not expressed directly as a position statement but far more subtly in queries or comments interpreted by clients as affirming or as disapproving a particular way of behaving or of being. This is particularly true of interventions in families where nods to one family member or quizzical looks to another are seen by clients as indications of approval or disapproval.

Values and Marital Integrity

Even the decision about appropriate treatment involves value choices on the part of the therapist as well as the clients. When Mrs. Jones calls with the complaint that "our marriage is going to hell and I'm going out of my mind about it—can you help me?" the therapist may respond, "I can give you an appointment" or, alternatively, "I can see you and your husband." The decision to see her alone or together with her spouse may have a decisive bearing on the ultimate result. Being seen alone or together reflects different "goods" and indicates the value placed on retaining the marriage. Suppose, as sometimes occurs, a wife who strongly desires more intimacy, more loving communications, and generally closer relations is married to a man who could not and apparently cannot supply what she wishes. What is to be done? A therapist may opt to try to moderate her demands or enhance the husband's capacities to meet them. To a degree, what a therapist opts for depends not only on what the client wishes, but also the value the therapist places on individual satisfactions as opposed to maintaining the integrity of the marriage. Stuart (1980) maintains that therapists' values about various aspects of marriage, including the permissibility of extramarital affairs, can have a critical bearing on the course of the family relationship. But, as he points out, rarely is an unequivocal value position expressed. He asks, "Is it going to be a meaningful decision for the individual if it is made by me?" (p. 129).

Some therapists take a moral position against divorces, citing empirical support that demonstrates that persons in intact marriages and families are mentally healthier than those who have divorced or are products of broken homes. One is Bergin (1985) who solicited the opinions of practitioners in his research on therapists' values. He reported that a majority of those interviewed espoused values of monogamy, fidelity, sobriety, and altruism. Bergin further maintains that there are data to prove that mental health of families is contingent on such normative values.

A couple may end up being treated by a therapist whose values are those of a Bergin, who will try very hard to persuade the family to stay together. They could, however, as readily be referred to the therapist who asserts, "If the patient is gravely unhappy in his marriage, . . . if the prognosis for the relationship and happiness is close to zero, then I accept the responsibility not only to advise the dissolution of the marriage, but also to help in every practical way to bring it about." Notwithstanding the declaration in the code of the American Association for Marriage and Family Therapy (1979) that in all circumstances therapists should unequivocally advise their clients that decisions to separate or to divorce are solely their own responsibility, therapists' values about such decisions can clearly play decisive roles.

As Jacobson and Margolin (1979) assert, couples are especially sensitive to cues that subtly reveal therapists' opinions about the validity of their marriages. In response to this very real problem, Berger (1979) and Gurman and Klein (1981) have some suggestions. They urge family therapists to take the time to review their own values and ask how they will affect their practices. If certain values will influence a particular case, they should make these values known to the clients. As Stuart (1980) says, "While [such] statements offer no fail-safe protection for clients, they do put client as well as therapist on notice of the possible directions of value-governed influence attempts, and these [may] help to limit any unwanted ill effects of clinical influence" (p. 25).

A survey by Knapp (1975) indicated that marriage counselors hold strong values about extramarital sex. Twenty-eight percent of the therapists surveyed approved of "open marriages," and 43 percent said they would even support this kind of arrangement for their clients. Bergin's findings, however, seemed to indicate support for more traditional values regarding sexuality and marital fidelity. Although spouses who accept the idea of extramarital affairs should not automatically be denied marital therapy, it is counterproductive for them to be treated by one who strongly disapproves of such behavior. A decision about how to treat a couple when one spouse is openly involved in an affair should never be determined solely by the therapist's values or predilections, but should take into account the client's views and understandings of appropriate and acceptable sexual behavior.

Values and Sex-Role Bias

In the course of family therapies such subtle nonverbal therapist behaviors as who is addressed when discussing significant family issues (e.g., money expenditures or concerns about proper child rearing) can communicate biases about sex roles and functions. In this connection it has been charged (Gurman & Klein, 1981; Hare-Mustin, 1978) that family therapists are likely to express directly or indirectly such biases as showing more interest in a husband's career issues than a wife's; deferring to the husband's needs; assuming that child rearing and children's problems are the wife's legitimate province and responsibility; perpetuating the society's double standard in regard to attitudes toward male versus female extramarital affairs; and assuming that continuation of an unsatisfactory marriage would result in better adjustment than separation or divorce.

The challenge to therapists is to be fully aware of their own biases and *not* to act on them. Ethical danger lies in therapist manipulation of patients so that they will conform to the therapist's biases.

Manipulation in Family Therapies; The Issue of Paradoxical Interventions

Psychotherapists have often been accused of manipulating their clients. By their selective queries and interpretations, they emphasize certain problems or suggest improvement in certain behavioral patterns. With extremely resistant or recalcitrant patients manipulative strategies are more likely to be employed, and since many therapy efforts are addressed to ambivalent participants, it is not surprising that therapists feel obligated to use such methods. These manipulative techniques are practiced in all systems, but they have achieved a certain salience in family work, probably because of the acknowledged difficulty in getting families to change their mutually aversive interactional patterns. Family therapists have been more explicit than others in discussing such strategies, and one technique that has gained prominence is paradoxical interventions.

The idea of paradox evolves partly from the double bind wherein the individual is told to continue with destructive or pathological behavior to force the person outside the pathological frame of reference. According to Watzlawick and his associates, if the individual complies, he no longer "can't help it; he himself is doing it." In other words, in a therapeutic double bind a client gains control over a symptom either by giving it up or enacting it. The key issue is that the individual now acknowledges control over doing or not doing.

A distinguished heritage is claimed for the use of paradox. Alfred Adler employed the technique by giving his patients "permission" to have their symptoms, getting them to exaggerate these symptoms and directing them to repeatedly engage in symptomatic behavior, suggesting that they even refine and "improve" their symptomatic performances by redefining such behaviors as positive rather than negative, and predicting the symptom's continuation. Opposition in the patients would impel them to disobey their therapist's instructions with consequent improvement.

According to Weeks and L'Abate (1982), a rationale for the success of such techniques was developed by Dunlap (1928, 1930), who called his method negative practice. He employed it effectively in cases of stuttering, enuresis, and compulsive nail-biting. In his 1946 book Dunlap stated that the general principle involved making efforts to do, instead of avoiding the things that one has been doing. It brings under voluntary control responses that have been until now involuntary. The analyst Rosen (1953) also used paradox with his psychotic patients, instructing them to act crazy. As he said, "Your boldness indicates to the patient that you are willing to take a chance [in] making him act crazy because you are convinced that he no longer can . . . perhaps it has to do with the patient's sense of choice when you ask him to do something foolish." Even the existential therapist Frankl (1960) endorsed forms of paradox for therapeutic work, saying that he sometimes urged his patients to "will" their symptoms to occur because "if we succeed in bringing the patient to the point where he ceases to flee from or to fight his symptoms, but, on the contrary, even exaggerates them . . . the symptoms may diminish and the patient is no longer haunted by them."

Paradoxical interventions may take extreme forms as in the techniques described by Farrelly and Brandsma (1974) who use such "humorous" instructions as telling a suicidal patient to place her arm in a vice to be better able to cut it off with a hacksaw. Of course, the intention is to get the individual to discontinue self-destructive behaviors when the therapist provocatively urges their exaggeration. They also purposely use ridicule, mimicry, sarcasm, and irony for the same goal.

As Stierlin (1974) points out, family therapists have been quite explicit about the use of paradox to change pathological patterns of interactions among family members. Probably more than others, they have emphasized this strategy, ostensibly for the benefit of family members and to counter the family's pathologic wielding of power and control over its members. Among family therapists, Selvini-Palazzoli and her group (1978) and Haley (1963, 1976) are probably best known for their uses of paradox. Weeks and L'Abate (1982) described the paradoxical techniques employed by family therapists; among them are "reframing" the victim's powerlessness by the device of congratulating the person on being able to take on status through martyrdom, suggesting only half in jest that the individual enjoys the feelings of potency in being a martyr and could do so even better. Other family members are encouraged to escalate their reciprocal role-fixed behaviors of "taking care of you as though you were a child."

Selvini-Palozzoli (1982) rationalized paradox as follows: "What we are interested in is that the family should receive information that shakes them up . . . when it is totally unexpected, it is stupefying and productive of effects." What is stupefying, of course, is the therapist's instruction or interpretation that is so in contradiction to the premises of family members. As the author says, "It places them (the family members) in checkmate."

Two different types of paradox are employed by family therapists. Compliance-based paradox is used so that the family will find it impossible to comply with the prescribed behaviors, or so the prescription creates an aversive or otherwise untenable situation. Defiance-based paradox is employed so that the family will actively oppose and deliberately sabotage the prescription. This is reckoned as a success because the therapist naturally does not want them to carry out the prescription.

Clearly, paradox is not resorted to when clients are cooperating in their treatments and where therapeutic alliances function well. Instead, it is used to break the repetitive destructive patterns that seem so recalcitrant, especially in families. Many family therapists believe that some families need to be jolted out of their pathological patterns. As Bloch (1983) notes, people in families do things that don't seem to make sense, and they are often insistent on frustrating their therapists. They must be routed out of their established behavior patterns because they cling to the very ones that make them miserable and incapacitate them. Papp (1983) says that the family often seems to have a strong investment in keeping its symptomatology and not openly acknowledging it. In her own modification of the Italian School of Family Therapy's approach to paradox in family therapy, Papp employs an observing group of professionals to amplify it or to add drama to the "enactments" of the family.

Such techniques inevitably raise the question of truthfulness in therapy. According to Papp and her associates, a therapeutic truth is not at all objective validity, but rather a truth found to be useful in promoting the therapeutic change deemed essential to the family's mental health or its individual members. Obviously, more sophisticated families may conclude that they are being conned, however benignly. Because they have confidence in their therapist, they are likely to decide, "OK, we'll play along because you seem to believe that it will help us with our problems."

Weeks and L'Abate (1982) acknowledge that many paradoxical prescriptions seem absurd and therapists who use them may have to suppress their own laughter when they give them. But they are serious about their purposes, cautioning, "We tend to appear very solemn in disclosing our own impotence to alter the pathology and in predicting relapses." Indeed, they suggest that novice "paradoxers" should perfect their role play through practicing in front of video cameras.

Family therapists do not all hold the same view of paradoxical strategies. For instance, those who emphasize building on trust and intimacy find such techniques altogether repugnant and unethical. For them they are the opposite of honest self-disclosure. Paradox is the epitome of controlling rather than cooperative relating. Whan (1983) criticizes the techniques as parodies of the same kinds of secretive and Machiavellian relations characteristic of pathological families. Maranhao (1984) accuses those who use such devices of dumping the ethical foundations of therapeutic values in their overeagerness to achieve pragmatic results. These techniques are clearly at odds with goals of promoting authentic relating among family members. That they appear to work does not, in itself, justify their use, according to Doherty (1985). Any decisions about a particular intervention should be based on careful consideration of its ethics, not just on a pragmatic basis that it does indeed move things along or shakes up the status quo.

The ethical problem becomes more sharply etched if one imagines being treated by such disingenuous methods. We might recall Hamlet's caustic retort to his two would-be helpers Rosenkranz and Guildenstern, "You cannot play upon this poor instrument, yet you would play upon me!" Perhaps as one of my interviewees, Frank Partin, a family therapist himself, suggests, the fear of being so manipulated is the reason family therapists themselves seek one-to-one therapy when they or their family members have psychological problems and avoid family therapies. Deception in a therapy context is not a trivial issue. Perhaps, as Rosenbaum (1982) observes, some family therapists aspire to be magicians who practice the trick of producing a wondrous array of rabbits and other surprises when they say they have nothing up their sleeves.

Weeks and L'Abate defend paradoxical therapy from the accusation that it encourages deceitfulness by saying that the purpose of a therapy intervention is, after all, to change a behavior. One does this by changing a frame of reference and consequently employs paradox to alter the meaning of an action. Although paradoxical statements may not be true, clients perceive them as benevolent lies used out of kindness. The problem, as they see it, is an empirical, not an ethical one. They argue that so-called linear therapists lie when they falsely offer an optimistic view of prognoses or when they employ methods that have little chance for success.

Despite such disclaimers, authenticity remains a serious ethical question. Can truthfulness be dismissed as impractical or irrelevant in such a vitally influential process as psychotherapy? Whether paradox is effective may be a technical question, but whether it should be employed at all is an ethical one. That all forms of psychotherapy may be guilty of employing subtly coercive methods and of degrees of subtle manipulation does not justify a blatant disregard for values of truthfulness and authenticity in the therapeutic relationship. It is, of course, important to recognize that not all users of paradox do so heedless of its possible adverse consequences. For example, the well-known family therapist Madanes (1981) urged her colleagues never to use such methods in families that had histories of violence and abusive behaviors toward one another because such families might latch on to the prescriptions as justification for even more destruction; she suggested reserving them instead for "helpful and loving" families. Of course, these are precisely the families one would have thought did not require such techniques to deal with their problems.

In Chapter 2 we examined the deterioration or negative effects that can result from therapists' interventions. Our discussion concerned casualties in various therapies, yet it is important to point out that Gurman and Kniskern (1978) found that from 5 to 10 percent of patients or marital or family relationships actually worsen in conjunction with their marital or family treatments. Although it is no more possible from their findings to indict therapists as directly responsible for these effects than it was from other studies of the occurrence of deterioration or casualties in psychotherapy, these figures are surely grounds for concern. And, as Gurman and Kniskern (1978) add, their figures may actually represent an under- rather than an overestimate since much of the research was done by professionals who are themselves strongly biased toward family therapy.

As in other deterioration effects studies, negative outcomes were associated with a therapist's poor interpersonal skills, a tendency to prematurely attack loaded issues, inadequate guidance, especially at the therapy's inception, lack of support for family members, and failures to intervene appropriately. We may add overly charismatic and cavalier attitudes and the unwarranted imposition of values on the family. To what extent casualties may result from such manipulative techniques as paradoxical interpretations is as yet unknown.

Family therapies pose difficult ethical dilemmas for the practitioner because they are treatments of a group of individuals with enduring vital relationships to one another. These therapies inevitably touch on core issues of fidelity and trust, dominance and submission, autonomy and control, and intergenerational commitments to love and caring. Families come with problems, and the "expert" has tremendous potential influence on them in their agonized search for solutions.

7

Ethical Issues in
Organizational Therapy

For many of us—perhaps most—the workplace is not merely the locale where we earn a living. It is also a significant social context—whether we wish it to be or not—an arena where our cooperative as well as competitive impulses are expressed, our competencies are tested, where we interact, often warily, with work associates, where we experience often rapidly alternating satisfaction and frustration. In large and small organizations multiple daily subtle and not so subtle exercises in attempts at dominance or experiences of submission result in psychic gain or pain. However disguised, vulnerability in terms of concerns about personal self-worth and others' responses is ever present.

Organizational therapies typically deal with problems of trust; intraorganizational, interdepartmental, and interpersonal conflict; and excessive competitiveness in the workplace. Walton and Warwick (1973) have identified some ethical issues confronted by those asked to intervene: (1) the provision of adequate and full information about the techniques to be employed; (2) equity among the various individuals and groups participating in an intervention; (3) avoidance of techniques that embarrass, humiliate, or denigrate; and, (4) assurance of confidentiality. Another ethical issue, identified by Miles (1979), is the manifestation of the intervenors' personal values in their activities to a greater degree than they acknowledge or even realize.

Values: Toward Organizational and Individual Fulfillment

What values guide a therapeutic intervention in organizations and how are they congruent with those that actually characterize its relationships, patterns of communication, decision making, and reward system? To what extent is the organization responsive to values important to individuals who are the targets of the proposed intervention? In their discussion of corporate culture Naylor and Mulligan (1986) stressed the need for articulation of the organization's values. They call for statements of corporate philosophy that would spell out the optimal working environment as envisioned by the organization. How will it encourage individual workers to find meaning and personal satisfaction in their work lives? They argue that workplace environments characterized by an emphasis on equity, fairness, cooperation, and trust would legitimize such personal concerns and create a more productive atmosphere. As an example of one organization's articulation of management purpose, Naylor and Mulligan cite the Lord Corporation's creed.

> We believe in the worth and dignity of each individual and in the need to provide an environment which encourages self-realization of individual potential.

> We expect that individuals and organizations will work together to fashion their own destinies and, in the pursuit of excellence, will develop an economy which provides maximum opportunity and freedom.

> We pledge that our business will be conducted with integrity and high ethical standards, incorporating a sense of community and civic responsibility which will balance the interests of all our stakeholders.

Such a philosophy could be a basis for greater cooperation between workers and management; however, adherence to such a creed in corporate cultures is a relative rarity. Members of many organizations are wary of management in the belief that verbalized aims and corporate actuality are frequently inconsistent. Workers fear manipulation and dissembling on the part of management, and consultants brought in by management to solve or ameliorate psychological problems are often viewed with profound distrust.

According to Miles, the functions of an intervenor ordinarily range from direct attempts at person-changing to task or structure-changing. Among the tools and techniques that may be applied are groups for collective self-analytic processes and self-reflection that can focus on group concerns, interpersonal issues, or individual problems. Individuals and groups might be coached to improve their function. The goal of the intervention would be to alter the organization's ways of accomplishing its tasks and collective planning and goal setting to chart the organizations's course. Intervenors use interview results or interpersonal check sheets filled out by employees to lend an air of objectivity and of worker participation.

According to Fullan, Miles, and Taylor (1978), the methods of modern organization intervention are: (1) the application of behavioral science concepts in implementing needed change; (2) the use of internal as well as external change agents to assist the process of diagnosis and change; and (3) self-analytic approaches involving the organization's members in data collection, diagnosis, and action directed toward improvement of the work environment. Its dual objectives are to improve not only organizational functioning, but also the quality of its members' work lives.

Therapeutic Goals of Interventions in Organizations

It is generally recognized that the workplace can become a source of intolerable psychological stress, an arena for abrasive and demoralizing interactions. Resultant symptoms may be marked withdrawal and apathy among workers, noncooperation among units that nominally collaborate for the good of the whole, and counterproductive competitiveness between individuals at all levels. Some individuals may quietly suffer their debilitating anxieties and stresses; however, inner conflicts, lowered self-esteem, frustrated ambitions, and various other life stresses will reduce personal productivity or even find expression in dysfunctional relationships with adverse effects on an entire organizational unit.

Therapeutic interventions in organizations attempt to ameliorate such problems or promote such goals as greater work satisfaction, usually in the interest of better morale and improved productivity levels. However, such intervention efforts—whether for remediation or for growth—are subject to even greater moral ambiguities than in psychotherapy. For example, intervention is almost invariably sponsored by authorities who have considerable "fate control" over the lives of participants. Often the targets of change do not participate in the choice of goals and the procedures do not accommodate their wishes or vulnerabilities. As Warwick (1978) points out, interpretation of the intervention consequences is also left to the intervenor or the sponsor, and it may be at odds with the perception of those who participate in and are most affected by the intervention.

Miles (1979) has outlined some of the most salient and complex ethical challenges concerning the goals of these interventions. Perhaps the most difficult question is whose goals are being worked at and whose agent the consultant really is. Intervenors may hold humanistic values regarding the quality of work life, the importance of individual needs, contrasts between authoritarian Theory X and democratic Theory Y managerial strategies, but management may simply be concerned with obtaining increases in productivity and hold a much lower priority for worker satisfaction.

The Background of Therapeutic Interventions in Organizations

Early psychological interventions in industry were characterized not by concern with ethical issues but rather with profits. The time and motion studies that typified the activities of industrial psychologists in the early decades of this century left an enduring legacy of suspicion and hostility to psychological interventions. Man–machine relationship studies and experiments also did not reassure workers that management held their welfare and job satisfaction as a high priority. On the contrary, workers were reinforced in their fears of exploitation.

Group formation techniques aroused heightened interest during World War II. For instance, studies of combat effectiveness had shown the importance of loyalty to small groups in the army (Back 1974; Greenbaum, 1979). Similarly, small group applied research was used in the war to integrate air crews in preparation for combat as rapidly as possible.

In the wake of World War II the discoveries of the mid-1930s that informal relationships among workers were important in determining levels of productivity were integrated with a heightened sense of the importance of democratic values. The small group's function as a strategic means to effect organizational change had been demonstrated earlier by the serendipitious findings of Mayo (1933) and Roethlisberger and Dickson (1939) who found that cohesion among workers influenced output and boosted productivity more than the improvements in lighting purposely designed to accomplish that goal.

Group dynamics, which had developed as an applied and research field shortly before and immediately after World War II, seemed to be even more relevant for industry than for other institutions (Back, 1974), and applied group dynamics appeared especially promising for improving labor relations and reducing intergroup tensions. In the postwar years and for at least two decades afterward, group methods to foster desired change were used in government, industries, and educational institutions, as well as in the armed forces. Individuals, acting together in subgroups, learned how to use their groups to try to change the larger social structures to which they belonged. Some efforts to counter the inertia of organizations were made by encouraging group attendance at workshops run by individuals from the same organization so that the participating subgroup could provide mutual support while the changes were instituted in the organization. An alternative was to conduct sessions with the entire organization at its various hierarchical levels, as exemplified by the Tavistock Institute (London) approach. The technique of treating the organization by dealing with various hierarchical levels is also often used today by some organizational development specialists in the United States (e.g., Blake & Mouton, 1968).

Participative Management: Therapeutic and Productive

Kurt Lewin conceived of the group as a unit structurally similar to a personality. Each place within the group is filled by a role necessary to the work of the group and, ultimately, to its survival. If the conflicts in these areas can be explored and worked through, and if the group can achieve a balance with respect to them, it can achieve a higher level of efficiency and productivity in relation to its tasks.

An underlying goal of the studies of Lewin and his students was to enhance the strength and vitality of democratic, rather than autocratic, forms of management (recall the postwar atmosphere of democratic optimism). From Lewin's point of view, it was important for individuals in organizations (whether large or small) to feel that they had a vital role in decision-making processes. Lewin's students also conducted experiments with groups to determine how group actions could be more effective. Bavelas (1950) and Leavitt (1951) found a hierarchical structure more efficient in finding solutions to simple problems quickly, but they discovered that such a structure also resulted in low morale in those not centrally involved in the decision-making process. Despite its reduced efficiency, the more complete communication structure, corresponding to the most democratic and participatory form of interaction, led to higher morale.

During the 1960s and early 1970s, some industrial and educational organizations were hiring consultants to conduct growth groups on the assumption that such experiences would benefit the organization. The explosive proliferation of these programs marked an increasing tendency to interpret workplace as well as personal problems in psychotherapeutic terms rather than as economic or social difficulties. Such interventions were intended primarily to foster growth rather than remedy malfunctioning and were initiated by many imaginative organizations.

However, the recreational ambience of some of these interventions was not concomitant with the original aims of the sponsoring organizations. Esalen, a resort in California, drew considerable criticism in the 1960s and 1970s for its growth groups for managers. There was much satire about "touchy-feely" groups, but managers also became fearful of the possibility of damaging psychological consequences to themselves and those who they referred for such programs. Unfortunately, the attributions of Esalen became attached to the whole idea of group interventions, and ultimately to almost all therapylike interventions in industry.

From their inception most group interventions were characterized by a dialectic of tension between a focus on individuals (feelings, attitudes, reactions, values) and a focus on process (communication patterns, sociometrically measured preferences, leadership and influence, roles taken or assigned). However, it proved easier to change one's own behavior and perhaps to influence others in one's personal sphere or family than to change workplaces or social institutions.

The original notion had been to change through experiential learning, allowing participants to experience their values along with improving their skills. This process was intended to enlarge individual autonomy, but it could also be used for other less desirable, unethical purposes. For instance, the methods employed by Albert Speer in organizing German armament industries for greater productivity during World War II were characterized as essentially democratic and participative. In reshaping the German armament industry, Speer, emphasizing norms of openness, participation, and flexibility, created a vital problem-solving and self-renewing organizational complex. There was, however, no questioning of moral issues or the worthiness of goals.

Those who apply therapies in organization contexts have remained primarily concerned with issues of motivation, conflict, and morale. The egalitarian values of many intervenors are buttressed by research demonstrating the frequent effectiveness of democratic group methods for mutual aid, especially morale raising. A coherent conception of therapeutic intervention in organizations arose in the 1960s called Organizational Development (OD). It is also currently known as Human System Development (HSD). Its methods are still applied in educational institutions, government departments, churches, hospitals, and even some branches of the military, as well as in the corporate settings where it originated. Because the OD or HSD efforts in the United States have been so influenced by ideological commitments to democratic change and shared leadership, its interventions are intended to be faciliative and consultative rather than authoritarian.

The National Training Laboratories in Washington, D.C., and the Tavistock Institute of Human Relations in London encouraged such interventions, because both organizations shared the assumption that participative decision making fostered a healthier work environment. In their view corporate mental health is attained when workers feel they are heeded by management and sense that they have considerable control over their work lives.

To their credit, group dynamicists initiated searches for answers to questions that remain of paramount importance. They have inquired, for example, what optimal group processes are and how they may be most effectively mobilized for the individual member's benefit. What are the group conditions that facilitate positive change, as opposed to those that generate negative outcomes? To what extent and how should the leader influence the group's processes, and in what ways can this function be shared with group members? How can the group best foster a useful carryover of individual gains to the workplace and to the personal lives of individual workers?

Organizational and Conventional Therapies: Similarities and Differences

As we know, psychotherapies are treatments of psychological dysfunction; however, the range of application of therapies has spread from traditionally recognized symptoms and syndromes—various forms of neuroses and psychoses—to encompass many other kinds of psychological distress, among them conflicting relationships, vocational frustration and disabling anxieties, personal alienation, and feelings of meaninglessness that dissatisfied workers experience. Psychotherapies in the various contexts in which they are administered, whether explicitly clinical or not, raise ethical issues because they are not merely technologies of change, but also systems of beliefs and values about how one should live and what constitutes mental healthy behavior.

An individual or an organization—a profit-making company, a government unit, an educational system—can alternatively be viewed as systems that may function well or badly. Even organizations in which participants have a relatively high degree of autonomy, (e.g., universities and research-oriented corporations) occasionally become the targets of therapeutic interventions by consultants when they experience inner turmoil and dissension. Even well-adjusted workers may feel excessive and debilitating stress and turn to the consultant just as an individual or family does when experiencing more conflict than they can handle. Emotional problems arise because some members may be more vulnerable to scapegoating or excessive competitiveness, or tend to greater self-criticism and be more preoccupied with concerns about status than others.

The issues that prompt psychological interventions for individuals, groups, or organizations almost always include intra- or interpersonal conflict. Therapeutic intervention involves the delicate task of developing more gratifying and personally effective ways of feeling and acting. Whether or not the change agent or consultant is a trained clinician (as many are), the intervention procedures and their life consequences are often indistinguishable from therapy techniques and their effects.

Although many organization consultants are themselves trained in a background of therapeutic theories or etiologies of conflict and strategies for change, it is understandable that they would not wish their clients to feel they are being dealt with as patients in need of treatment. There are sound ethical and strategic reasons for maintaining clear distinctions unless, of course, evidence of identifiable pathology presents itself. For this reason it is important to understand similarities and differences between the therapeutic context where acknowledged psychotherapy-seekers voluntarily participate in treatment and the organization context where consultant therapists operate under the sponsorship of authorities, but influence a broad range of individual and system behaviors. It would not be ethical to practice therapy on organization members under the guise of problem solving or training.

To understand how ethical issues surface in interventions that take place in organizations, let us consider further differences between other types of psychotherapies and organizational interventions.

1. In organizations the decision to intervene is usually made by management; individuals in therapy typically enter into it voluntarily. (The exception is family therapy where the decision is made by parents.) This difference may affect motivation to participate in organization interventions, sometimes resulting in resistance, whether passive or active, noncooperation, and even dissembling.

2. In psychotherapies the therapist is usually the agent of the help-seeker, committed to helping realize that individual's legitimate goals. (Exceptions occur in the treatment of incapacitated persons, minors, prisoners, and individuals who pose a danger to themselves or others.) In organizations management sponsors the intervention. Since the fees are almost always paid by management, the intervenor must feel an obligation to serve its interests. Such an obligation leads to a considerable amount of ambiguity about workers' interests. Where there are conflicting interests, workers are justifiably concerned that their own may be overlooked.

3. A therapeutic alliance—mutual confidence about the parties' interests—is expressed in conjoint formulation of goals by therapists and their clients. Where such an

alliance is achieved, there is likely to be more wholehearted collaboration toward mutually desired goals. However, this is not likely in the organization context, given the problems of voluntary versus "coerced" participation.

4. Individual and group happiness is not in itself a goal of the organization. By contrast, goals of traditional therapies are almost always couched in terms of greater gratification, improved interpersonal relations, self-fulfillment, and self-esteem.

5. In organizations, a norm of competitive aggressiveness is linked with ambition. Hence, a characteristic problem in many corporations and institutions is distrust and suspicion because of excessive competitiveness. In therapies, ambivalent motives are explored to lessen their abrasive effects on self-esteem and interpersonal relationships. The problem in organizations is often one of moderating competitiveness so that individuals and units may cooperate effectively.

6. Factors of organization structure, such as complex chains of command, inadequate communication channels, and multiple decision points, may add to the feelings of frustration. But there is comparatively little concern with structure itself in therapy contexts; the emphasis is primarily on feelings and attitudes. A roughly analogous difficulty may be encountered in some family cases in which one parent sabotages another's disciplinary efforts or children are faced with contradictory demands, resulting in confusion about authority in the family.

7. Although third parties (e.g., relatives and work associates) may be affected by an individual's therapy, many more people will feel the effects of interventions in organizations, even when these effects may be less directly traceable to the intervention itself. For instance, individuals may be promoted or demoted or have their status changed.

8. Issues of confidentiality pose an ethical problem in any intervention that elicits feelings, personal disclosures, and exposes interpersonal conflicts. These involve special dangers in organizations because of the control of some individuals over the destinies of others. The cogent comparison is once again with family therapies where violations of confidentiality can have serious life consequences.

9. Responsibility for a therapy is vested in the therapist who can accelerate or slow down the process to meet the needs of the client. However, control over procedures and pace or interventions in organizations is often shared only with management.

10. Explorations of individuals' roles in organization interventions often involve issues of technical function and effectiveness, not only feelings about those roles. Thus the reactions of others to effectiveness or competence, or their lack, are a legitimate aspect of the intervention. In psychotherapies, role explorations focus mainly on feelings and attitudes about the demands of the various social roles in which the individual functions, with special attention to stresses encountered in them.

Ethical Issues in Interventions in Organizations

Rosenthal (1984) has criticized behavioral sciences for the murkiness of some of its most frequently used descriptors for "desired" social and emotional states. Warwick (1978) points out the ambiguity of terminology about goals for those who are the targets of organizational change. Such words as trust, authenticity, and designations such as a healthy organization are not conceptually precise and are amenable to widely varying definition and interpretation. The phrase quality of working life is no more operational than the concepts self-realization or self-fulfillment. Such ambiguities become especially problematic when an intervention is launched to enhance trust or create a healthier work environment. The language and terminology used in therapeutic interventions in organizations are particularly subject to misuse because the real power relations governing the organization may be masked by seemingly benign therapeutic language such as problem-solving or improved effectiveness.

Warwick (1978, pp. 131–32) suggests that the intervenor should be alert to the following concerns in launching an intervention.

1. Clarification and candor about whose interests are being served by the intervention and whose will be neglected or damaged. As Miles has pointed out, the tricky questions are: Whose goals? Managers'? Certain subordinates'? An entire subsystem's? Whose interests are to be served? Which parts of the system will have their interests met?
2. Planning and design of the intervention in relation to the needs and wishes of its intended targets, not only in response to the dictates of management.
3. Taking care that consent to participate is truly an informed consent, or at least that the intervenor has tried to respond to inquiries about processes and likely consequences. Above all, one should avoid or prevent coerced participation.
4. Consideration of long-range as well as short-term consequences for participants, including open examination of the risks regarding the confidentiality of disclosures in the course of the intervention.
5. Careful evaluation of the possible aversive consequences of loss of status or diminished esteem, which should be weighed against possible benefits from the intervention.

Forbes (1977) says he has found that consultants often function as restabilizing agents rather than change agents, and Miles concurs that consultants are frequently brought in to minimize disruptive forces and stabilize, affirm, and strengthen the existing order. Their real purpose in the organization is not to foster growth and improvement, but to restore homeostatic balance.

Total System Interventions

As Back (1974) observed, change agents have repeatedly discovered that it is easier to change oneself than to change the social units, families, groups, or organizations one belongs to. Programmatic changes, in particular, may conflict with the established order of relationships and values in those social units, especially when the change agent seeks to revolutionize customary modes of communication and decision making, as illustrated by the following case of organization intervention.

> A parochial school system director had attended an encounter group workshop conducted by a psychologist, nationally known as an exponent of encounter experience. The director was deeply impressed by the workshop and thought that the process could be effective in bringing about desirable change in her school system (consisting of elementary and high schools and a college). She believed that it could be a means of renewal and revitalization for the entire system. So she contracted for a series of encounter experiences with her entire staff. A team of group leaders, which did not include her former group leader, conducted the sessions. There ensued a period of great turmoil in the organization, marked by resignations and firings. The entire system was shaken to the point of near collapse. Among the less bitter criticisms was the reiterated comment that the leaders had no idea of how the system conducted its affairs. Demands

for openness, trust, and sharing of feelings were bound to be resisted or responded to as coercive in this hierarchically organized school system. The director, however, never lost faith in her mentor-leader and insisted that had he personally conducted the group meetings, good results would have been achieved.

The ethical point is that the director should not have allowed her enthusiasm about the method to blind her to the obstacles to its use in her own system. For their parts, the intervenors did not seem to take into account the system's culture and needs, but pushed ahead with their own methods. Prior to launching their intervention the consultants should have considered whether these methods were really appropriate and which organizational variables could be changed without damage to members' esteem. Such preintervention assignment might have prevented the disastrous outcome. Tichy and Hornstein (1976) have shown that selection of just which organization variables are important, salient, and changeable is very powerful in intervention planning.

Golembiewski, Carrigan, Munzenrider, and Blumberg (1972) reported an intervention intended to ease the pain of demotion for 13 regional managers from the marketing department of a major firm. Several complained that participation in the project, which involved "induced" catharsis, among other things, implied that they were not being treated as adults able to take the demotion without having to participate. One of them referred to the sessions as coddling and hand-holding. The authors defended this kind of intervention as helpful, and validated their opinion through the use of tests. However, in commenting on this intervention from the ethical perspective, Kramer (1972) asked, "And does the morality of making demotions less painful convert the applied social scientist into an agent of management, an anesthetist, or a 'cooling-out' functionary?" Walton (1978) adds that although the consultants may have been genuinely concerned with both organization achievement and the alleviation of human pain, a broader humanistic concern would have required attention to the fairness of the decisions leading to the demotions, including questions about the criteria for the decision and the review and appeal mechanism, if any, used in the process. Moreover, an overriding ethical issue is that the demotees were apparently *required* to participate.

Targets of Change

Bermant and Warwick (1978) note that the alliance of the sponsor with the intervenor (who has strong power deriving from professional image, knowledge, and expertise as well as an obvious inside track to management) may be viewed and experienced as an unfair coalition because the participants usually are the sponsor's subordinates. Although the intervenor may be committed to free choice and to the idea that all parties to a problem situation must be involved in diagnosing and improving it, in fact, subordinates may not have a real choice to decline.

> A large oil company in Britain had cut its personnel by 10 percent in an across-the-board reduction. The ensuing demoralization was so great that even acts of petty sabotage occurred at a number of the company's installations. A drop in productivity and sudden increases in absenteeism also convinced top management that they needed to restore confidence in the company's future. They engaged a team of consultants from a well-known institute of human relations. The intervention consisted of "open" group sessions for all levels, in the course of which employees were encouraged to air their concerns. The atmosphere was like that of a difficult group therapy session, characterized by a profound lack of mutual trust. The group leaders were not really in a position

to explain, much less defend, management's original reduction in force. While the overall process doubtless was intended to reassure the workers, it actually alarmed them that more firings were in prospect.

The ethical question is whether the intervenors should have accepted this assignment, knowing they could have no influence over the decisions management had already taken. As with the demotees, it would seem that these consultants, no matter how well meaning, were being used as management's agents to calm disgruntled employees.

The Choice to Enter or Depart

Walton and Warwick (1973) observe that once an intervention process is underway, it is difficult to withdraw from it. We must recognize the nature and power of conformist pressures a group almost invariably brings to bear on potentially deviant members. As in therapy groups, departures almost always alarm other group members, and pressure is exerted on the member to remain at least ostensibly involved. Such pressures sometimes have the effect of intensifying the difficulties that led the person to wish to leave in the first place.

Those who are targeted for interventions face several problems. First, the organization is an explicitly hierarchical situation in which not all share equal vulnerability. Obviously, those in a situation of dependency on others higher in the hierarchy may have more to lose from any changes, especially individuals involved in personnel promotion or demotion. Second, persons lower in the organization's hierarchy will usually be told, not asked, what to do. Consequently, informed consent emerges as a major ethical issue. Third, spread of information about participants is likely because of the many informal as well as formal communication channels in any organization. Confidentiality leaks have many serious negative consequences for some participants. Fourth, there is a danger of provocative maneuvers by consultants who have knowledge about workers on the basis of preintervention interviews, or from managers' complaints about specific persons included in the intervention procedures.

The following intervention was brought to my attention because of its presumed ethical ambiguity, not because of a poor outcome. Pamela Shreve, a vice president of a large utilities firm, tells of her colleagues' experiences at the hands of a group of consultants engaged by the company's chief executive officer. The consultants interviewed all the middle- and upper-level managers over several months.

> Very quickly, the interviews moved from technical and organization functions to their personal lives. Managers were also asked to describe their subordinates, events in their childhood, characteristics of their mothers and fathers, siblings, spouses, as well as their own goals. Two remembered questions were "How would you want your mate to change?" and "How would your mate want you to change?" My colleagues were fearful for their jobs. As one said to me, "We weren't programmed for this!" Their permission of informed consent had not been asked. The CEO had simply hired the consultants to do the job.

The aspect that most disturbed this individual was a tactic the intervention team used that she described as insidious. "Just when you thought you were all finished and were just 'chewing the fat' they suddenly asked you some question of a very personal kind." She felt the consultants offered no therapy, but would point out what "you seem to need." "This is what you have to work on to improve yourself, to become more effective," then they would ask, "Are you surprised?" Many organization personnel felt they were being manipulated to let down their guards.

The most frequent reactions among her management colleagues were hurt, disappointment, but also fear. They wondered, "Why does he (the CEO) have to put us through this?" They concluded that he wanted to use it to justify getting rid of some people, but didn't want to confront them on traditional productivity issues. Employees decided the boss was storing the information for subsequent "riffing" and the consultants were a way of conveying critical messages to subordinates because he hadn't the stomach for doing it himself. Participation was voluntary in the sense that one was encouraged to sign up early. Failure to do so resulted in a memo reminding the employee of "the opportunity"! Small wonder that this opportunity was greeted with anxiety, suspicion, and fear.

Intervention Means

As Walton and Warwick (1973) point out, many intervenors rely on standard prescriptions. In recent years intense group experiences involving interpersonal confrontations have been used, sometimes without adequate justification. The problems may not be appropriately treated by that method; one example was the parochial school case cited above. Indiscriminate use of group methods when carried out with colleagues can have undesirable side effects such as polarizations and enduring animosities. Moreover, the choice of group methods almost invariably focuses primarily on interpersonal issues, thereby obscuring possibly more relevant interdepartmental conflicts, technology issues, or other structural problems. Continuing to prescribe group interactions as curative in all situations is unethical because it may exacerbate existing problems and produce others rather than resolve or alleviate them.

Manipulation and Threat: Winners and Losers

Kelman and Warwick (1978) comment that some interventions involve threats of deprivation to induce action that would not be undertaken willingly plus manipulation (restriction of choice often without full awareness) and excessive degrees of exhortation. Particular procedures may be perceived as especially coercive, either because they require behavior members would not spontaneously or easily perform or because they fear retaliation from superiors for refusing to participate. An example is a technique in which members were asked to arrange themselves in a power ladder, a ranking of influence—with one end reserved for those "most influential in the system," and, at the other end, "losers," the least effective. Participants only belatedly recognized how painful the technique was. One member who had placed himself low on the ladder had bitter afterthoughts. A consultant should plan interventions carefully and be vigilant about their hurtful as well as coercive effects; both should be minimized to the fullest possible extent.

Richard Mills, a professional consultant, is a skilled negotiator and arbitrator, adept at resolving disputes. He also espouses humanistic concerns and values of trust and openness in his frequent presentations. Unfortunately, he also sometimes compulsively kindles conflicts that smoulder in the organizations he consults with. His own part in stimulating these conflicts rarely becomes apparent; his unfailing good humor and friendly demeanor belie his sublimated aggression. Probably Dr. Mills is unconscious of his mixed motives, but he is ethically dangerous because he convincingly uses the terms and upholds the values that would lead others to trust him.

Confidentiality

The consultant is often placed in a difficult position regarding the confidentiality issue. It is easy for intervention participants to get carried away by the chance to talk about troubling problems and reveal more than they realize, with potentially damaging consequences for them or others when data are reported back to supervisors. Walton and Warwick (1973) also report examples where managers requested information from intervenors about subordinates' responses as an aid in making personnel decisions. This is easier to refuse if one's prior commitment to confidentiality has been clear.

The degrees and conditions of privacy must be established. The ordinary commitment is that all those who provide data should receive feedback, but circumstances arise that could inhibit this. For example, a manager insisted that data making him look bad be excluded; the intervenor, to maintain the consultative relationship, assented. Should potentially harmful material be excised? How can one know what consequences will ensue if the information is fed back to bosses, to other members—even to intimates of a person described in negative terms? Is there any protection for participants?

Miles (1979) reports that in the course of a research project involving a school system, he purposely deleted some negative faculty reactions to the administrator because it would make the latter "look bad to the central office." He justified this action because he wanted to protect the research relationship, which would have been in jeopardy. What are the limits to candor and openness, especially when it is not always possible to explain mitigating circumstances or affect a superior's judgment on the basis of feedback received from others who participated in an intervention?

Walton and Warwick (1973) report a number of instances where managers demanded information about employees from consultants who had conducted interventions involving the subordinates. They wanted to use this information as data for personnel decisions. Where the consultants had a clear and firm commitment to confidentiality they could easily refuse. However, the problem became more complex when information, unknown to the managers, about the incompetency of the individuals in question came to the surface. Should intervenors make managers aware of such instances? One internal consultant, Henry Rolfs, faced this problem when he discovered that a person whom he was treating for a psychological dysfunction, a manager slated for a promotion that would place him in an even more powerful position in the firm, was actually dangerously mentally ill. In the opinion of the therapist-consultant, the individual was harmful to himself and potentially to others. The consultant urged the individual to agree to be hospitalized, promising to facilitate the procedure, but also threatening that he would act to inform top management if he refused.

The ethical dilemma is similar to that often encountered in a clinic or private practice of psychotherapy when a potentially dangerous situation is revealed. How likely is the danger to occur? Who will suffer the consequences of the individual's action? A therapist is ethically and legally obligated to act in certain situations to prevent damage or even to warn third parties who could be harmed. Clearly, in the organization setting, coworkers and subordinates would be at risk if an individual were allowed to continue, especially if promoted to a position of power and influence when he or she was mentally ill and potentially destructive. The careful judgment and evaluation of the consultant have to serve as the basis for an ethically responsible decision.

Differential Status and Power

Mirvis and Seashore (1982) say that when behavioral scientists leave their clinical practices or university functions to work with an organization they are not fully prepared for the challenge of being ethical in their new contexts. One consequence is that the intervenor may become entangled in a network of multiple roles and functions—both their own and those of the client system—and in conflicting images derived from them. The more parties holding conflicting expectations, the more stressful the situation becomes. It is important to clarify intervenor roles regarding labor and management, supervisors, and subordinates, competing departments, and other interests. The following case involves conflicting interests of a consultant who is an internal employee and conducts an in-house counseling service for his company.

> As an employee of the organization, Ted Jackson is in charge of a counseling staff (six full-time counselors) that deals with the psychological problems of employees, who may apply for help at any time with assurances of confidentiality of records and with no penalty for missed work hours. J has sponsored an internship program in cooperation with a nearby university for training advanced graduate students in industrial counseling. Several interns use their training opportunity and the contact it provides with workers to agitate against production of one of the company's products, an addictive pathogen. They urge employees to protest against its continued manufacture. When management becomes aware of this, J discontinues not only the student interns, but also the cooperative internship program.

What should be done when policies or products that are part of an organization are objectionable from the intervenor's value framework? Is an intervenor justified in trying to change such policies or products? Is infiltration and working from within ethically justified? Is it unethical to try to undermine an organization's policies regarding its products?

Miles (1979) was sought as an intervenor by the Army Corps of Chaplains to conduct a program aimed at reducing race prejudice in the armed forces during the Vietnam war. Miles opposed the U.S. involvement in Vietnam and stated so to the representatives of the military who interviewed him. Were he to be involved in the effort, he would be working to raise participants' awareness about the undesirability of the war and, in his view, its differential impact on blacks. The coordinator of the program declined his services.

In contrast to the behavior of the interns described in the case above, Miles's position was ethically sound. He was straightforward and left the coordinator with no doubt about what he would do. Regardless of whether one agrees with his position on the Vietnam war, it is evident that he neither equivocated nor dissembled, but clearly stated the values that would guide him. One might say that regardless of what one may feel about the interns' objections to the company's product, the fact is that they were aware of it prior to their acceptance in the organization and had raised no objection when they sought their positions. Trying to affect change in the way they did would be viewed by many as unethical and disloyal.

Max Pages, a European consultant (cited in Tichy 1974), declared, "I do not have goals for the organization, except possibly to destroy it . . . my main wish is not to comfort the organization, not to try to reach a new equilibrium. . . . I want to work more on mobilizing people's wants . . . [they want] the opportunity to express their needs. They want not to be bossed; they want to enter into relationships that will not be possessive. This is what I wish to mobilize when I work with people."

Obviously, this forcefully stated position would probably not be endorsed enthusiastically by many managers. It is certainly not a popular opinion, for, as Petrella (1977) says, "Most organizations are 'about' output and productivity. How satisfied people are in their work is really a secondary value . . . if you want to be shown the exit, start talking about humanizing work or the quality of working life without showing that you are deeply concerned about productivity." The ethical challenge for practitioners is in finding a balance between the needs and aims of the organization and the legitimate needs and aspirations of individuals in the work setting.

Consequences of Intervention

The ethical problems encountered in real-life settings take on unique and disconcerting features in the context of an organization. Its workers have positions in a hierarchy, as well as relationships with different groups including consumers, unions, and other institutions and their hierarchical relationships within the organization. Thus, employees behave within an interdependent framework of rights and responsibilities, and their overlapping interests are often in conflict. Consultants constitute only a weak force with limited means for affecting this field of powerful, often conflicting forces.

Bermant and Warwick (1978) agree with Mirvis and Seashore (1982) that consultants often enter such a complex situation without a real understanding of whom they are working for and the potential conflicts of interest. They emphasize the need for truthfulness about possible dangers as well as expected benefits, and for being candid about the risks with regard to confidentiality. Clients and client organizations should be informed in as much detail as possible how the intervention will work, expected results, and what influence they may have on intervention planning and process. Such understanding is the best protection against unethical outcomes.

Intervenors have a clear obligation to be sure that their own preferred diagnoses (such as mistrust, lack of interpersonal skills, or power maldistribution) are tested as *one* possible description of affairs, but not the only one; that data from different parties are included in the diagnostic study; and that subordinates are asked for their views and interpretations of the issues that trouble the organization.

Levinson (1980) points out that we have ample evidence of the pathology that can result from lowered self-esteem and loss of community and peer support. Organizational emphasis on winners and losers and unrelenting pressures for production can and do produce feelings of resentment, helplessness, and apathy. He draws a sobering parallel with those animal studies that show consequences of withdrawal or even death for defeated and demoralized members of the species. It is undoubtedly true that lower status members experience a good deal of stress and perhaps more pathology than those above. But there are no easy solutions to such pathology-generating elements of organizational life. Naive attempts to provide cure-alls such as greater participatory management may result in weakening leadership. The consequent absence of effective guidance can result in even greater individual and group demoralization.

In concluding his critical review of interventions in organizations Miles (1979) says, "We are talking about people's work lives and how they live them, and about the expenditure of lots of time and money. We are also concerned with an emerging profession that is trying to deal with ancient and near-intractable issues in a competent way. The stakes are not small." Clearly it is essential to consider, and to reconsider, the values guiding an organization intervention, because the conceptions of values held by management—the "goods" worth pursuing—may not be identical with those of workers or the consultant. Values are implicit in the methods chosen to implement the intervention and change process. From this perspective, deception, manipulation, and coercion are morally dangerous methods. Consequences must also be viewed with special ethical concern. Losses in self-esteem by individuals whose competence has come under scrutiny should always be a matter of primary concern for intervenors.

Toward Ethical Responsibility in Organization Therapies

Meltzer and Stagner (1980) make the point that organization interventions ultimately affect individuals, no matter how complex the structures that compose the context in which they are applied: "It is the individual who experiences fear, anxiety, hostility, resentment, insecurity, and the other assorted emotions of which the species is capable" (p. 496). The impact of interventions on human beings demands an understanding of the sources of frustration and aggression before the application of technologies of change. The dialectical interaction between individuals and the organization they work in must be clearly understood to influence it ethically. Interventions should seek to moderate the abrasive effects of the power inherent in the hierarchical structure of the organization and to strive for the achievement of work conditions that nurture feelings of positive self-worth. William Gellerman and Mark Frankel (personal communication) are currently conducting a project to assess ethical issues in organizational interventions. Their goal is to contribute to the development of ethical guidelines for practitioners and organizational researchers. The project is intended to

1. Increase professional consciousness of ethical issues and ethically responsible practice by

   a. Stimulating a widespread discussion of values and ethics underlying organization interventions.
   b. Examining different perspectives on values and ethics in such activities and trying to resolve differences.
   c. Identifying those values and ethical guidelines that are generally accepted—and which could guide professional practice and relevant preparation for careers in organization interventions.

2. Enable professional organization consultants to meet ethical challenges more effectively by making more informed ethical choices about their intervention strategies.
3. Contribute to helping organization development professionals achieve excellence in their functioning.

Their project invites organization intervenors to examine their own values and the ethical challenges they confront; its aim of developing a code through participation of those active in the field is laudable. Such a statement of ethics can result only after studying cases that include the ethically mixed bag of intentions, values, interests, and consequences. Because of the complexity of ethical decision making and the contradictory value positions frequently encountered when working with subjects as complex as most organizations, there will be a continuing need for professional education that focuses on case-by-case analyses of ethically ambiguous situations. The egregiously unethical practices and gross violations of normative codes of conduct are easily spotted, and their perpetrators do not long enjoy the confidence of their clients. But sensitivity to the ethically ambiguous and equivocal procedures must be developed for intervenors, their sponsors, and the targets of their interventions.

8

Legal and Ethical Issues

What Constitutes Malpractice

The inclusion of this chapter on legal issues is prompted by reports of increasing legal actions brought against therapists for malpractice. Although most suits are for allegedly wrongful treatments in inpatient settings and treatment contexts outside our scope of voluntary outpatient therapies, some therapists in private practices have been prosecuted for malpractice in the purely verbal therapies.

Many therapists are not clear about the precise definition of malpractice. According to legal usage, if you even unintentionally hurt or damage someone and if it can be shown that you failed to act in the way any reasonable and prudent person might have acted in similar circumstances, you are said to be negligent. Malpractice is a form of negligence applied to professionals. Like all other citizens, professionals owe to their fellow humans a duty of care, but in rendering their professional services, they are moreover obliged to perform in a manner consistent with the way a reasonable and prudent professional who practices in their profession would act under similar circumstances. If it can be shown that a professional therapist failed to meet this standard (i.e., in caring for a patient or client), then malpractice is said to have occurred.

According to Cohen and Mariano (1982) malpractice comes under tort law, which in turn is subsumed under civil law. There are three broad bases for liability in tort law: intentional torts, negligent torts (unintentional actions for which one may be held liable), and torts based on strict or absolute liability. Negligent torts, the basis for most current malpractice suits, include the breach of a duty of care, negligent misrepresentations, negligence causing emotional distress, negligent invasion of privacy, and negligent failure to act.

The bases necessary for successfully pursuing a malpractice action are the same as those needed to establish negligence. The plaintiff must prove that

The professional owed a duty of care to the patient or client.
The professional breached that duty.
Some harm or injury befell the patient or client.

The harm or injury was factually and proximately the result of the professional's breach of duty.

This last element, proximate cause, is defined as "that cause which as a natural and continuous sequence, unbroken by an intervening cause, produces the injury without which it would not have occurred" (Furrow, 1980). In malpractice litigation the issue of forseeability is frequently involved and entails the question of whether the practitioner knew or should have known that his or her actions would result in a specific outcome.

Despite the acknowledged difficulty of establishing negligence in outpatient, mainly verbal, psychotherapies, former clients who feel they have been maltreated are increasingly seeking redress by engaging attorneys and bringing actions against their former therapists. Such malpractice suits invariably accuse the defendant therapist of breaching professional standards of conduct. These plaintiffs often report negative changes in their lives and mental status as the direct and indirect consequences of the bad treatment they claim to have received. Such negative changes include marital or family disruption, depressions (often resulting in self-destructive acts), job and income loss, and required hospitalization.

According to the American Psychological Association (1986), more people are bringing suits against therapists than ever before. Although the frequency of legal actions is still far below that experienced by other health professionals, the drastic increase in recent years has caused the costs of professional liability insurance to soar. Like other concerned citizens, therapists view this trend with mixed feelings. Some see it as evidence of greater maturity on the parts of patients and clients who rightly demand that mental health care should be held to high standards of practice characterized by competence and ethical responsibility; others decry this development as an example of the increasing proclivity to use litigation to redress real grievances or profit from imagined ones. Pope, Simpson, and Weiner (1978) and Kermani (1982) are among many who interpret this trend as a warning to mental health practitioners to review and correct ethically equivocal practices and effectively monitor and eliminate therapist abuses. However, legal critics of the mental health professions regard the trend as healthy. Lacking faith in the capacity or the willingness of the mental health establishment to police its members, they see litigation as a necessary step toward reform (see Cohen & Mariano, 1982; Furrow, 1980; Robitscher, 1980).

The most frequent causes of malpractice suits are faulty or negligent rendering of services, negligence leading to suicide, badly advised or poorly supervised treatments (medications or techniques with somatic effects are frequent causes), failure to appropriately supervise a patient known to be disturbed, failure to consult, abandonment, and improper or unprofessional conduct on the part of the therapist. The criteria for therapists' techniques or actions are that the therapists must have the knowledge and learning, skills and abilities that others in similar practices ordinarily possess; that the therapists must exercise due care and diligence in applying this professional knowledge and skill; and that they must use reasonably good judgment in carrying out the duties of a credentialed therapist.

The Standard of Care: Court Rulings and Therapeutic Techniques

As Furrow (1980) points out, it is frequently difficult to state to a reasonable degree of (medical) certainty whether the application or omission of a particular procedure at a specified time caused mental injury to the patient. Thus the plaintiff who complains of exclusively mental injuries may have a difficult time proving the element of damages. Not only are the allegations intangible and difficult to demonstrate to the judge and jury, but they also tend to be somewhat speculative because of the state of knowledge about mental illness. The task is simplified in cases where the alleged negligence has caused or encouraged the patient to sustain or inflict personal injuries on self and others.

Because the bulk of psychotherapy consists of verbal communications between therapists and their clients, as Edelwich and Brodsky (1982) suggest, judicial regulation may not be able to reach the heart of the problem. Until 1979 there were no reported legal decisions in which a therapist was successfully sued for what was said to a client in the course of therapy sessions. The therapies that Hogan (1979) surveyed included a broad range of primarily verbal techniques, mainstream systems as well as some at the outer limits, such as encounter and sensitivity training groups, est seminars, and others that might be classified as fringe therapies. So long as the treatments were restricted to talk (i.e., probes, clarifications, interpretations, advice, and the like), their conductors remained immune from suits, no matter how damaging the probes and clarifications, how incorrect the interpretations, or how poor the advice (Hogan, 1979). However, this situation is changing, and therapists may find themselves in increasing danger of being sued for malpractice not only for what is said and its consequences, but also for failure to seek and obtain the client's informed consent to the treatment the therapist intends to provide.

Courts have traditionally not taken positions about the preferred treatments of psychological disorders. One can readily appreciate the complexity of trying to do so in view of the multiple methods currently available, each with its advocates and adherents. Establishing a standard, particularly in the mental health field, is virtually impossible. Consequently, the law has traditionally judged practitioners against the standards of the practitioner's own school of treatment. In the past any treatment would be considered legitimate provided that it was a method supported by at least "a respectable minority of the profession." However, in several cases, courts have shifted the burden to the therapist to justify the use of unorthodox methods, and even voluntary outpatient procedures may now be construed as coercive or punishing.

Coercion

The suits brought to courts and many of those settled out of court involved issues of contested hospitalization, inappropriate administration of medications, other somatic procedures such as shock therapies or psychosurgeries, and inpatient coercive treatments. Until fairly recently, the courts were relatively reluctant to judge a therapy as coercive in the absence of particularly objectionable conditions. According to Friedman (1975, p. 62) such conditions had to be "shocking to the conscience," "barbarous," that is, physically or mentally abusive in such base and inhumane proportions as to shock and offend the court's sensibilities. An example of such treatment is the following.

> Two residents of the Iowa Security Medical Facility (ISMF) brought suit against the staff and the state because of their subjection to apomorphine, a morphine-based vomiting-inducing drug, as part of an aversive conditioning program to deal with behavioral problems. The drug was injected for such infractions as not getting up, for swearing, lying, giving cigarettes to other patients without permission, even for talking without

permission. The court refused to accept ISMF's assertion that administration of the drug, in the absence of informed consent, was acceptable treatment, adding in its judgment, "whether it is called aversive stimuli or punishment, the act of forcing someone to vomit for a fifteen-minute period for committing some minor breach of rules can only be regarded as cruel and unusual unless the treatment is being administered to a patient who knowingly and intelligently has consented to it" (*Knecht v. Gillman*, 1973).

In this case there appeared to be some confusion between treatment and punishment in the minds of the therapists. Some overlap exists even in verbal psychotherapies. But as Finkel (1982) notes, the layperson has little problem in distinguishing between therapy and punishment even though experiencing some difficulty in putting this distinction into words. It is quite clear that one helps while the other hurts. One is undertaken in the name of rehabilitation; the other seems to serve the purpose of retribution. Finkel asserts that some therapists who use primarily verbal therapies seem to mix opposites—therapy and punishment—in the name of benevolence to the point where courts are asked to look into the "haze, maze, irony, and poignancy" of "therapy-punishment." Psychological, as well as physical, coercion can be hurtful to the patient. Although psychological coercion poses significant ethical problems, as we have seen in our discussion of the various therapies, these have rarely been grounds for legal actions. More frequently there is psychological persuasion or intimidation that eventually veer toward physical coercion or abuse.

Therapeutic Abuse and Sexual Exploitation

Negligence, coercion, and abuse are, of course, not the same, but angry and upset clients may not make these distinctions. Verbal abuse in the past has not been held to constitute evidence of malpractice.

> As a patient, Mr. Hess claimed in his suit against Dr. Frank, his psychotherapist, that the latter had repeatedly uttered obscenities at him. But the court dismissed the claim since, according to its judgment, the psychiatrist had, in fact, rendered the services agreed on. In an appellate court ruling, it was held that negligence implies the failure to exercise requisite skills, but that abusive language, in and of itself, may not be the test of the use of requisite skills.

Courts have usually relied on prima facie evidence of malpractice in the absence of documentation of malpractice. For instance, under the doctrine of Res Ipsa Locatur—the thing speaks for itself—in the case of *Hammer v. Rosen*, where the therapist had been seen to strike the patient on a number of occasions, the ruling was that the acts were inherently negligent and did not require expert testimony to establish negligence. The ruling took into account, but dismissed, the therapist's claim that his methods, however seemingly violent, had been highly effective in other cases and were necessary for successful treatment (see Cohen, 1979, Cohen & Mariano, 1982).

According to recent surveys of practitioners, a significant number of therapists, between 5 and 10 percent of males and a much smaller proportion of females, engage their patients in erotic contact, many to the point of sexual intercourse. The most recently reported survey, done by psychiatrist Nanette Gartrell and her associates and published in the September 1986 *American Journal of Psychiatry,* establishes that 6.4 percent of men (out of 1423 respondents) admitted having sexual contact with their patients. The characterization of the contact was "contact to satisfy sexual desire in the patient, in the therapist, or in both.'' This is only the latest in a series of equivalently revealing studies of the problem of sexual relations during therapy contacts (or immediately following them) between therapists and their clients. Psychologists have obtained similar figures for their profession (Holyroyd & Brodsky, 1977). The numbers themselves are widely considered under- rather than overestimates because of the shame and humiliation involved for patients as well as therapists in revealing such information.

Therapists of all orientations are aware of the temptations that exist in all psychotherapy contexts. These temptations and their associated ethical dangers are most salient in the intimacy generated in individual therapy, but they can be part of any therapy contact. They become especially conspicuous in the feelings that inevitably are generated in sympathetic and caring exchanges between patient and therapist.

This caring can certainly be described as a loving relationship, but it is a special kind of loving. Although therapy may involve a form and quality of love, it depends for its therapeutic efficacy on a strong and abiding commitment not to become involved with the other aspects of caring, especially physical expressions of affection, that are normally expressed in a love relationship. Brownfain (1971) examined the legal actions brought against psychologists between 1961 and 1971 for alleged sexual improprieties. He asserted that the majority of such cases occurred because women patients had felt rejected when they discovered that the therapeutic relationships were to be maintained on a professionally correct level. These suits were largely unsuccessful, but they emphasize the significance of the patient's erotic transference-based fantasies and wishes.

According to Kermani (1982), lawsuits are increasingly brought against therapists not because of refusal, but because of complicity. It is, of course, well understood by therapists that sexual arousal in response to the attractiveness or emotional appeal of the client is a common experience in the cozy, seclusive, and physically attractive setting in which therapy takes place. As treatment progresses, it becomes difficult to abide by the professional imperative to maintain the distinction between a therapeutic and a personal interest in the patient.

Marmor (1976) charged that therapists who allow their countertransference feelings to determine their behavior with clients to the extent that they become involved in love or sexual relationships with them have failed in their professional responsibility. In response to the claim (which he dismissed as hypocritical and self-serving) that sexual activity with patients was engaged in for their benefit, Marmor caustically noted that it was almost never elderly or unattractive patients who were thus ''treated,'' but rather youthful and attractive ones. While many therapists who confessed sexual involvement admitted that they had been feeling especially lonely, emotionally vulnerable, and needy at that point in their own lives, others said they felt fatherly toward the individuals with whom they became sexually involved. In response to this claim, Marmor asserted that it is precisely because of the qualities of a parental relationship that erotic exchanges with patients cannot be justified. As Marmor asks, ''Since when is it necessary for a parent to have sex with his child in order to achieve emotional or sexual maturity for the child?'' He asserts that such a relationship may be compared with incest at a dynamic level and is therefore an equivalent dereliction of professional duty and obligation.

Some therapists have defended the legitimacy of sexual and romantic involvements with former clients after therapy has been terminated. Indeed, any therapist can point to marriages of former patients with their therapists. Although, as Gartrell et al. point out, it is tempting to try to devise some pragmatic solution to the requisite time period after therapy's termination when such relationships would no longer be an ethical infraction, it is difficult to do so. As Annette Brodsky, a psychologist, asserts, "father-daughter incest does not become acceptable one year after the daughter has left home". It seems that transference as well as countertransference feelings that make therapist-patient sex incestuous are not likely to be bound to specific time schedules. Another reason for restraint is that many patients return to treatment with the same therapist more than once in their lives.

Terms such as transference and countertransference, once quite unfamiliar to judges and juries, have now become part of the language of litigation in cases involving alleged malpractice by psychotherapists. In given cases, the attorneys and the judge will inquire about the dynamics of therapist-patient interactions. They may specifically question the therapist's handling of the patient's transference reactions. They will wish to establish whether the defending therapist could be judged to have reasonable control over personal countertransference impulses, as any professional therapist should.

Several landmark cases involve legal actions against therapists in which judgments were made against the defendants. Our consideration of this topic is necessarily brief and selective. However, the reader is cautioned that the cases cited are dated and presently pending court actions may alter the picture they portray of the bases for rulings for or against psychotherapists.

Cohen and Mariano (1982) have described the legal as well as professional obligation of therapists to provide treatments that are well-fitted to the problems or illness of the particular patient. Mrs. Zipkin's complaint against Dr. Freeman indicates procedures used with her that could not be justified in a court of law. It is unlikely that any treatment involving sexual relations with a therapist could be.

> In the course of therapy, Mrs. Zipkin apparently made declarations of love to Dr. Freeman, her therapist, who responded with his own confession of love. Their subsequent relationship included nude swimming parties and sexual intercourse. On the therapist's advice, she attempted to divorce her husband, and she brought suit against her brother with regard to certain financial disagreements. The presiding judge declared that the therapist's acts had been willfully malicious, having no reasonable connection with professional services. An expert witness psychiatrist testified that this therapist's actions constituted gross mismanagement of transference reactions in the patient and should be viewed as improper treatment. In the final ruling it was noted that "the therapist mishandled the transference phenomenon, which is a reaction that psychiatrists antici-pate and which must be handled properly. . . . Damage would have been done to Mrs. Zipkin even if the trips outside the state had been carefully chaperoned, if the swimming had been done with suits on, and if there had been ballroom dancing instead of sexual intercourse."

It is clear that sexual involvements, having been proscribed by all the professional therapists's associations, will be cited as prima facie evidence of malpractice when damage to the client is established. Davidoff (1973) noted another landmark case involving inappropriate relating to a patient on the part of a therapist, that of *Werner v. Landau.*

> It appears that the therapist, Werner, met with the patient, Landau, in social gathering places and in her home. Despite Miss Landau's expression of shame about her feelings of love for him, and despite the therapist's acknowledgment that the feelings were likely transference-based, he urged her to continue treatment with him. Although there was no finding about actual sexual relations, they had talked of going off together for weekends. The patient subsequently attempted suicide, sought consultation, and ultimately returned

to Dr. Werner in her attempt to "resolve the transference." The court held that the therapist had made a "tragic mistake" by introducing social contact, even though he may have had good intentions. The plaintiff was awarded monetary damages for her injuries which left her unable to function normally. The therapist was faulted for thinking it desirable to take her out when she was already in a highly emotional state and in love with him. The court remarked that he should have referred the patient to another therapist, and the social contact was judged to be the cause of the individual's deterioration.

Proof of social contact with the patient, manipulation of the individual's outside life, and certainly sexual relations may be sufficient to create a prima facie case for a plaintiff even without the use of expert testimony. If the patient or client's condition worsens as a result of the therapist's mishandling of personal feelings, it is arguable that the therapist has breached the fiduciary duty of care. Therefore, the therapist must always be vigilant about countertransference reactions to the patient (Furrow, 1980). The following case further illustrates the consequences of unchecked countertransference.

In the case of *Wilkinson v. Anclote Manor* (see Cohen & Mariano, 1982), the defendant psychiatrist treated the patient with psychotherapy during a period of two years at a psychiatric hospital. It appears that the therapist proposed marriage and said that he would divorce his wife. (The wife subsequently committed suicide after divorcing the therapist.) In her subsequent suit for damages against the therapist, the plaintiff's expert witnesses testified that the therapist had essentially acted out his countertransference feelings toward the patient, and that his conduct was below acceptable practice standards for psychiatrists. The court held the psychiatrist guilty of malpractice and liable for damages.

An even more flagrant violation of standards of practice is evident in the case of *Roy & Hartogs,* in which the therapist was charged with damaging his patient by convincing her to have sexual relations as part of treatment.

The patient had sought help because of her sexual problems. The parties had sexual relations over a thirteen-month period, and in the course of this "treatment" the patient's condition worsened to the extent that she required hospitalization on two occasions. In this case the defendant attempted to establish that his patient was suffering from paranoid delusions, that she had assented to sexual relations with him, and that he was actually physically incapable of performing sexually. The court rejected his contentions and found him guilty. A significant element in the ruling was the conception that a therapeutic relationship is analogous to a guardian-ward relationship and that a guardian cannot claim that his ward consented to a sexual relationship.

The lesson for avoiding charges of malpractice based on inappropriate contact with clients is clear: confine relationships to the office, except for clearly defensible and specific treatment indications. One should keep hands off patients, except for the kinds of greetings, comforting responses, and the like that one would engage in before others. Any physical contact should be in the service of an acceptable therapeutic aim and rationale. When sexual or other strong feelings are evoked or elicited toward a patient, a therapist should seek consultation with those who can be counted on to provide objective guidance and good advice. If the feelings cannot be readily overcome, the patient should be referred to another therapist or agency.

Although there are not, as yet, legal requirements for consultation with other professionals in the event of experiencing strong attraction or other powerful emotions, it seems clear that such consultation could help avert not only injury to the client, but also prevent damage claims against the therapist. Such consultation—and possible referral— may be essential because of a subsequent judgment of negligence in the event of a suit. Just as a therapist's response to an extremely hostile or aggressive client may cause the therapist to feel so threatened that he or she responds in a manner that triggers a deterioration in the person, so may a reaction to a seductive patient present a high risk of involvement.

Informed Consent in Psychotherapies

The origins of the doctrine of informed consent may be traced to the rights of individuals to be free from coercion and unwarranted interference. As Justice Benjamin Cardozo enunciated the principle, "Every human being of adult years and sound mind has a right to determine what shall be done with his own body" (1914). The requirement of a patient's permission before undertaking an intended procedure reconfirms the status of the individual as a thinking person, capable of sharing in the decision making. To fail to disclose the risks and possible consequences of a treatment to the patient is to reduce the person to dependency and render a judgment of incapacity. Informed consent doctrine is both a legal constraint on an overreaching paternalism—through fear of litigation—and an ethical model that should be internalized as one of the values of conscientious practitioners. Furrow (1982) argues that informed consent should be taken as a model for mental health practitioners and that it is likely to pervade consumer awareness so that patients will increasingly ask for more information about proposed treatments.

As we have seen with respect to each therapeutic modality discussed in this book, providing opportunities for informed consent is rarely easy. Indeed, as Furrow acknowledges, the problem of obtaining it is perhaps the most anxiety-provoking issue in the therapist-patient relationship. Most therapists would object that even if they were able to explain complex treatment procedures in everyday terms, and even if it were beneficial for patients to understand them *prior* to undergoing them, those expected to understand and give their informed consent are not really competent to do so not only because of the knowledge necessary, but also because of the typically upset states they are in when they come for psychotherapy.

The ethical and legal dilemma is significant. On the one hand, since a therapeutic partnership is at the heart of psychological treatment, probably more so than in any other form of health care, and because informed consent encourages that kind of joint responsibility and mutual scrutiny that is earnestly called for by ethical psychotherapists (see Goldberg, 1977; Levine, 1972), it would appear vital for noncoercive ethical psychotherapy. On the other, obtaining truly informed consent poses unique problems for psychotherapists. Besides considerations of the upset state of the client, the problem is that the concepts of psychotherapy are difficult to communicate. Most therapists believe that therapy procedures begin to make sense only in the course of experiencing them. Moreover, dynamically oriented therapists take account of a natural defensiveness and ambivalence about entering into therapy that will only be exacerbated by explanations likely to obstruct rather than facilitate its progress.

To such objections, legal critics of psychotherapy counter that more responsible practices will inevitably result from obtaining informed consent; its difficulties will prompt the field as a whole to take a hard look at the relative merits of the variety of treatment techniques; and that techniques that cannot be explained should be reexamined for their appropriateness, utility, and relative effectiveness. Moreover, informed consent will provide patients with more realistic expectations regarding probable treatment outcomes, thus avoiding injuries caused by exaggerated and unrealistic hopes and expectations. If a therapist leaves the nature of therapy undefined, he or she may stimulate magical wishes and fantasies, resulting in deterioration in the patient's condition when these prove unfounded.

Dyadic Therapies

A recent case involving the psychoanalytic treatment of a depressed individual suggests that the doctrine of informed consent is likely to have an increasingly strong influence on what therapists do or fail to do. It illustrates how legal actions in the future may be undertaken because informed consent was not obtained.

> A physician, Dr. Osheroff, suffering from depression and treated by psychoanalytic methods at the Chestnut Lodge, one of the most prestigious psychoanalytic centers in the country, brought suit against it alleging malpractice. According to his suit, he was suffering from a clinical depression with sleep disturbance, excessive agitation, weight loss, and disturbances of mood. He claimed that Chestnut Lodge failed to correctly diagnose his condition and that the "confrontational" psychotherapy given him inappropriately aimed at restructuring his personality, resulting in deterioration of his condition. One of the salient points in Dr. Osheroff's suit is that he had neither been asked for, nor had he given his *informed consent* for the treatment he received.

Other important legal-ethical issues are involved in this landmark case. It is the first ruling of neglect involving a purely "talking therapy." The finding of a violation of standards of care is based on the notion that the appropriate treatment of severe depressive illness involves drug treatments included in or together with any psychotherapy that may be provided. In the past, the "respectable minority rule" has formed the basis of defense against charges of malpractice. The remarkable aspect of this case is that once a large enough consensus exists about a particular treatment for a particular disorder, a practitioner who falls below that standard will no longer be protected by the respectable minority rule, unless that practitioner had obtained the informed consent of the patient. Such consent would, of course, entail disclosure of treatment alternatives.

This case is still in adjudication because the hearings were not held in a court of law but before the Maryland Mental Health Arbitration Office. However, expert witness psychiatrists testified on behalf of the defendants as well as for the plaintiff, and it can be anticipated that the ruling, if sustained in appeals, will have enormous effects on treatment procedures in the future which we will examine in the next chapter. Until now, informed consent would not have been thought to be a crucial factor in the therapist-patient legal considerations. Also, the treatment of clinical depression with psychotherapy alone rather than with the aid of psychotropic drugs would previously have been thought to fall within the respectable minority rule. One has only to consider the difficulties in distinguishing among types of depression, and the fact that so many help-seekers describe their condition as depressed, to imagine the extent of the potential problem, legal as well as ethical. Because the Osheroff case may have an enormous impact on how practitioners treat any case in which depression plays a significant part, it will be closely followed as the appeal process works its way through the courts.

Besides disclosures about intended techniques and associated risks, practitioners should be prepared to discuss referrals, the limits of confidentiality, criteria for progress, the potential for medications or for medication evaluation, and any other contingencies that may occur. It is also wise to establish a time frame for therapy so that client and therapist may together evaluate at certain fixed points whether progress is being made and if therapy should be continued or terminated. A growing number of therapists are using some form of memorandum or agreement or contractural form that requires the client's written consent.

At a symposium during the 1978 annual convention of the American Psychological Association, Cohen discussed the significance of a requirement to obtain informed consent for practitioners.

> I would agree that patients' informed consent to psychotherapeutic treatment should be ethically, if not legally mandated. However, I have grave doubts about how theory can be put into practice in this context . . . how much information is necessary to make a consent fully informed? Perhaps the most basic question concerns the incapability of psychotherapists to predict changes in their patient's lives that were not targeted for change when therapy was begun . . . how precise or accurate can a therapist be in forecasting to his clients possible outcomes? . . . Judicious use of the principles of informed consent may be just the answer to the difficult questions attendant to the issue of control in psychotherapy.

Multiperson Therapies

In discussing the ethical issues characteristic of the various therapies, it became clear that those involving groups, families, and organizations pose especially complex problems in obtaining truly informed consent. The most difficult are families and organizations, because members of groups may, for purposes of informed consent, be treated just as individual patients are (although explaining what will go on in groups often taxes the ingenuity of group therapists). Because family therapies involve each of several family members, including minor children, it is necessary to try to explain to each within the limits of likely comprehension what the procedures and their associated risks will be. Everstine et al. (1980) include the following among the information provided the family members: qualifications of the therapist(s), descriptions of the procedures, explanation of how the therapist(s) will function, benefits reasonably to be expected, discomforts and risks to be anticipated, alternative treatments available, statements regarding the availability of the therapists to answer client inquiries in the course of treatment, and unequivocal assurance that the family or its members may terminate when they choose. Among the risks listed for families and couples is the possibility that therapy could lead to outcomes viewed as undesirable from the point of view of one or another family member, such as separation or divorce, or changes in power and authority status within the family.

Breaches of Confidentiality and Privileged Communication

The concept of confidentiality is based on the right to privacy, which recognizes the individual's freedom to pick and choose the time, circumstances, and particularly the extent to which the individual wishes to share with or to withhold from others attitudes, beliefs, behavior, and opinions (Shah, 1969). The concept of privilege involves the right of the individual to refuse to disclose certain information. Patients of mental health professionals have a right to expect that the confidentiality of their relationship and their communications will be assured. In many states therapists have been granted the same right to privileged communications as physicians and lawyers. However, many therapists as well as their clients are unaware of the important distinction between these concepts. Whereas confidentiality concerns matters of communications outside courtrooms, privilege protects clients from disclosure in judicial proceedings (Jagim et al., 1978).

Although it is commonly believed that privilege applies to all therapist-patient communications, laws vary from state to state and apply differently to the various professions practicing therapy. For instance, in several states a social worker doing the same kinds of therapy as a psychiatrist would be denied the privilege granted to the psychiatrist. Therapists must become familiar with the laws governing their profession in the specific locale in which they practice.

Breaches of confidentiality constitute one of the most frequent causes of legal actions against therapists. The principles of the American Psychiatric Association reflect the stands of the various professional associations regarding confidentiality.

> A physician may not reveal the confidences entrusted to him in the course of medical attendance or the deficiencies he may observe in the character of the patient unless he is required to do so by law, or unless it becomes necessary to protect the welfare of the individual or the community. Where the psychiatrist is ordered by a court to reveal the confidences entrusted to him by patients he may comply, or he may ethically dissent within the framework of the law. When the psychiatrist is in doubt, the right of the patient to confidentiality and, by extension, to unimpaired treatment, should be given priority. In the event that the necessity for legal disclosure is demonstrated by the court, the psychiatrist may request the right to disclosure of only that information which is relevant to the legal question at hand (American Psychiatric Association, 1973, p. 1063).

Similar positions have been adopted by the American Psychological Association (1981) and by the American Personnel and Guidance Association (1981).

Thus, although the therapist-client privilege is not absolute, there is a duty on the part of mental health professionals not to disclose information obtained in the course of the therapeutic relationship. This duty is an affirmative one imposed on the practitioner, and its breach constitutes an invasion of the patient's right to privacy. The waiver of privilege is the right of the client, not the practitioner, and this right is enforceable by the client. Examples of legal actions brought against practitioners for breaches of confidence are illustrated in the following cases.

> The case arose out of the disclosure by Dr. Patton, defendant to the plaintiff's employer, of certain information acquired in the course of treatment, contrary to the expressed instructions of patient Horne. The complaint asserted that the alleged conduct of the therapist in disclosing the information constituted a breach of fiduciary duty and an invasion of the plaintiff's right of privacy. In citing precedent rulings, it was noted, "The relationship of physician and patient is necessarily a highly confidential one. It is often necessary for the patient to give information about himself which would be most embarrassing or harmful to him if given general circulation. . . . A wrongful breach of such confidence, and a betrayal of such trust, would give rise to a civil action for the damages naturally flowing from such wrong" (*Horne v. Patton,* 291 Ala. 701, 287 So.2d 824 [1973]).

In another relevant citation the precedent ruling referred to disclosure of information about the patient to his insurer. "When a patient seeks out a doctor and retains him, he must admit him to the most private part of the material domain of man. . . . To promote full disclosure (in treatment), the profession extends the promise of secrecy. . . . But the disclosure is certainly intended to be private. If a doctor should reveal any of [the patient's] confidences, he surely effects an invasion of the privacy of his patient. We are of the opinion that the preservation of the patient's privacy is no mere ethical duty . . . there is a legal duty as well. The unauthorized revelation of medical secrets, or any confidential communication given in the course of treatment, is tortious conduct which may be the basis for an action in damages" (cited from *Hammonds v. Aetna Casualty and Surety Co.*, 243 F. Supp 793 (N.D. Ohio, 1965)).

As difficult as it might be to maintain confidentiality and to clarify the limits of privilege in dyadic, one-to-one psychotherapy, it is far more difficult in group therapies where privilege and the constraints of confidentiality are ill-defined. For instance, are statements made in the presence of other group or family members confidential? The following case illustrates the problem with respect to marital and family therapies.

> When a New Jersey couple who had been treated in marital therapy decided to divorce, the therapist was subpoenaed by the husband's lawyer to testify in court about the contents of their conjoint therapy sessions. The wife refused to waive her right to privilege. Consequently, the therapist refused to testify, claiming confidentiality and professional privilege. It happens that the status of psychologist-patient relations was not covered by privilege statutes in that state at the time. Nevertheless, the judge ruled to protect the wife's confidentiality on the basis of laws that governed not psychotherapists, but marriage counselors and their clients in that state.

As noted earlier, however, therapists may not assume that other jurisdictions will be similarly accommodating. Whereas New York and Tennessee courts have maintained privilege in similar cases, Virginia judges have denied it. Herrington (1979) reported a ruling by a Virginia judge in which he ruled that "when a husband and a wife are in a counseling session with a psychiatrist . . . there is no confidentiality because the statements made there were not made in private . . . but in the presence of the spouse."

Bersoff and Jain (1980) put forward a "solution" to this problem, suggesting that because in many states privilege is extended to those aiding in the therapeutic procedures of medical practitioners, for example, nurses, technicians, family members, or fellow group members present when confidential materials are divulged, they should be regarded as agents of the therapist. It is doubtful that such a definition would be acceptable to courts of law. Obviously, there can be no guarantee that none of those present when confidential material is disclosed will ever call on a therapist to testify in the event of litigation between them.

An inevitable ambiguity also exists regarding the confidentiality of children's communications (Minuchin, 1974; Hines and Hare-Mustin, 1978). It is the therapist's responsibility to protect the parent's confidentiality with respect to their children, yet the limits of confidentiality of the child's communications are uncertain. In some states parents have no legal right to demand that therapists reveal what the child has communicated. It is unclear how a therapist may act when a child specifically requests that certain things not be revealed to the parents.

As Keith-Spiegel and Koocher (1985) comment, ambiguity regarding the therapist's obligation to maintain confidentiality is especially great in group therapies. Although the situation is rapidly changing, few rulings have been made about materials disclosed in group sessions. Slovenko (1977) was impressed by the remarkable lack of concern of the group members he interviewed about the possibility—indeed the likelihood—of breaches of confidentiality about revelations in group sessions. As one of Slovenko's interviewees, herself a therapist, stated: "If somebody in the group would talk about me, I would talk about them. I mean that it's the same kind of thing that worked since I was in grade school. If you shut up about me, I shut up about you." Slovenko was amazed at this seeming indifference to possible violations of confidentiality and the position of apparent mutual deterrence that governed the exchange of confidences. When he pressed further and inquired what would be their responses if an intended criminal action were revealed, the group members persisted in their avowal that they would maintain confidentiality, but would be guided by the therapist as to whether confidentiality should be breached.

The legal status of confidentiality and privilege in multiperson interventions is unclear and likely to remain so in the absence of rulings on actual cases. Some group therapists (Morrison, Frederick and Rosenthal, 1975) suggest contracts between group members that specify fines or other punitive consequences for breaches of confidentiality (see Slovenko, 1977). However, the legal standing of such a contractual arrangement has not, to my knowledge, ever been tested. In a similar vein, Moreno once proposed a code of ethical conduct for all group members. This early pioneer and innovator designed group therapy as a mutual curative experience in which each member shared responsibility for the group's ethical conduct. His code, in greatly modified form, was published by his widow, Zerka (1978); however, its legal status has never been established and is unlikely to be.

The Duty to Protect; The Duty to Warn

The Duty to Warn

The duty to maintain confidentiality may conflict with a duty to warn or protect in the likelihood of physical harm or injury. In the landmark case of *Tarasoff v. Regents of the University of California*, the issues concerning the therapist's duty to the patient versus the duty to society at large were discussed at length, and the court concluded that a therapist is obliged to keep communications confidential "unless . . . disclosure is necessary to avert danger to others." In the words of Justice Tobriner, "Protective privilege ends where the public peril begins" (17 Cal.3d 425, 131 Cal. Rptr. 14, 551 P.wd 334 [1976] P.wd 334 [1976]).

> A student in therapy had made threats on the life of a young woman in the course of a therapy session. The therapist judged the young man to be dangerous and communicated this judgment to his supervisor, and subsequently to the police, but not to the intended victim or her family. The intended victim was subsequently killed and the family brought suit. The court held that a therapist treating a mentally ill person who could injure others must use reasonable care to prevent such injury. Specifically, threatened persons should be warned, or such precautions as are necessary to prevent such injury must be taken.

As Stone (1984) noted, no other state has adopted the Tarasoff requirement and even California's ruling was equivocal in many respects (dissenting judges argued that confidentiality is so central to the practice of therapy that the duty to warn could cripple its effectiveness). Tarasoff, however, has created a powerful precedent whose consequences are yet unknown.

Therapists have, of course, had the right to breach confidentiality under conditions of seeming imminent danger, but with the implications of the Tarasoff decision it would appear that they have a legal obligation to do so or face prosecution themselves. With the often-encountered problem of "false positives"—countless clients in therapy give vent to extreme hostile fantasies or expressions of lethal feelings about many people—and the acknowledged difficulties in predicting dangerous behavior, it is likely that therapists will defend themselves by overreporting. Therapists would thus be encouraged to violate their patients' confidences. Obviously, an unwanted result would be that many potentially violent individuals would avoid therapy altogether. Others would be hesitant about making disclosures that might be essential for successful therapy.

Since the Tarasoff ruling, many therapists have pondered its implications and the dilemmas they could find themselves in when confronted by a client threatening violence. Bersoff (1976) and Lane and Spruill (1980) are among many who considered that therapists could end up curtailing rather than enhancing the liberties of their clients, because typical errors among mental health practitioners are in over- rather than underprediction of danger. But assuming a considered judgment of danger, neither the courts nor legal codes instruct what to do. Although warning a potential victim may seem feasible, who should do it? Therapists, like other citizens, turn to the police when violence threatens. Thus, the function of the therapist might be to consult with police in given instances. But such consultation did not excuse the therapist in the Tarasoff case. That decision had the effect of placing therapists in a double bind. If they do not warn a potential victim, and assault takes place, they may be liable for failure to protect the intended victim; if they do warn and nothing takes place, they could be sued by their patient. Alternative strategies are scarcely fail-safe or original, but therapists are well advised to consider such actions as continuous monitoring and surveillance, enlisting family members, consultation for medications if indicated, and changes in locale for the client. Until legislation is enacted that will protect therapists in such circumstances, hospitalization may be the safest intervention. But none of these strategies eliminates the possibility of being sued. Unfortunately, whenever there is a question about an individual's potential danger the courts are likely to impose on therapists a social control function, whether or not therapists resist it (see Halleck, 1971).

The Duty to Protect

A duty to protect extends to patients who are at risk for injury to themselves. Courts have noted that the outpatient setting differs greatly from inpatient settings and that the duty to protect and liability in not protecting are greater in a hospital. But failure to take appropriate preventive measures could still give rise to damage suits. The precautionary steps are a matter for resolution at trial based on expert testimony as to good general measures for preventing suicide, given that a patient is acknowledged to be dangerous. Apparently, however, courts have thus far rejected Tarasoff as a precedent for requiring warnings to parents or relatives that would breach the patient's confidences. It has been held that Tarasoff is limited to a disclosure requirement "when the risk to be prevented thereby is the danger of violent assault, and not when the risk of harm is self-inflicted harm or mere property damage." In short, they declined to further extend the holding of Tarasoff.

Furrow (1980) predicts that the range of liability for failure to prevent suicide of outpatients is likely to remain small, primarily because of the limited availability of precautionary steps. As he observes, psychiatric hospitalization is a difficult and cumbersome procedure in most states, and therapists other than psychiatrists would have trouble invoking such procedures. However, situations can readily be imagined (and they are known to occur) where patients call therapists to express suicidal feelings or speak about them in sessions; the therapist may brush them aside or fail to attempt preventative action, such as additional meetings, consultation with colleagues, supplemental monitoring, hospitalization, etc. Such avoidance of the problem may give rise to liability. Of course, where evidence exists that a therapist has acted in such a way as to precipitate a suicide attempt, either through failure to perceive the reality of the riskiness of an intervention or through misuse of a specific technique, liability is likely to be established (see Farberow 1974, and Stone, 1971).

The interested reader may wish to refer to the *Legal Guidebook in Mental Health*, edited by Cohen and Mariano (1982), for detailed treatment of multiple other legal issues such as liability for negligence of associates and assistants of therapists, liability arising from referrals to other practitioners, and other infractions leading to possible legal consequences.

As noted, legal critics are increasingly pessimistic about the capacities of professional therapists to monitor themselves. Furrow (1980) holds that the services provided by therapists expose patients to distinctive and significant risks of harm, and that harm (the deterioration effect) can be of sufficient magnitude to warrant serious consideration of extended tort liability to psychotherapists. What he advocates is the application of a "strict liability model" to therapy to pressure the professions to accelerate research on risks and efficacy in therapies. Under this model, courts could find the therapeutic services, not just the therapist's conduct, defective. Crude though legal control through litigation might be, in his view it would convey a message in the dollar costs of judgments and the psychic costs of being sued and put through the judicial process.

Strict liability involves circumstantial proof, applied when common experience suggests a substantial, if indeterminate probability of negligence. It bears a similarity to product liability and assumes that therapy is an instrument under the control of the therapist; the accident (deterioration effect) would not have occurred if the therapist had used proper care. In the past, offering goods for sale has been distinguished from professional services, and the professional is not considered (as is the manufacturer or marketer) able to detect or eliminate defects in the service offered. But Furrow's model would hold the therapist liable for the quality of the therapy.

In defense of this radical departure from practice, Furrow argues that such a move would offer aggrieved clients a more effective legal avenue for redressing their grievances; it would create safety incentives by putting greater financial and social pressures on therapists to use or develop safer methods. They would also doubtless be more cautious about patient selection, and would carefully consider whether their preferred methods of treatment are appropriate to a given case.

According to Furrow's description, in his hoped-for consequences of such a shift from negligence to strict liability the therapist would have to consider the following.

1. Whether the service (the therapy treatment) generates a significant risk of harm to a class of consumers (individuals, families, organizations, members).

2. Whether the risk is one not anticipated by the typical service consumer (the client) and is therefore not a risk that is guarded against.
3. Whether the existence of the risk threatens established consumer (client) expectations regarding the service (therapy) and its expected level of performance.
4. Whether in supplying the service (therapy) the service provider (therapist) has either knowingly or unknowingly generated the consumer's (patient's) expectations or (has) taken advantage of the social context in which the demand (need) for the service (therapy) exists.

In their *North Carolina Law Review* article, Feldman and Ward (1979) discuss the legal aspects of the therapist's responsibility to patients. In their view, the therapist must avoid any conflict (of interest), dishonesty, or other interference with the discharge of duties as one who has a contractual obligation to treat with skill and care. Their examples of potentially breaching activities are: a group therapy in which the therapist has included the patient solely to achieve optimal size (or for pecuniary reasons) without reference to the individual's needs; exploring an innovative treatment and applying it to a patient in the interest of research rather than the person's care; maintaining a therapy relationship (overlong) without informing the patient that the dynamics of the techniques being used had run their course; becoming emotionally or sexually involved with the patient.

Although Furrow credits Feldman and Ward with the laudable purpose of wishing to protect against "overzealous, irresponsible, or self-serving practitioners," he notes that the majority of damages occurring in therapy do not arise from deliberate choices by badly intentioned therapists, but from factors over which therapists apparently have little control or about which they as yet know little. For this reason he wants to see the principle of strict liability established, in which the mere fact of patient or client injury establishes a prima facie case of liability if causation (the therapist's precipitating role) or other type of negligence can be shown. The therapist's burden of responsibility would require the therapist to justify his or her actions as those of a good-faith practitioner. If testimony is clear and cogent, in Furrow's opinion, the therapist will most likely be vindicated.

Benjamin Schutz, a clinical psychologist who has written about legal liability in psychotherapy (1982), attempts to anticipate near-future trends in legal actions against therapists; the following are among his predictions.

1. Plaintiffs will use intentional torts and contract law to avoid the pitfalls of proximate cause and standards of care that are the downfall of so many malpractice actions.
2. Increased use will be made of the informed consent doctrine in negligence cases, especially with verbal psychotherapies (the kinds we have been focusing on in this book) and with the potentially noxious effects of cathartic therapies.
3. Malpractice suits will be more effective with directive and behavioral therapies because of the relative ease of establishing proximate cause.
4. Suits charging undue influence will increase as a result of increasing employment of psychotherapy with the aging and very elderly.
5. Family therapy will generate suits by family members dissatisfied with outcomes . . . approaches that focus solely on the family system may lose sight of the rights of individual members and thus risk injuries to them.
6. Insurance peer-review actions may prompt suits. If a claim for reimbursement or payment is rejected for a client because a treatment plan is found inadequate, the client may try to recover fees paid for services from the practitioner.

7. Therapists may be sued because, in the wake of increasing use of short-term or time-limited therapies, the decision not to apply such therapies could be interpreted as negligence in some cases.
8. Another possible development is one Furrow has recommended, namely a shift to strict liability or "product liability." This is especially likely in the cases of therapists employing such devices as biofeedback machines; it may also be extended to purely verbal therapies.

Another possible development stems from the Osheroff case, should the findings of the Maryland Mental Health Arbitration Council be upheld in other courts. It is that therapists will incur the burden of establishing that a self-described "depressed" patient or client does not require pharmacological intervention. Since the vast majority of people who present themselves for psychotherapy complain first and foremost that they are depressed, the term, in itself, is not diagnostically clear or specific. Nevertheless, it is conceivable that upholding Osheroff will lead to suits against therapists who have conducted purely verbal therapies.

Schutz (1982) recommends the inclusion of legal issues and considerations in the training and continuing education of practitioners. As he notes, psychotherapy's step into the legal limelight, no matter how unwelcome, is an irrevocable one, and cannot be ignored in preparing psychotherapists to take on their roles. For continuing education, workshops sponsored by the various professional societies, together with collegial mutual monitoring perhaps in small groups of four or five, should focus on risks of legal actions and how best to avoid them.

Pope, Simpson, and Weiner (1978) could rightly claim that the psychotherapist is less often sued than the practitioner of impersonally administered, highly technologized health care methods. They could fairly state that the likely reasons were that emotional damage is more difficult to assess than physical damage; that there are no standards of practice for psychotherapy and therefore no measures of the adequacy of a therapist's management of a case; and that, most of all, the psychotherapist is able to establish a "working human relationship" with the patient. In the future, it seems, the two last reasons are much less to be relied on than previously. Standards of care are likely to be imposed on, if not initiated by, the professions that provide therapy services. Moreover, the working human relationship may not be an adequate defense in the event of claimed harms or injuries. Nevertheless, despite the rapidly shifting situation and the increasingly litigious atmosphere in the society, therapists may avoid malpractice or negligence actions in the following ways.

> [Therapists should] keep up with developments in diagnosis and treatment. Do an adequate examination and periodically reexamine the patient/client to evaluate progress. Give adequate warning of possible consequences of suggested diagnostic and treatment procedures. Have a sound rationale for the proposed treatment. Use consultants, peer supervision, and case conferences, especially when in doubt about the treatment indicated, when treatment is stalled, or when the individual may be worsening. In all instances, protect the patient's privacy. Obtain written consent for treatment, as well as for recording, release of information, and publishing case reports (even though the individual's identity is appropriately disguised). Take appropriate action, if necessary, direct action, when a patient endangers himself or others. Warning a threatened third party may be necessary (at least, in California), but in all instances take such steps as are reasonable to protect all parties involved. Become aware of those aspects of your demeanor or other aspects of your intervention style that superfluously irritate or

frustrate and try to modify these. Do not, under any circumstances, become sexually involved with clients. Confine your relationship with them to the therapy setting, except for situations with specific treatment requirements that could be justified. In general, keep hands off patients for other than ordinary greetings or in service of an acceptable therapeutic rationale. In the event you do not wish to continue with a client, for whatever reason, try to find an appropriate referral (Pope, Simpson, & Weiner, 1978).

Their advice is sound, and those who follow it are unlikely to risk harming or injuring their patients or the suits for legal damages that could ensue from claims about such harms or injuries. However, in the absence of leadership from professional training programs and practitioner associations, courts are likely to become increasingly involved in setting not only the outside limits of acceptable practice, but even the standards of practice, however undesirable this may be from the point of view of the practitioners (Harris, 1973).

9

Where We Are Now,
Where We Go from Here

We have seen that practitioners face a number of ethical dilemmas that apply equally to all psychotherapy systems and all the treatments derived from them. Most concern the values and needs each partner brings to the therapy process. We began by examining illustrations of unethical or ethically equivocal conduct as reported by practitioners themselves. These garden-variety ethical dilemmas confronted daily by ordinary practitioners provide a base from which to view the concrete issues and questions encountered by all therapists.

Deterioration effects, bad outcomes for those seeking psychological relief, are difficult to quantify. Although attempts at evaluative research do not indicate either the precise number of such unfortunate outcomes or the processes by which harms and injuries result instead of therapeutic change, we have seen that knowledgeable and experienced theoreticians and practitioners agree that a significant number of therapy casualties may be attributed to ethically questionable practices. Multiple reasons may be given for failures of therapy to help, but a significant proportion of negative effects is judged to have been directly or indirectly caused by unwarranted and unethical interventions. Such actions arouse concern not only among consumers, but also in the professional associations responsible for the training and oversight of therapists, and they will be derelict in their responsibilities if serious prevention attempts are not made.

In trying to understand the sources of therapists' intervention—the legitimacy of their interpretations and suggestions—we have explored some predominant values and philosophic stances of mainstream systems of therapy. Recognizing that no system of psychotherapy is value-free, we still find it remarkable that professional associations of therapists have not stimulated reflection on the values embedded in each. Such value systems do not stand by themselves; each is subject to translation and interpretation by individual therapists who filter their ideologies through their personal values. Consequently, an ethical stance by a therapist requires awareness not only of those values in the concepts of the therapist's orientation, but also acknowledgment of personally held biases. How can therapists be made more aware of the elements that shape their interventions without becoming paralyzed?

Structural and ideological elements in therapies are ethically significant and may be abused to the detriment of the patient's psychological state. Differences in behavior can reflect the structure of the therapeutic relation. Individual, group, family, and organizational contexts do not present drastically varying ethical problems—the ethical imperative "do no evil" is applicable to each—but ethical problems surface differently in each, disguised by the differences in numbers of persons treated, the relationships among them, or the specific strategies employed because of their presumed greater effectiveness in those contexts.

The impact of threatened and actual litigation on practitioners and on modes of practice is undeniable. Although comparatively few suits against therapists were successful in the past, there is a significant surge of litigations at present. A survey of professional therapists' journals yields a clear impression of growing anxiety among practitioners about present and future trends. Some may discount the seriousness of the threat to their professional integrity; others warn their colleagues about its likely aversive consequences. Those who pooh-pooh the seriousness of the problem believe that the current spate of litigious activity is caused by widespread consumer resentment against medical practitioners, but there is ample evidence that consumers of therapy services are also becoming aroused about what they regard as inferior treatment, not to mention instances of outright malpractice. It is not possible to forecast future trends of legal actions; however, if the recent past is any indication, therapists are right to consider preventive action and to pay closer attention to any ethical infraction by colleagues. Damage to the field is already evident in the defensive practices of some therapists who avoid clients they consider capable of employing litigation.

Power of the Therapist; Freedom of the Client; Accountability of the Therapy

In their discussion of the general question of ethics in social intervention strategies, Bermant and Warwick (1978) use three themes. They begin with a consideration of power differentials between helper and help-seeker and then examine the constraints placed on the help-seeker's freedom; they conclude by considering the kind of accountability therapists may be held to. Honorable rather than dishonorable intentions are assumed: the therapist intends to act ethically. The ambitions of the therapist for the patient are beyond reproach, neither corrupt and venal nor beset by unresolvable conflicts of interest. Therapists, like other effective social intervenors, have the expertise—the resources—to act on their intentions of changing their clients in significant ways. This intention to produce change, based on their acknowledged expertise can become an exercise in power.

Freedom of the client is defined as the capacity of the individual (or group) to choose the degree of participation in the change process or to decline to take part at all. It also involves the opportunity to set or alter goals, to be informed about procedures employed, and to withdraw without undue pressure to continue. In response to these criteria of freedom from coercion and constraint, the doctrine of informed consent, previously manifested mostly in medical treatments and biological experimentation, inescapably becomes an important feature of voluntary participation in any form of psychotherapy.

The requirement of accountability most clearly relates to the need to protect the individual or group's freedom from coercion, that is, from unwarranted uses of power by therapists. It prevents not only careless care, but also abuses of the power inherent in the therapist's position vis-à-vis the client. Bermant and Warwick note that numerous professionals, notably attorneys, doctors, engineers, and others, have been forced by the increased incidence of malpractice to avoid those tactics that could be considered marginally ethical or unethical. As a result, many professional associations are reconsidering their codes of conduct and are becoming concerned about how to educate practitioners in their fields toward greater ethical awareness and responsibility.

How may the power vested in the therapist be abused to the detriment of patients? We have seen that the opportunities for such abuse are most clearly evident in dyadic therapies, less obvious, but plentifully available in multiperson contexts. One with potentially disastrous consequences is the organizational intervention involving an employee who objects to a procedure and will likely be in a minority position holding an "untenable" reservation about processes defined as developmental, team-building, organizationally healthy, or in the pursuit of excellence. As we have seen, definitions of health by managers and subordinates can be very different. The use of professional jargon and various terms dear to practitioners' hearts may mystify rather than clarify goals and procedures for potential participants. The doctrine of informed consent, difficult though it may be to negotiate, appears essential to mitigate the unwarranted effects of power differentials in this modality, as in the others. Could potential therapy clients follow the advice given by Bermant and Warwick (1978) for all targets of helping interventions?

> Get completely clear on what problem is to be solved (addressed, ameliorated, resolved) and about who has defined the problem. Insist that the intervenor do the same. Set forth the objectives to be achieved and the criteria by which they are to be measured. And— let no mystique surrounding a profession or an institution replace or suppress discussion about the precise reasons for change (p. 384).

The authors might well have added the advice to consider the techniques by which change is to be brought about. Moreover, these should not be one-shot considerations. For multiple reasons—emotional upset, ambiguities in therapist's communication, difficulty in comprehension, unfamiliarity with the procedures—clients may not be in a position to make informed judgments about participation on the basis of a single explanation. Periodic restatements of purpose and review of procedures are necessary to insure ethically responsible conduct of the change process and adequate consideration of the client's changing needs. What prevents therapists from "laying all the cards on the table?"

The unyielding reluctance to provide fully informed consent as a condition for entrance into therapy is not attributable to unethical impulses among therapists, nor to a lack of concern for patient welfare. I share with my fellow practitioners the well-founded fears that full disclosure presents very real problems to the most ethical therapist. Concerns about the impact of such disclosure on emotionally overwrought clients are legitimate, but the most widely held reservation is that many clients must—repeat, must— react to such disclosure with attempts to counteract the tactics that will be employed. In other words, advance information about intended procedures will undercut some, if not all, the intended effects of such procedures.

What is to be done? As Widiger and Rorer (1984) and Lebensohn (1977) have suggested, there can be deleterious effects on help-seekers if they have to be warned of the difficulties of getting better, the possibilities of getting worse, and the complexities of likely transference reactions (not to mention countertransference responses from the therapist!). Not only behavioral, strategic, or social influence therapists consciously manipulate patient's beliefs; so also do dynamically oriented ones. Indeed, Frank has convincingly argued that all therapies manipulate hope and beliefs in the interest of helping the individual recover. One can argue that it is more important to be therapeutically effective in relieving the help-seeker's distress than to be completely truthful and informative but of no help. Similar arguments have been advanced by Gillis (1974) who claimed that it was justifiable to use ploys worthy of the used-car salesman, such as flattery, no-miss interpretations, and even confusion tactics to bring about desirable change.

My own reservations about full disclosure and informed consent notwithstanding, it seems that the ethical pitfalls of avoiding it outweigh the tactical disadvantages that, at least initially, result from such communication to patients. Some patients can absorb and consider much information of this kind and will welcome it; others may not understand at first. Some therapists may even offer sample sessions or short courses on what will occur. Group therapy is sometimes introduced in this way because many people find the idea of multiperson treatment confusing. An obvious case where full disclosure and informed consent are essential is organizational intervention. Objections, reservations, and second thoughts at an early stage could prevent the harms that result from ill-advised, inappropriate, premature implementation of treatment procedures.

The therapist is personally, professionally, and legally accountable. As all the codes of professional therapists' associations hold, practitioners are bound to abide by accepted moral principles in carrying out their work. Moreover, they have special obligations to consider as a supreme value the client's or patient's welfare and not attempt to gratify personal needs or wishes at their expense. We are also becoming increasingly aware of legal accountability, even though until now psychotherapies have not been held to levels of accountability as powerful or as pervasive as those regulating medicine or law. It remains to be seen how this will affect practice. Many fear that the issue of legality will only undermine the crucial bases of trust and confidence without which psychological treatment cannot be effective. On the other hand, there is widespread recognition that extant codes provide only the most general guidelines for ethical conduct and are ambiguous when it comes to specific cases. Although therapists must use codes to guide their behavior, the burden of decision throws them back on their own ethical sense and rules-of-thumb. The question that demands attention is whether there can be effective training in ethical sensitivity that would translate these general guidelines into more meaningful applications to specific incidents and cases.

In considering the ethical issues involved in clinical practice, I have been repeatedly challenged by a seeming discontinuity between competence and ethicality apparent in the responses of some practitioners. Often they were themselves troubled by a lack of connection between these concepts. Could not a poor intervention be the result of misdiagnosis, a misapprehension of what the person, group, family, or organization needed—a mistake in judgment—rather than being self-serving or malicious? Even when they acknowledged ethically equivocal actions, interviewees were typically quick to amend their statements by suggesting that they had made a misjudgment or, at worst, had suffered a transient lapse. They did not consider themselves really unethical.

Competence must be defined in terms of ethical actions as well as the requisite knowledge and skills needed to perform therapeutic tasks; seeing clients with problems one is not trained to treat or using procedures one is unfamiliar with cannot be ethical. Competence may not be separated from ethical conduct. To the degree that power and authority are inherent in the therapist's role and function, these must be exercised with care and constant awareness of the pitfalls of injudicious interventions. Because therapists are charged with responsibility for their clients, they must be constrained by knowledge and awareness of how their interventions could harm or injure them.

Given the current diversity of therapeutic orientations, the best that can be achieved, according to Widiger and Rorer (1984) is tolerance for various ethical stances and principles. This kind of ethical relativism is in their view necessary because ethical problems are unique in each philosophical position. It is not possible to establish one comprehensive set of ethical principles, but there can be orientation-specific guidelines by which a therapist of a given approach should judge the appropriateness of interventions. The markedly different standards pertaining to truthfulness, degree and kinds of disclosures, and attitudes toward obtaining informed consent underscore the problem. This view, of course, differs from one that permits a therapist the therapeutic privilege of withholding information that is likely to seriously upset a client.

The prospect of each therapist's acting in terms of individual standards (assuming these could be concretely specified) has a certain appeal. If the philosophic and value implications of each approach were clearly understood by its adherents (an essential ethical requirement for therapists of all orientations), such an approach would have the advantage of defining ethical responsibility in ways that would be shared among a number of practitioners. Each therapist could have on file with a designated ethics committee a statement of principles to which he or she would be held accountable, and one that could be made available to potential patients or clients.

Whether a comprehensive set of ethical principles could be equally applicable to all therapies and all treatments remains a serious question for practitioners as well as for theorists of psychotherapies. Would abusive behavior in one be therapeutic in another? Are there no ethical stances that could be required of all therapists, regardless of their orientations? Flanagan and Liberman (1982), in discussing the ethics of behavioral therapies, argue that the ethical problems behavioral therapists confront are identical with those of other mental health practitioners. They involve the judgments of treatment objectives, intervention strategies, respect for the well-being of clients, and sensitivity to the often conflicting interests of individuals in treatment, their families, and associates. Like others, behavioral therapists have become sensitized to ethical issues because of abusive practices in the field, misinterpretation of the therapy in the popular literature, and its potential for misuse. Flanagan and Liberman insist that any therapy, seen as a technology for producing behavior change, is subject to misapplication and to misuse.

Implications for Training and Continuing Education in Ethical Awareness

The therapists whose interviews are included in Chapter 1 were also asked for their suggestions for preventing unethical conduct and enhancing ethical awareness and sensitivity. Although their responses were brief, they are, I believe, important viewpoints of people who struggle with these issues on a daily basis.

Is Psychotherapy for the Therapist a Requirement for Ethical Practice?

Leonard Bernard discusses his requirement that residents have the experience of personal therapy.

> I insist that my psychiatric residents have personal therapy—I don't tell them with whom or what kind. That is the only way I can be reasonably confident that their own problems

won't get into their treatments and mess up their patients. Now I know it may sound dictatorial—maybe it is—but I think it's essential for good practice. I tell them, "Look, you are just another human being who is probably screwed up like everybody else—like the people you'll see, and probably in the same ways too. So you are going to have to be aware of how the way you are screwed up is going to influence those you're working with." By being in therapy they are going to become more vigilant about ways they react to their patients.

Probably most therapists would agree with the advisability of experiencing personal therapy not only as a basis for understanding what the client goes through—how the procedures are perceived—and as corrective for the therapist's personal problems, but also to prevent unethical exploitation of the client. Since Freud's dictum about the importance of analysis for the analyst, many dynamically oriented therapists have asserted that it is essential for preventing any distortion of the therapy process because of countertransference needs or motives in the therapist.

In his description of training criteria for psychotherapists, Grayson (1982) strongly advocates personal therapeutic experience, but only as one of a number of criterial suggestions, which include better selection procedures, greater awareness by teachers of therapy of their modeling effects on students, and a demand that unbiased introductions to therapeutic systems and treatments other than locally favored ones be given to render the therapist less rigid and doctrinaire.

It is easy to understand why personal therapy is high on the list of educational as well as remedial actions that should be taken to assure ethical therapy practice. Therapists as a group are so likely to view deviance in terms of psychopathology that psychotherapy seems a natural and appropriate preventive or remedy. However, personal experience would appear to be the most powerful and persuasive ethical education that can be offered. As patients themselves, intending therapists would experience many, if not all, of the discomforts, emotional trials, and anxieties of the clients they will treat. A genuine therapeutic experience, at the very least, should render the therapist more sensitive to the feelings associated with being on the other side, with the emotional consequences of patient status.

Raising Ethical Consciousness Among Trainees

Multiple opportunities exist for considering ethical therapeutic practice in the course of training in any mental health profession besides the time-consuming and expensive process of personal therapy. Some of the interviewees for this book are themselves teachers and trainers of therapists, and several described ways in which they try to build ethical considerations into their teaching. One of them, Yaakov Frank, states what he does by way of alerting his residents to potential unethical actions.

> In the residency training case conferences, or any other chance I get, I just tell them straight out: here are the pitfalls; here's where you could get the patient and yourself into big trouble. I just say it plain—no physical contact! Don't get them too dependent. You might have to be confrontative, but watch out. Don't overdo it. Remember, your patient is very vulnerable to you.

A similar point is made, if less assertively, by the supervising therapist, Ellen Boltax, in her case conferences with her students.

> I try to brainstorm the likely ethical issues with the students. Whenever it seems relevant, I ask them to consider how a particular strategy could get you into ethical problems. For

instance, the question might be what do you do if you sense the patient is trying to "put the moves on you"? How do you handle it? What might you say? At what point should you take up the question with somebody like me or another supervisor? How do you handle the issue of referring to somebody else?

Both peer supervision—consultation opportunities—and peer pressure to assure quality control were mentioned by interviewees as desirable means for preventing unethical conduct. These are not limited, of course, to trainees but might involve experienced practitioners in the field as well. Michael Dichter and his colleagues set up such a small group of colleagues, and his experience may be instructive.

> We tried to get this thing going, and it lasted for a time with, I really believe, pretty good results. But it broke down because of schedule conflicts. I realized that people won't stick with a thing like that unless it is a requirement from top down. Obviously, I couldn't make it a requirement all on my own. But I really think it ought to be—and I mean from the profession. Professional associations should demand it; It would certainly help get quality control, which we really need. If everybody who practices was in some kind of consultation group, they could monitor and help each other. Some ethical question one guy couldn't see because he's too close and personally involved would come up for discussion because the others would catch it. I really think it's the only way to avoid ethical problems.

Unfortunately, peer supervision and monitoring have become increasingly linked only to problems of cost-control—whether a particular therapy is justified, the number of sessions necessary—rather than for improving practice. Those supervisory groups stemming from the PSRO, the Professional Standards Review Organization Act of 1972 (which subsequently gave way to the PROs—Professional Review Organizations in 1982), are almost exclusively concerned with cost-containment and have evidenced few initiatives to improve the quality or the ethicality of treatments.

Profession-endorsed and sponsored peer-consultation groups seems an excellent suggestion. Composition of such groups could take into account differing ideological commitments and not insist on either extreme of homogeneity or heterogeneity of views. To begin the process, such groups might well be within-school, but ultimate heterogeneity of membership might be a good way to begin breaking down the barriers of ideological— even disciplinary—boundaries. It might be a path toward the evolution of comprehensive ethical principles for all therapy practitioners.

Can Therapeutic Ethics Be Taught?

Robert Michaels, a dynamically oriented psychiatrist, has discussed the problems of teaching ethics to therapists (1981). He points out that the professions and the public, while increasingly troubled by problems that practitioners face (and produce), rarely consider how to alter behaviors that eventuate in ethical concerns. There are differences among teachers of therapists, among the interviewees, on how to approach the question of unethical practices and how to teach ethical sensitivity. Indeed, some believe that the problem is really selection of people with good characters rather than an inculcation of ethical awareness. Others claim that, personal therapy aside, good supervision that models ethical concern is the best instruction. As for formal teaching of ethics, one obstacle is that therapists who may be excellent teachers of clinical methods may not have the knowledge required to teach about ethics, while moral philosophers are not typically competent or appropriate as instructors concerning therapy questions.

The training regimen itself is an obstacle. In dynamically oriented programs the trainee's attention is focused on acquiring the paradigms of treatment according to the concepts being taught. As Michaels says, this seems to demand a suspension of the more customary framework of ideas about behavior and its consequences—the everyday commonsense approach that includes a considerable amount of moral judgment. At times, training leads to a seeming amorality that seeks to understand all kinds of behaviors while suspending judgment about their moral implications. In the effort to absorb the new paradigms, to understand the psychological determinants of a given behavior, the trainee is in the position of trying to learn a foreign language. One may have to stop using one's native tongue for a time. In the jargon of the field, concern about ethical issues at this point could be used as a defense or resistance against learning about psychodynamics. Michaels is, however, optimistic that just as it is possible that learning a new language can enhance one's understanding of a familiar one, so these two different frameworks for considering human behavior—the psychological and the moral—can each clarify and explicate the characteristics of the other.

In considering formal courses in ethics for preprofessional training, a basic requirement, according to Michaels, is understanding moral reasoning, types of justification for actions, and the history of such conceptions. The teacher of ethics must be prepared to deal with the larger questions of metaethics. Discussions of the relationships between individual autonomy, rights to treatment, and involuntary treatments can be used to illuminate the relationships between utilitarian and absolutist modes of ethical reasoning. What therapists ought to do and why involves normative rules, standards and codes of the therapy professions. Important related issues of law, politics, and social policy also affect therapist's practices. Many topics such as invasive treatments, coercion, problems in seeking and obtaining informed consent, questions of agency, privacy, and confidentiality, issues of guardianship and responsibility, constraints on patient autonomy, and other ethically sensitive issues could be explored in terms of the values and ethical decisions they entail. Although the skills of diagnosis and effective strategies to move therapy are an essential ingredient of training, so are trainees' abilities to recognize ethical problems that arise in therapy and to reason about them in a coherent and useful way.

Unfortunately, as Michaels acknowledges, few therapists are able to teach this type of material without the collaboration of philosophers. Such courses can easily degenerate into moralistic sermons—a result that would have counterproductive consequences in terms of ethical consciousness. (As we will see, this indeed has been the outcome for some interviewees.) Ethics for therapists are best taught in terms of their application to concrete cases and their direct and indirect effects on patients and clients, especially regarding harms and injuries.

Ethical considerations may be introduced into training seminars, carefully conducted courses, grand rounds, case conferences, and group as well as individual supervision. Ethical issues thus are brought into central elements of training where trainees have the most emotional investment. The point is to enable trainees and students to recognize the universality of ethical issues as a necessary framework for understanding their roles and functions as psychological healers.

Some practitioners are less than enthusiastic about the usefulness of courses and seminars about ethics for therapists, as evidenced in Peter Williams' comment.

If a guy is psychopathic, you aren't going to knock it out of him in any courses. Supervision—good supervision—is the only ticket. You get some of these so-called ethicists—they are so pompous and narcissistic themselves that they turn you off. I figure you have to first find a way to exclude the people who shouldn't get through, shouldn't be doing therapy at all. Then you have to provide decent supervision to cover discussions of this kind of stuff and you have to have personal therapy. Basically, acting ethically comes down to good supervision and peer pressures. You have to have small enough groups of people who would make it their business to meet regularly and talk about their cases with each other—yeah, and their countertransference reactions too.

But peer pressures have their problems too, just as courses and seminars may not achieve their intended goals. Jane McNamara expresses her reservations as follows.

Sure it's a good idea to talk about instruction in ethical decision making in therapy, but I think there can be a danger that you could make it impossible for people to learn from making mistakes—their own mistakes, even ethical ones. You can easily produce a situation where the novice therapist would be so inhibited by this and that prohibition that he or she would be almost paralyzed. I mean, you don't want them thinking, "I shouldn't even be feeling this, or I shouldn't want something."

Personal reservations about the value of peer group discussions are also expressed by Alex Clement.

I get uptight about talking about what I'm ashamed of or anxious about in front of other people. I just don't feel free enough to do it honestly. I consult with one other colleague on a regular basis. We meet for lunch once a week and really open up to each other. I trust him and he trusts me. We both feel free to talk about what troubles us about cases, or anything else, for that matter. But I can see the value of a small group talking about what they're worried about in their work. It could be a kind of support group—a sort of group therapy for us. Maybe it would be good for me, but it has to be the right group, and I haven't found it yet.

The same interviewee expressed doubts about the value of formal courses. He felt they would be less helpful than individual supervision. It is probably true for many that ethical abstractions are not helpful, and ethical issues can be understood best when concretely represented in actual case materials. Courses and even peer consultations may seem too far removed from the contexts in which therapy occurs—where actual decisions affecting the clients must be made. If courses are given, care must be taken to avoid turning off their intended beneficiaries. Nancy Rogow comments that her own exposure to a course in ethical issues in therapy left her dissatisfied, to say the least.

There should be some way to talk about these problems without sounding like you're preaching or that you have some kind of God-given wisdom about it. The trouble is that I did have a course in ethics but the guys who taught it came across as holier-than-thou. I hated it. I realize that a lot of us in the field are struggling with problems of how to operate in decent ways, and I wish there were readings and decent courses that would address those concerns.

Alvin Barry is convinced that his own exposure to ethical issues in a seminar devoted to the topic was quite helpful.

We had case materials and lectures and the participants could bring up their own cases for discussion. In each session, the person who conducted it would have stop-places so that we were asked what our own tactics would be and why. We had to defend what we wanted to do ethically as well as in terms of strategy. The lecturers were some of the most experienced therapists around, but we also had several lawyers come in who had been involved in some cases involving abuse or malpractice. I still think of it now and then because it was very helpful. I particularly recall one presentation on the problem of handling being sexually attracted and how to respond. I've used lots of the stuff I learned there. I think that both APAs should require courses like that one.

The recommendations of practitioners and theoreticians for ethical consciousness raising and for preventive education for therapists focus on the following experiences.

1. Personal psychotherapy for the trainee or the practitioner already in the field has the value of developing greater awareness of client's and patient's emotional states as well as ameliorating the therapist's personal problems that could be potential sources of ethical misconduct in a therapy relationship. While not a sure preventive, personal therapy is nevertheless the single best way to gain self-understanding and self-awareness. Because personal therapy, in most cases, demands self-scrutiny in all aspects of one's life, it can help in developing the ethical consciousness necessary for ethical behavior.

2. Courses and seminars focused on ethical issues in therapy practice should be an integral part of preprofessional training, but they must be carefully designed to involve plentiful discussion of case materials, preferably those regarding individuals being treated at the time by seminar and course participants. As we have seen, the matter of who conducts these seminars is not easily resolvable. Professional philosophers and ethicists whose expertise does not extend to therapy practice and techniques may not be the best persons to teach them. For similar reasons, lawyers may also be inappropriate instructors. The most effective teachers of ethics would be therapists able to discuss philosophical and ethical implications of practice from a perspective closer to the student's, or, at least, one informed by pragmatic considerations of effectiveness in the therapeutic role.

3. It is clear that ethical problems do not begin or end with novices in the field; there is a pressing need for continuing education. Where are the workshops in ethical consideration in the proliferating weekends devoted to developing additional clinical skills? What can professional associations do to promote the idea of peer-consultative as well as review groups for enhancing the prospects of quality assurance? The conviction of practitioners that such programs must be initiated from the top down poses an obligation for these associations. On the other hand, to the degree that such peer consultative groups could be heterogenous in terms of disciplinary affiliation and system or school adherence, they might also function to stimulate useful consideration of differences in values, not only techniques and procedures. A possible by-product of great social significance would be the evolution of a comprehensive set of ethical principles applicable to all psychotherapies.

Our consideration of ethical issues in the psychotherapies has taken us into value and moral questions as well as techniques and procedures, topics previously not high on the priorities of therapy training programs for experienced practitioners. We have examined hard questions to which few unequivocal answers can be given. And yet the inquiry may not be abandoned. Such is the importance of psychotherapists in contemporary society that, in the words of Perry London (1986), they fill a moral vacuum in modern life, acting as moral arbiters, instructors in how to live one's life, authorities in areas once dominated by religious leaders or philosophers. Serving as healers of psychological suffering and pain, they are turned to for guidance in the difficult spiritual matters once the province of pastor or rabbi: how to conduct oneself, how to relate to others, how to think about one's life. But therapists must draw on their knowledge and understanding of human sciences.

Unlike shamans, clerics, and gurus who may believe they can confidently prescribe how to live the good life and achieve the rewards it brings, psychotherapists must speak with far less certainty about how to live. Even though they cannot be fully competent in matters of moral concern to their patients and clients, they may not dismiss them as being of no professional concern or relevance. As London says, learning what people are like tells us what we may help them to become. As knowledgeable healers of the mind, heart, and soul, therapists can lend a thoughtful voice to the many soul-destroying concerns people bring to them.

Efforts to make psychotherapy for better and not for worse, to achieve good and not ill effects, must be unremitting. If ethical problems arise in everyday therapy encounters, then it is in daily concrete steps that ethical solutions must be found. Self-scrutiny for psychotherapists is not limited to trainees but extends through a lifetime of therapeutic practice. As a therapist, one assumes a unique ethical charge and responsibility. Professional self-respect as well as the trust of patients and clients demand that it be honorably fulfilled.

References

Chapter 1

Baeyer-Katte, W. V. (1982). Das socialistische patient kollektiv in Heidelberg, Spk. In W. V. Baeyer-Katte, D. Claessens, H. Feger, & F. Neidhardt (Eds.), *Analysen zum terrorismus gruppenprozess* (Vol. 3, 184–306). Opladen, West Germany: Westdeutscher Verlag.

Bergin, A. E. (1985). Proposed values for guiding and evaluating counseling and psychotherapy. *Journal of Counseling and Values, 29*(2), 99–116.

Dahlberg, C. C. (1970). Sexual contact between patient and therapist. *Contemporary Psychoanalysis, 6*(2), 107–124.

Davidson, V. (1977). Psychiatry's problem with no name: therapist-patient sex. *American Journal of Psychoanalysis, 37*(1), 43–50.

Edelwich, J., & Brodsky, A. M. (1982). *Sexual dilemmas for the helping professional.* New York: Brunner/Mazel.

Gartrell, N., Herman, J., Olarte, S., Feldstein, M., & Localio, R. (1986). Psychiatrist-patient sexual contact. *American Journal of Psychiatry, 143*(9), 1126–1131.

Gurman, A. S., Knudson, R. M., & Kniskern, D. P. (1978). Behavioral marriage therapy IV: Take two aspirin and call us in the morning. *Family Process, 17*(2), 165–180.

Hare-Mustin, R. T. (1978). A feminist approach to family therapy. *Family Process, 17,* 131–194.

Hart, J., & Corriere, R. (1977). *The dream makers: Discovering your breakthrough dreams.* New York: Funk and Wagnalls.

Holyroyd, J. C., & Brodsky, A. M. (1977). Psychologists' attitudes and practices regarding erotic and nonerotic physical contacts with patients. *American Psychologist, 32,* 843–849.

Jacobson, N. (1983). Beyond empiricism: the politics of marital therapy. *American Journal of Family Therapy, 11*(2), 11–24.

Liberman, R. P., & Raskin, D. E. (1971). Depression: A behavioral formulation. *Archives of General Psychiatry, 24,* 515–523.

London, P. (1986). *Modes and morals of psychotherapy* (2nd ed.). New York: Hemisphere.

Margolin, G. (1982). Ethical and legal considerations in marital and family therapy. *American Psychologist, 37,* 788–801.

Murray, E. J. (1956). A content-analysis method for studying psychotherapy. *Psychological Monographs, 70.*

O'Leary, K. D., & Turkewitz, H. (1978). Treatment of marital disorders from a behavioral perspective. In T. J. Paolino & B. S. McCrady (Eds.), *Marriage and the treatment of marital*

disorders: Psychoanalytic, behavioral and systems theory perspectives. New York: Brunner/
Mazel.

Parloff, M. B., Goldstein, N., & Iflund, B. (1960). Communication of values and therapeutic
change. *Archives of General Psychiatry, 2,* 300–304.

Parloff, M. B., Iflund, B., & Goldstein, N. (1957). Communication of "therapy values" between
therapist and schizophrenic patients. Paper read at American Psychiatric Association annual
meeting, Chicago, IL, May 13–17.

Tarasoff v. Regents of the University of California, 13. Cal. 3rd 425, 131 Cal. Reptr. 14, 551 P.
2nd 334 (1976).

Traux, C. B. (1966). Reinforcement and nonreinforcement in Rogerian psychotherapy. *Journal of
Abnormal Psychology, 71,* 1–9.

Vitz, P. C. (1985). The dilemma of narcissism. *Journal of Social and Clinical Psychology, 3,* 9–14.

Walton, R. E., & Warwick, D. P. (1973). The ethics of organizational development. *Journal of
Applied Behavioral Science, 9,* 681–698.

Wendorf, D. J., & Wendorf, R. J. (1985). A systematic view of family therapy ethics. *Family
Process, 24,* 443–453.

Wolfe, B. E. (1977). Moral transformations in psychotherapy. In R. Stern, L. S. Horowitz, & J.
Lynes (Eds.), *Science and psychotherapy.* New York: Raven.

Chapter 2

Bergin, A. E. (1971). The evaluation of psychotherapy outcomes. In A. E. Bergin, & S. Garfield
(Eds.), *Handbook of psychotherapy and behavior change.* New York: Wiley.

Bergin, A. E., & Lambert M. J. (1978). The evaluation of psychotherapy outcomes. In A. E.
Bergin, & S. Garfield (Eds.), *Handbook of psychotherapy and behavior change* (2nd ed.).
New York: Wiley.

Bouhoutsos, J., Holyroyd, J., Lerman H., Forer, B., & Greenberg, M. (1983). Sexual intimacy
between psychotherapists and patients. *Professional Psychology, 14,* 185–196.

Dahlberg, C. (1970). Sexual contact between patient and therapist. *Contemporary Psychoanalysis,
6,* 107–124.

Davidson, V. (1977). Psychiatry's problem with no name: Therapist-patient sex. *American Journal
of Psychoanalysis, 37,* 43–50.

Feldman-Surmess, S., & Jones, G. (1984). Psychological impacts of sexual contact between
therapists or other health care practitioners and their clients. *Journal of Consulting and Clinical
Psychology, 52,* 1054–1061.

Freud, S. (1910). The future prospects of psychoanalytic therapy, *Collected papers,* Vol. II.
London: Hogarth Press (1953).

Furrow, B. (1980). *Malpractice in psychotherapy.* Lexington, MA: Lexington Books.

Gartrell, N., Herman J., Olarte, S., Feldstein, M., & Localio, N. (1986). Psychiatrist-patient
sexual contact, I. *American Journal of Psychiatry, 143*(9), 1126–1131.

Glidewell, J. C. (1978). Ethical issues in and around encounter groups. In G. Bermant, H. C.
Kelman, & D. P. Warwick (Eds.), *The ethics of social intervention* (pp. 67–102). New York:
Wiley.

Hart, J., Corriere, R., & Binder, J. (1975). *Going sane.* New York: Dell.

Holyroyd, J. C., & Brodsky A. M. (1977). Psychologists' attitudes and practices regarding erotic
and nonerotic physical contact with patients. *American Psychologist, 32,* 843–849.

Kaplan, R. E., Obert, S. L., & Van Bluskirk, W. R. (1980). The dynamics of injury in encounter
groups: splitting, resistance and the misuses of power. *Conference of American group
Psychotherapy Association,* February 16, 1980, Los Angeles.

Kardener, S. H., Fuller, M., & Mensh, I. N. (1973). A survey of physicians' attitudes and practices
regarding erotic and nonerotic contact with patients. *American Journal of Psychiatry, 130,*
1077–1081.

Lakin, M. (Ed.). (1979). What happened to small group research? [Special issue]. *Journal of Applied Behavioral Science, 15.*

Lakin, M. (1985). *The helping group.* Reading, MA: Addison-Wesley.

Lambert, M. J., Bergin, A. E., & Collins, J. L. (1977). Therapist-induced deterioration in psychotherapy. In A. M. Gurman, & A. M. Rogers (Eds.), *The therapist's contributions to effective treatment.* New York: Pergamon.

Langs, R. (1985). *Madness and cure.* Emerson, NJ: Newconcept Press.

Lieberman, M. A., Yalom, I. D., & Miles, M. B. (1973). *Encounter groups: First facts.* New York: Basic Books.

Los Angeles Times. July 16, 1981.

Marantz, P. J. (1986). Personal communication.

Marmor, J. (1976). Some psychodynamic aspects of the seduction of patients in psychotherapy. *American Journal of Psychoanalysis,* 319–323.

Moore, R. A. (1985). Ethics in the practice of psychiatry: Update on the results of enforcement of the code. *American Journal of Psychiatry, 142,* 1043–1046.

Pope, K. S., Levenson, H., & Schover, L. R. (1979). Sexual intimacy in psychology training: Results and implications of a national survey. *American Psychologist, 34,* 682–689.

Psychiatric News. September 19, 1986, p. 14.

Redlich, F., & Mollica, R. F. (1976). Overview: Ethical issues in contemporary psychiatry. *American Journal of Psychiatry, 133,* 125–136.

Riskin, L. L. (1979). Sexual relations between psychotherapists and their patients: Toward research or restraint. *California Law Review, 67,* 1000–1027.

Robitscher, J. (1980). *The powers of psychiatry.* Boston: Houghton-Mifflin.

Schmideberg, M. (1963). Letter to the editor. *American Journal of Psychiatry,* 899.

Schutz, W. (1975). Not encounter and certainly not facts. *Journal of Humanistic Psychology, 15*(2), 7–18.

Stone, A. A. (1971). Suicide precipitated by psychotherapy: A clinical contribution. *American Journal of Psychotherapy, 25*(18), 26.

Stone, A. A. (1984). *Law, psychiatry and morality.* Washington, DC: American Psychiatric Association Press.

Strupp, H. H., Hadley, S. W., & Gomes-Schwartz, B. (1977). *Psychotherapy for better or worse.* New York: Aronson.

Webb, W. L., Jr. (1986, September 19). How to report offenders. *Psychiatric News,* p. 14.

Wheelis, A. (1973). *How People Change.* New York: Harper & Row.

Yalom, I. D., & Lieberman, M. A. (1971). A study of encounter group casualties. *Archives of General Psychiatry, 25,* 16–30.

Chapter 3

Antze, P. (1976). The role of ideologies in peer psychotherapy organizations: Some theoretical considerations and three case studies. *Journal of Applied Behavioral Science, 12,* 323–346.

Bakan, D. (1966). *The duality of human existence.* Chicago: Rand McNally.

Bandura, A. (1969). *Principles of behavior modification.* New York: Holt, Rinehart and Winston.

Barton, A. (1974). *Three worlds of therapy.* Palo Alto, CA: Mayfield.

Bellah, R. N., Madsen, R., Sullivan, W. M., Swidler, A., & Tipton, S. (1985). *Habits of the heart.* Berkley, CA: University of California Press.

Bergin, A. E. (1980). Psychotherapy and religious values. *Journal of Consulting and Clinical Psychology, 48,* 95–105.

Bergin, A. E. (1985). Proposed values for guiding and evaluating psychotherapy. *Journal of Counseling and Values, 29*(2), 99–116.

Bergin, A. E., & Garfield, S. (Eds.). (1973). *Handbook of psychotherapy and behavior change* (rev. ed.). New York: Wiley.

Callahan, D. (1973). *The tyranny of survival and other pathologies of civilized life.* New York: Macmillan.

Campbell, D. T., & Specht, J. C. (1985). Altruism: Biology, culture, and religion. *Journal of Social and Clinical Psychology, 3,* 33–42.

Drane, J. F. (1982). Ethics and psychotherapy: A philosophical perspective. In M. Rosenbaum (Ed.), *Ethics and values in psychotherapy* (pp. 15–50). New York: Free Press.

Englehardt, T. H. (1973). Psychotherapy as meta-ethics. *Psychiatry, 36,* 440–445.

Erikson, E. H. (1964). *Insight and responsibility: Lectures on the ethical implication of psychoanalytic insight.* New York: Norton.

Erikson, E. H. (1976). Psychoanalysis and ethics—avowed and unavowed. *International Review of Psychoanalysis, 3,* 409–415.

Freud, S. (1949). Future of an illusion. New York: Liveright.

Hurvitz, P. (1974). Peer self help groups: Psychotherapy without psychotherapists. In P. Roman, & H. Trice (Eds.), *The sociology of psychotherapy* (pp. 9–138). New York: Aronson.

Lasch, C. (1979). *The culture of narcissism.* New York: Norton.

Lazare, A. (1973). Hidden conceptual models in clinical psychiatry. *New England Journal of Medicine, 288,* 345–351.

Lazarus, A. A. (1981). *The practice of multimodal therapy.* New York: McGraw-Hill.

Levine, M. (1972). *Psychiatry and ethics.* New York: Braziller.

London, P. (1964). *The modes and morals of psychotherapy.* New York: Holt, Rinehart and Winston.

London, P. (1986). *The modes and morals of psychotherapy* (2nd ed.). Washington, DC: Hemisphere.

Low, A. A. (1950). *Mental health through will-training.* Boston: Christopher Publishing House.

MacIntyre, A. (1981). *After virtue.* Notre Dame, IN: Notre Dame Press.

Mechanic, D. (1981). The social dimension. In S. Block & P. Chodoff (Eds.), *Psychiatric ethics* (pp. 46–60). New York: Oxford University Press.

Meichenbaum, D. (1977). Cognitive-behavior modification: An integrative approach. New York: Plenum Press.

Menninger, K. (1958). *Theory of psychoanalytic techniques.* New York: Basic Books.

Menninger, K. (1978). *Whatever became of sin?* New York: Bantam Books.

Mowrer, O. H. (1980). Integrity groups. In R. Herink (Ed.), *The psychotherapy handbook.* New York: New American Library.

Mowrer, O. H., Vattano, A. J., Baxley, G., & Mowrer, M. (1975). *Integrity groups: The loss and recovery of community.* Urbana, IL: Integrity Groups.

Murray, E. J. (1956). A content-analysis method for studying psychotherapy. *Psychological Monographs, 70.*

Musto, D. (1982). A historical perspective. In S. Bloch & P. Chodoff (Eds.), *Psychiatric ethics* (pp. 13–30). New York: Oxford University Press.

Parloff, M. B., Goldstein, N., & Iflund, B. (1960). Communication of values and therapeutic change. *Archives of General Psychiatry, 2,* 300–304.

Parloff, M. B., Iflund, B., & Goldstein, N. (1957, May). Communication of "therapy values" between therapist and schizophrenic patients. Paper presented at the meeting of the *American Psychiatric Association,* Chicago, IL.

Rieff, P. (1966). *The triumph of the therapeutic: Uses of faith after Freud.* New York: Harper & Row.

Rieff, P. (1978). *Sigmund Freud: The mind of the moralist* (3rd ed.). Chicago: University of Chicago Press.

Robitscher, J. (1980). *The powers of psychiatry.* Boston: Houghton-Mifflin.

Rogers, C. (1951). *Client-centered therapy.* Boston: Houghton-Mifflin.

Rogers, C. R., and Skinner, B. F. (1956). Some issues concerning the control of human behavior: A symposium. *Science, 124,* 1057–1066.

Rosenthal, P. (1984). *Words and values*. New York: Oxford University Press.

Rychlak, J. F. (1973). *Introduction to personality and psychotherapy*. Boston: Houghton-Mifflin.

Seligman, E. R. (Ed.). (1967). *Encyclopedia of social science*. New York: Macmillan.

Shostrom, E. (Producer). *Three approaches to psychotherapy, I*. [Film]. Psychological and Educational Films. 3334 E. Coast Hwy., Corona Del Mar, CA.

Skinner, B. F. (1953). *Science and human behavior*. New York: Macmillan.

Skinner, B. F. (1958). Reinforcement today. *American Psychologist, 13*, 3.

Spiegler, M. D. (1983). *Contemporary behavioral therapy*. Palo Alto, CA: Mayfield.

Stolz, S. B. (1978). Ethical issues in behavior modification. *Report of the American Psychological Association Commission*. San Francisco: Jossey-Bass.

Stone, A. A. (1984). *Law, psychiatry and morality*. Washington, DC: American Psychiatric Association Press.

Szasz, T. S. (1963). *Law, liberty and psychiatry: An inquiry into the social uses of mental health practices*. New York: Macmillan.

Szasz, T. S. (1965). *The ethics of psychoanalysis*. New York: Basic Books.

Szasz, T. S. (1970). The manufacture of madness: A comparative study of the inquisition and the mental health movement. New York: Harper & Row.

Szasz, T. S. (1971). The ethics of suicide. *The Antioch Review, 31*, 7–17.

Szasz, T. S. (1974). *The myth of mental illness*. New York: Harper & Row.

Szasz, T. S. (1975). *Psychiatric justice*. New York: Macmillan.

Traux, C. B. (1966). Reinforcement and nonreinforcement in Rogerian psychotherapy. *Journal of Abnormal Psychology, 71*, 1–9.

Vitz, P. C. (1977). *Psychology as religion: The cult of self-worship*. Grand Rapids, MI: William Erdmans.

Vitz, P. C. (1985). The dilemma of narcissism. *Journal of Social and Clinical Psychology, 3*, 9–14.

Wachtel, P. L. (1977). *Psychoanalysis and behavior therapy: Toward an integration*. New York: Basic Books.

Wallach, M. A., & Wallach, L. (1983). *Psychology's sanction for selfishness*. San Francisco: W. H. Freeman.

Wolfe, B. E. (1977). Moral transformations in psychotherapy. In R. Stern, L. S. Horowitz, & J. Lynes. (Eds.), *Science and psychotherapy* (pp. 177–189). New York: Raven.

Wolpe, J. (1973). *The practice of behavior therapy* (2nd ed.). New York: Pergamon Press.

Yablonsky, L. (1965). *Synanon: The tunnel back*. New York: Macmillan.

Zilboorg, G., & Henry, G. W. (1941). *A history of medical psychology*. New York: Norton.

Chapter 4

Barton, A. (1974). *Three worlds of therapy*. Palo Alto, CA: Mayfield.

Bayles, M. D. (1981). *Professional ethics*. Belmont, CA: Wadsworth.

Bloch, S., & Chodoff, P. (1981). *Psychiatric ethics*. New York: Oxford University Press.

Carotenuto, A. (1985). *The vertical labyrinth*. Toronto, CA: Inner City Books.

Chesler, P. (1972). *Women and madness*. Garden City, NY: Doubleday.

Davanloo, H. (1980). *Short-term dynamic psychotherapy*. New York: Jason-Aronson.

Edelstein, L. (1967). The hippocratic oath, text translation and interpretation. In O. Temkin, & C. L. Temkin (Eds.), *Ancient medicine*. Baltimore: The Johns Hopkins Press.

Edwards, R. B. (1982). *Psychiatry and ethics*. Buffalo, NY: Prometheus Books.

Englehardt, T. H. (1973). Psychotherapy as meta-ethics. *Psychiatry, 36*, 440–445.

Frank, J. D. (1974). *Persuasion and healing* (rev. ed.). New York: Schocken Books.

Furrow, B. (1980). *Malpractice in psychotherapy*. Lexington, MA: Lexington Books.

Gartrell, N., Herman, J., Olarte, S., Feldstein, M., & Localio, R. (1986). Psychiatrist-patient sexual contact. *American Journal of Psychiatry, 143*(9), 1126–1131.

Gillis, J. S. (1974). Social influence therapy: The therapist as manipulator. *Psychology Today, 8*(December), 90–95.

Grayson, H. (1982). Ethical issues in the training of psychotherapists. In M. Rosenbaum (Ed.), *Ethics and values in psychotherapy* (pp. 51–66). New York: Free Press.

Hobson, R. F. (1985). *Forms of feeling.* London: Tavistock.

Holyroyd, J. C., & Brodsky, A. M. (1977). Attitudes and practices regarding erotic and nonerotic contacts with patients. *American Psychologist, 32,* 843–849.

Horowitz, M., Marmor, C., Krupnick, J., Wilner, N., Kaltreider, N., & Wallerstein, R. (1984). *Personality styles and brief psychotherapy.* New York: Basic Books.

Kardener, S., Fuller, M., and Mensh, I. (1973). A survey of physicians attitudes and practices regarding erotic and nonerotic contact with patients. *American Journal of Psychiatry, 130,* 1077–1081.

Keith-Spiegel, P., & Koocher, G. P. (1985). *Ethics in psychology: Professional standards and cases.* New York: Random House.

Lakin, M. (1985). *The helping group: Therapeutic principles and issues.* Reading, MA: Addison-Wesley.

Langs, R. (1985). *Madness and cure.* Emerson, NJ: Newconcept Press.

Levine, M. (1972). *Psychiatry and ethics.* New York: Braziller.

Levitt, E. E. (1977). Unpublished paper on sexual transgressions between physician and patient presented at AMA annual convention, San Francisco, June 21, 1977.

London, P. (1964). *The modes and morals of psychotherapy.* New York: Holt, Rinehart and Winston.

Marmor, J. (1976). Some psychodynamic aspects of the seduction of patients in psychotherapy. *American Journal of Psychoanalysis, 36,* 319–323.

Musto, D. (1981). A historical perspective. In S. Bloch and P. Chodaff (Eds.), *Psychiatric ethics* (pp. 13–30). New York: Oxford University Press.

Raths, L., Hamrin, M., & Simon, S. (1978). *Values and teaching* (2nd ed.). Columbus, OH: Merrill.

Robinson, D. N. (1973). Therapies: A clear and present danger. *American Psychologist, 28,* 129–133.

Robitscher, J. (1980). *The powers of psychiatry.* Boston: Houghton-Mifflin.

Rogers, C. R. (1951). *Client-centered therapy.* New York: Houghton-Mifflin.

Rosenbaum, M. (1982). *Ethics and values in psychotherapy.* New York: Free Press.

Sifneos, P. E. (1972). *Short-term psychotherapy and emotional crisis.* Cambridge, MA: Harvard University Press.

Spacks, P. A. (1985). *Gossip.* New York: Knopf.

Stone, A. A. (1984). *Law, psychiatry, and morality.* Washington, DC: American Psychiatric Association Press.

Strupp, H. H., & Binder, J. L. (1984). *Psychotherapy in a new key.* New York: Basic Books.

Szasz, T. S. (1961). *The myth of mental illness: Foundations of a theory of personal conduct.* New York: Hoeber-Harper.

Szasz, T. S. (1971). Involuntary commitment: A form of slavery. *The Humanist, 31,* 11–14.

Szasz, T. S. (1977). The concept of mental illness: Explanation or justification? In H. T. Englehardt, Jr., & S. F. Spicker (Eds.), *Mental health: Philosophical perspectives* (pp. 235–250). Dordrecht, Holland: D. Reidel.

Van Hoose, W. H., & Kottler, J. A. (1985). *Ethical and legal issues in counseling and psychotherapy* (2nd ed.). San Francisco: Jossey-Bass.

Weinberg, G. H. (1984). *The heart of psychotherapy.* New York: St. Martin's Press.

Wendorf, D. J., & Wendorf, R. J. (1985). A systematic view of family therapy ethics. *Family Process, 24,* 443–453.

Chapter 5

Asch, S. E. (1956). Studies of independence and conformity: A minority of one against a unanimous majority. *Psychological Monographs, 70*(416).

Cartwright, D. (1966). Achieving change in people. In W. G. Bennis, K. D. Benne, & R. Chin (Eds.), *The planning of change.* New York: Holt, Rinehart & Winston.

Cohen, A. M., & Smith, R. D. (1976). *The critical incident in growth groups.* La Jolla, CA: University Associates.

Corsini, R., & Rosenberg, G. (1955). Mechanisms of group psychotherapy. *Journal of Abnormal and Social Psychology, 51,* 406–411.

Erikson, E. H. (1976). Psychoanalysis and ethics: Avowed or unavowed. *International Review of Psychoanalysis, 3,* 409–415.

Glidewell, J. C. (1978). Ethical issues in and around encounter groups. In G. Bermant, H. C. Kelman, & D. P. Warwick (Eds.), *The ethics of social intervention* (pp. 69–102). New York: Wiley.

Guidelines for group leaders. (1980). Association of specialists in group work. New York: American Personnel and Guidance Association.

Gunther, B. (1968). *Sense relaxation: below your mind.* New York: Macmillan.

Hart, J., Corriere, R., & Binder, J. (1975). *Going sane.* New York: Dell.

Haskell, R. E. (1975). Presumptions of group work: A value analysis. *Small Group Behavior, 6,* 469–488.

Jourard, S. M. (1971). *The transparent self: Self-disclosure and well being.* Princeton, NJ: Van Nostrand.

Kaplan, H. I., & Sadock, B. J. (1972). *New models for group therapy.* New York: Dutton.

Kopp, S. B. (1977). *This side of tragedy.* Palo Alto, CA: Science and Behavior Books.

Levine, M. (1972). *Psychiatry and ethics.* New York: Braziller.

Levy, J. (1971). Group responses to simulated erotic experiences in a theatrical production. *International Journal of Group Psychotherapy, 21,* 3, 275–87.

Lieberman, M. A. (1976). Change induction in small groups. *Annual Review of Psychology, 27,* 217–250.

Lieberman, M. A., Yalmon, I., & Miles, M. B. (1973). *Encounter groups: First facts.* New York: Basic Books.

MacIntyre, A. (1981). *After virtue.* Notre Dame, IN: University of Notre Dame Press.

Parsons, T. (1951). *The social system.* Glencoe, IL: Free Press.

Sherif, C. W., Sherif, M., & Nebergall, R. E. (1965). *Attitude and attitude change: The social judgment-involvement approach.* Philadelphia: W. B. Saunders.

Spitzer, A. (1983). *Psychotherapy: A chronicle of psychotherpeutic abuse.* Clifton, NJ: Human Press.

Strupp, H. H., Hadley, S. W., & Gomes-Schwartz, B. (1977). *Psychotherapy for better or worse: The problem of negative effects.* New York: Jason Aronson.

Yalom, I. D. (1975). *The theory and practice of group psychotherapy.* New York: Basic Books.

Chapter 6

Barton, C., & Alexander, J. F. (1981). Functional family therapy. In A. S. Gurman, & D. P. Kniskern (Eds.), *Handbook of family therapy.* New York: Brunner/Mazel.

Beels, C. C., & Ferber, A. (1966). Family therapy. *Family Process, 8,* 280–318.

Berger, M. (1979). Men's new family roles—some implications for therapists. *The Family Coordinator, 28,* 638–646.

Bergin, A. E. (1985, April). Proposed values for guiding and evaluating counseling and psychotherapy. *Counseling and values, 29*(2), 99–116.

Bersoff, D., & Jain, M. (1980). A practical guide to privileged communication for psychologists. In G. Cooke (Ed.), *The role of the forensic psychologist.* Springfield, IL: Charles C. Thomas.

Bloch, D. A. (1983). Foreword to Papp, P. *The process of change.* New York: Guilford Press.

Bodin, A. M. (1981). The interactional view: Family therapy approaches of the Mental Research Institute. In A. S. Gurman, & D. P. Kniskern (Eds.), *Handbook of family therapy* (pp. 267–309). New York: Brunner/Mazel.

Boszormenyi-Nagy, I., & Framo, J. (1965) (Eds.). *Intensive family therapy.* New York: Hoeber.

Boszormenyi-Nagy, I., & Krasner, B. R. (1980). Trust-based therapy: A contextual approach. *American Journal of Psychiatry, 137,* 767–775.

Boszormenyi-Nagy, I., & Ulrich, D. N. (1981). Contextual family therapy. In A. S. Gurman, & D. P. Kniskern (Eds.), *Handbook of family therapy.* New York: Brunner/Mazel.

Briar, K. H. (1978). *The meaning of work and its implications for social work education.* Paper presented at the annual meeting of the Council on Social Work Education, New Orleans, LA.

Doherty, W. J. (1985, October). Values and ethics in family therapy [Special issue]. *Counseling and Values, 30*(1).

Dunbar, K. (1928). A revision of the fundamental law of habit formation. *Science, 67* (April 6, 1928), 360–362.

Dunbar, K. (1930). Repetition in the breaking of habits. *Scientific Monthly, 30,* 66–70.

Dunbar, K. (1946). *Personal adjustment.* New York: McGraw-Hill.

Everstine, L., Everstine, D. S., Heymann, G. M., True, R. H., Frey, D. H., Johnson, H. G., & Seiden, R. H. (1980, September). Privacy and confidentiality in psychotherapy. *American Psychologist, 35*(9), 828–840.

Fahs-Beck, D., & Jones, M. A. (1973). *Progress in family problems.* New York: Family Service Association of American.

Farrelly, F., & Brandsma, J. (1974). *Provocative therapy.* Fort Collins, CO: Shields Publishing.

Frankl, V. (1960). Paradoxical intervention: A logotherapeutic technique. *American Journal of Psychotherapy, 14,* 520–535.

Goldberg, C. (1977). *Therapeutic partnership: Ethical concerns in psychotherapy.* New York: Springer.

Gross, M., & Wilson, W. (1974). *Minimal brain dysfunction.* New York: Brunner/Mazel.

Grosser, G. H., & Paul, N. L. (1964). Ethical issues in family group therapy. *American Journal of Orthopsychiatry, 34,* 375–884.

Guerin, P. J., Jr. (1976). *Family therapy: Theory and practice.* New York: Gardner Press.

Gurman, A. S., & Klein, M. H. (1980). The treatment of women in marital and family conflict. In A. M. Brodsky, & R. T. Hare-Mustin (Eds.), *Research on psychotherapy with women* (pp. 159–188). New York: Guilford Press.

Gurman, A. S., & Klein, M. H. (1981). Women and behavioral marriage and family therapy: An unconscious male bias? In E. Blechman (Ed.), *Contemporary issues in behavior modification with women* (pp. 170–189). New York: Guilford Press.

Gurman, A. S., & Kniskern, D. P. (1978a). Research on marital and family therapy: Progress, perspective and prospect. In S. L. Garfield & A. E. Bergin (Eds.), *Handbook of psychotherapy and behavior change* (2nd ed.). New York: Wiley.

Gurman, A. S., & Kniskern, D. P. (1981). *Handbook of family therapy.* New York: Brunner/Mazel.

Gurman, A. S., & Kniskern, D. P. (1978b). Deterioration in marital and family therapy: Empirical, clinical and conceptual issues. *Family Process, 17,* 3–20.

Haley, J. (1963). *Strategies of psychotherapy.* New York: Grune and Stratton.

Haley, J. (1976). *Problem solving therapy.* San Francisco: Jossey-Bass.

Hare-Mustin, R. T. (1978). A feminist approach to family therapy. *Family Process, 17,* 181–194.

Hare-Mustin, R. T. (1980). Family therapy may be dangerous to your health. *Professional Psychology, 11,* 935–938.

Herrington, B. S. (1979). Privilege denied in joint therapy. *Psychiatric News, 14*(9), 1–9.

Hines, P. M., & Hare-Mustin, R. T. (1978). Ethical concerns in family therapy. *Professional Psychology, 9*, 165–171.

Hurwitz, N. (1967). Marital problems following psychotherapy with one spouse. *Journal of Consulting Psychology, 31*, 38–47.

Jacobson, N. (1983). Beyond empiricism: The politics of marital therapy. *American Journal of Family Therapy, 11*, 11–24.

Jacobson, N. S., & Margolin, G. (1979). *Marital therapy: Strategies based on social learning and behavior exchange principles.* New York: Brunner/Mazel.

Johnson, H. (1986, July-August). Emerging concerns in family therapy. *Social Work,* 299–306.

Kaplan, H. I., & Sadock, B. J. (1971). *Comprehensive group psychotherapy.* Baltimore, MD: Williams and Wilkins.

Kaslow, F. W., & Steinberg, J. L. (1982). Ethical divorce therapy and divorce proceedings: A psychological perspective. In L. L'Abate (Ed.), *Ethics, legalities, and the family therapist* (pp. 67–74). Rockville, MD: Aspen Systems.

Kluckhohn, I., and Spiegel, J. K. (1954). *Integration and conflict in family behavior.* Report No. 27 of the Group for the Advancement of Psychiatry, August.

Knapp, J. J. (1975). Some non-monagomous-marriage styles and related attitudes and practices of marriage counselors. *The Family Coordinator, 24*, 505–514.

Lansky, M. R. (1981). *Family therapy and major psychotherapy.* New York: Grune and Stratton.

Levine, M. (1972). *Psychiatry and ethics.* New York: Braziller.

Lewin, K. (1951). *Field theory in social science.* New York: Harper & Row.

Lewin, K. (1952). *Group decision and social change.* In G. E. Swanson, T. M. Newcomb, & E. E. Hartley (Eds.), New York: Holt.

Lieberman, M. A., Yalom, I. D., & Miles, M. B. (1973). *Encounter groups: First facts.* New York: Basic Books.

Lo Cicero, A. (1976). The right to know: Telling children the results of clinical evaluations. In R. Koocher (Ed.), *Children's rights and the mental health profession.* New York: Wiley.

Madanes, C. (1981). *Strategies of family therapy.* San Francisco: Jossey-Bass.

Maranhao, T. (1984). Family therapy and anthropology. *Culture, Medicine and Psychiatry, 8*, 225–279.

Margolin, G. (1982). Ethical and legal considerations in marital and family therapy. *American Psychologist, 37*, 788–801.

Minuchin, S. (1974). *Families and family therapy.* Cambridge, MA: Harvard University Press.

Napier, A., & Whitaker, C. (1972). A conversation about co-therapy. In *The book of family therapy* (pp. 480–506). New York: Science House.

Papp, P. (1980). The Greek chorus and other techniques of family therapy. *Family Process, 19*, 45–57.

Papp, P. (1983). *The process of change.* New York: Guilford Press.

Patterson, G. R., Reid, J. B., Jones, R. R., & Conger, R. E. (1975). *A social learning approach to family interventions.* Eugene, OR: Castalia.

Rosen, J. N. (1953). *Direct analysis: Selected papers.* New York: Grune & Stratton.

Rosenbaum, R. L. (1982). Paradox as epistemological jump. *Family Process, 21*, 85–90.

Ryder, R. G. (1985). Professionals' values in family assessment. *Counseling and Values, 30*(1), 24–34.

Selvini-Palozzali, M., Boscolo, L., Cechin, G., & Prater, G. (1978). *Paradox and counter paradox.* New York: Aronson.

Sider, R. C., Clements, C. (1982). Family or individual therapy: The ethics of modality choice. *American Journal of Psychiatry, 139*, 1455–1459.

Stanton, M. D. (1981). Strategic approaches to family therapy. In A. S. Gurman, & D. P. Kriskern (Eds.), *Handbook of family therapy.* New York: Brunner/Mazel.

Stein, H. F. (1985, October). Therapist and family values in a cultural context. *Counseling and Values, 1*, 35–46.

Stierlin, H. (1974). *Separating parents and adolescents: A perspective on running away, schizophrenia, and waywardness.* New York: Quadrangle/New York Times Books.

Stone, A. A. (1984). *Law, psychiatry and morality.* Washington, DC: American Psychiatric Press.

Strupp, H. H., Hadley, S. W., & Gomes-Schwartz, B. (1976). *Psychotherapy for better or worse.* New York: Aronson.

Stuart, R. B. (1980). *Helping couples change: A social learning approach to marital therapy.* New York: Guilford Press.

Triplett, N. (1897). The dynamogenic factors in pacemaking and competition. *American Journal of Psychology, 9,* 507–533.

Wallerstein, R. S. (1976). Symposium on ethics, values and psychological interventions. *International Review of Psychoanalysis, 3*(4), 369–372.

Walsh, F. (1983). Normal family ideologies in J. C. Hansen, & C. J. Falicov, (Eds.), *Cultural perspectives in family therapy.* Rockville, MD: Aspen.

Watzlawick, P., Beavin, J. H., & Jackson, D. D. (1967). *Pragmatics of human communication: A study of interactional patterns, pathologies, and paradoxes.* New York: Norton.

Watzlawick, P., Weakland, J., & Fisch, R. (1974). *Change: Principles of problem formation and problem resolution.* New York: Norton.

Weeks, G. R., & L'Abate, L. (1982). *Paradoxical psychotherapy: Theory and practice with individuals, couples and families.* New York: Brunner/Mazel.

Weiner, J. P., & Boss, P. (1985). Exploring gender bias against women: Ethics for marriage and family therapy. *Counseling and Values, 30*(1), 9–23.

Wells, R., & Dezen, A. (1978, September 17). The results of family therapy revisited: The non-behavioral methods. *Family Process, 17,* 251–274.

Wendorf, D. J., & Wendorf, R. J. (1985, December 24). A systematic view of family therapy ethics. *Family Process, 24*(4), 443–453.

Whan, M. (1983). Tricks of the trade: Questionable theory and practice in family therapy. *British Journal of Social Work, 13,* 321–337.

Whitaker, C. (1976). The hindrance of theory in clinical work. In P. J. Guerin (Ed.), *Family therapy: Theory and practice.* New York: Gardner Press.

Chapter 7

Back, K. W. (1974). Intervention techniques: Small groups. *Annual Review of Psychology, 25,* 367–388.

Bavelas, A. (1950). Communication patterns in task-oriented groups. *Journal of the Acoustical Society of America, 22,* 725–730.

Bermant, G., & Warwick, D. P. (1978). The ethics of social intervention: Power, freedom and accountability. In G. Bermant, H. Kelman, & D. P. Warwick (Eds.), *The ethics of social intervention* (pp. 377–418). New York: Wiley.

Blake, R., & Mouton, J. (1968). *Corporate excellence through grid organization development.* Houston: Gulf Publications.

Forbes, R. L., Jr. (1977). Organization development: Form or substance? *OD Practitioner, 9*(2), 12–13.

Frank, J. D. (1974). *Persuasion and healing* (rev. ed.). New York: Schocken Books.

Fullan, M., Miles, M. B., & Taylor, B. (1978). *OD in schools: The state of the art* (Final Rep). National Institute of Education, Ontario Institute for Studies in Education.

Gellerman, W., & Frankel, M. (1986). (Personal communication). Values and ethical issues in the organization and human system development profession.

Golembiewski, R. T., Carrigan, S. B., Munzenrider, R., & Blumberg, A. (1972). Toward building new work relationships: An action design for a critical intervention. *The Journal of Applied Behavioral Science, 8*(2), 135–148.

Greenbaum, C. W. (1979). The small group under the gun: Uses of small groups in battle conditions. In M. Lakin (Ed.), What happened to small group research? *Journal of Applied Behavioral Science, 15*(3), 392–409.

Kelman, H. C., & Warwick, D. P. (1978). The ethics of social intervention: Goals, means and consequences. In G. Bermant, H. C. Kelman, & D. P. Warwick (Eds.), *The ethics of social intervention* (pp. 3–33). New York: Wiley.

Kramer, H. (1972). A letter to the editor. *The Journal of Applied Behavioral Science, 8*(1), 63.

Lakin, M. (1985). *The helping group.* New York: Addison-Wesley.

Leavitt, H. J. (1951). Some effects of certain communication patterns on group performance. *Journal of Abnormal and Social Psychology, 46,* 38–50.

Levine, M. (1972). *Psychiatry and ethics.* New York: Braziller.

Levinson, H. (1980). Power, leadership and the management of stress. *Professional Psychology, 11*(3), 497–508.

Lewin, K. (1947). Frontiers in group dynamics I: Concept, method and theory in social science. *Social Equilibrium Human Relations, 1,* 5–40.

Lieberman, M. H., Yalom, I., & Miles, M. B. (1973). *Encounter groups: First facts.* New York: Basic Books.

London, P. (1964). *The modes and morals of psychotherapy.* New York: Holt, Rinehart and Winston.

Mayo, E. (1933). *The human problems of an industrial civilization.* New York: Macmillan.

Meltzer, H., & Stagner, R. (1980). Organizational development and change. *Professional Psychology, 11*(3), 495–496.

Miles, M. B. (1979). Ethical issues in OD interventions. *The OD Practitioner,* 1–10.

Mirvis, P. H., & Berg, D. N. (1977). *Failures in organization development and change.* New York: Wiley-Interscience.

Mirvis, P. H., & Seashore, S. E. (1982). Creating ethical relationships in organizational research. In J. E. Sieber (Ed.), *The ethics of social research.* New York: Springer.

Naylor, T., & Mulligan, T. (1986). *Corporate philosophy, culture and strategy.* Durham, NC: Duke University. Mimeo unpublished.

Petrella, T. (1977). Cold cash, cold logic and 'living in the hollows of our hands.' *OD Practitioner, 9*(4), 2.

Roethlisberger, F., & Dickson, W. (1939). *Management and the worker.* Cambridge: Harvard University Press.

Rosenthal, P. (1984). *Words and values.* New York: Oxford University Press.

Strupp, H. H., Hadley, S. W., & Gomes-Schwartz, B. (1977). *Psychotherapy for better or worse.* New York: Jason Aronson.

Szasz, T. (1960). The myth of mental illness. *American Psychologist, 15,* 113–118.

Tichy, N. (1974). An interview with Max Pages. *Journal of Applied Behavioral Science, 10*(1), 8–26.

Tichy, N., & Hornstein, H. (1976). Stand when your number is called: An empirical attempt to classify types of social change agents. *Human Relations, 29*(10), 945–967.

Walton, R. E. (1978). Ethical issues in the practice of organization development. In G. Bermant, H. C. Kelman, & D. P. Warwick (Eds.), *The ethics of social intervention* (pp. 121–145). New York: Wiley.

Walton, R. E., & Warwick, D. P. (1973). The ethics of organization development. *Journal of Applied Behavioral Science, 9*(6), 681–698.

Warwick, D. P. (1978). Moral dilemmas in organization development. In G. Bermant, H. C. Kelman, & D. P. Warwick (Eds.), *The ethics of social intervention* (pp. 147–159). New York: Wiley.

Weisbord, M. (1977). How do you know it works if you don't know what is? *OD Practitioner, 9*(3), 1–9.

Chapter 8

American Personnel and Guidance Association. (1981). *Ethical standards.* (Since July 1983 American Association for Counseling and Development.) Washington, DC.

American Psychiatric Association. (1973). Principles of medical ethics with annotations especially applicable to psychiatry. *American Journal of Psychiatry, 130,* 1058.

American Psychological Association. (1981). *Ethical principles of psychologists.* Washington, DC.

American Psychological Association Monitor. (1986, April). Vol. 17 (4), p. 1.

Anclote Manor Foundation v. Wilkinson. (1972). 263 SO. 2nd. 256 (Fla. Dis. Ct. Dpp).

Bergin, A. E., & Lambert, M. J. (1978). The evaluation of therapeutic outcome. In A. E. Bergin & S. L. Garfield (Eds.), *Handbook of psychotherapy and behavior change: An empirical analysis* (2nd ed.). New York: Wiley.

Bersoff, D. N. (1976). Therapists as protectors and policeman: New roles as a result of Tarasoff. *Professional Psychology, 6,* 267–273.

Bersoff, D., & Jain, M. (1980). A practical guide to privileged communication for psychologists. In G. Cooke (Ed.), *The role of the forsenic psychologists.* Springfield, IL: Charles C. Thomas.

Brodsky, A. (1986). *Psychiatric News,* Sept. 19, 14.

Brownfain, J. J. (1971). The APA Professional Liability Insurance Program. *American Psychologist, 26,* 648–652.

Cardozo, B. N. (1914). In *Schloendorfs v. Society of New York Hospital* 211, N.Y. 125,105 N.E. 92,93.

Cohen, R. J. (1979). Malpractice: A Guide for Mental Health Professionals. New York: Free Press.

Cohen, R. J., & Mariano, W. E. (1982). *Legal guidebook in mental health.* New York: Free Press.

Cohen, R. N. (1978). Tarasoff v. Regents of the University of California. The duty to warn. Common law and statutory problems for California psychotherapists. *California Western Law Review, 14,* 153–182.

Davidoff, D. J. (1973). *The malpractice of psychiatrists: malpractice in psychoanalysis, psychotherapy, and psychiatry.* Springfield, IL: Charles C. Thomas.

Edelwich, J., & Brodsky, A. (1982). *Sexual dilemmas for helping professionals.* New York: Brunner/Mazel.

Ellis, A. (1971). *Growth through reason: Verbatim cases in rational-emotive therapy.* New York: Science and Behavior Books, p. 228.

Everstine, L., Everstine, D. S., Heymann, G. M., True, R. H., Frey, D. H., Johnson, H. G., & Seiden, R. H. (1980, September). Privacy and confidentiality in psychotherapy. *American Psychologist, 35*(9), 828–840.

Farberow, N. L. (1974). *Suicide.* Morristown, NJ: General Learning Press.

Feldman, S. R., & Ward, T. W. (1979). Psychiatric injury: reshaping the implied contract as an alternative to malpractice. *North Carolina Law Review, 58,* 63–96.

Finkel, N. J. (1982). *Therapy and ethics: The courtship of law and psychology.* New York: Grune and Stratton.

Friedman, P. R. (1975). Legal regulations of applied behavior analysis in mental institutions and prisons. *Arizona Law Review, 17,* 39–104.

Furrow, B. R. (1980). *Malpractice in psychotherapy.* Toronto: D. C. Heath and Co.

Gartrell, N., Herman, J., Olarte, S., Feldstein, M., & Localio, R. (1986, September). Psychiatrist-patient sexual contact. *American Journal of Psychiatry, 143*(9), 1126–1131.

Gaylin, W., Glasser, I., Marcus, S., & Rothman, D. (1978). *Doing good: The limits of benevolence.* New York: Pantheon Books.

Goldberg, C. (1977). *Therapeutic partnership: Ethical concerns in psychotherapy.* New York: Springer.

Halleck, S. L. (1980). Law in the practice of psychiatry. *A handbook for clinicians.* New York: Plenum.

Hammer v. Rosen. (1960). New York, 2nd 376, 198 N. Y. S. 2nd 65.

Harris, M. (1973). Tort liability of the psychotherapist. *University of San Francisco Law Review,* *8,* 405–436.

Herrington, B. S. (1979). Privilege denied in joint therapy. *Psychiatric News, 14*(9), 1–9.

Hess v. Frank. (1975). 367 N. Y. S. (2nd) 30 Supreme Court of N. Y. Appellate Division.

Hines, P. M., & Hare-Mustin, R. T. (1978). Ethical concerns in family therapy. *Professional Psychology, 9,* 165–171.

Hogan, D. B. (1979). The regulation of psychotherapists. *A review of malpractice suits in the United States* (Vol 3). Cambridge: Bollinger.

Holyroyd, J. C., & Brodsky, A. M. (1977). Psychologists attitudes and practices regarding erotic and nonerotic physical contacts with patients. *American Psychologist, 32,* 843–849.

Horne v. Patton, 291 Ala. 701, 287 So 2nd 824 (1973).

Jagim, R. D., Wittman, W. D., & Noll, J. O. (1980). Mental health professionals' attitudes toward confidentiality, privilege, and third-party disclosure. *Professional Psychology, 9,* 458–466.

Kaplan, R. B. (1975). Psychotherapists, policemen, and the duty to warn—an unreasonable extension of the common law. *Golden Gate University Law Review, 6,* 229–648.

Keith-Spiegel, P., & Koocher, G. P. (1985). *Ethics in psychology.* New York: Random House.

Kermani, E. J. (1977). Psychotherapy: Legal aspects. *Psychiatry Digest, 38*(9), 33–39.

Kermani, E. J. (1982, April). Court rulings on psychotherapists. *American Journal of Psychotherapy, 36*(2), 248–255.

Knapp, S. (1980). A primer on malpractice for psychologists. *Professional Psychology, 11,* 606–612.

Knecht, v. Gillman. 488, F, 2nd 1136 (8th Cin, 1973).

Kozal, H., Boucher, R., & Garofolo, R. (1972). The diagnosis and treatment of dangerousness. *Crime and Delinquency, 18,* 371–392.

Lane, P. J., & Spruill, J. (1980). To tell or not to tell: The psychotherapist's dilemma. *Psychotherapy: Theory, Research and Practice, 17*(2), 202–209.

Lazare, A. (1973). Conceptual models in clinical psychiatry. *New England Journal of Medicine, 238,* 133–150.

Levine, M. (1972). *Ethics and psychiatry.* New York: Braziller.

Marmor, J. (1976a). Sexual acting out in psychotherapy. *American Journal of Psychoanalysis, 32,* 3–8.

Marmor, J. (1976b). Some psychodynamic aspects of the seduction of patients in psychotherapy. *The American Journal of Psychoanalysis, 36,* 319–323.

Minuchin, S. (1974). *Families and family therapy.* Cambridge, MA: Harvard University Press.

Moreno, J. L. (1962). Code of ethics for group psychotherapy and psychodrama. *Psychodrama and group psychotherapy.* Monograph #31. Beacon, NY: Beacon House.

Moreno, Z. T. (1978). Psychodrama. In H. Mullan & M. Rosenbaum, *Group psychotherapy: Theory and practice* (2nd ed.). New York: Free Press.

Osheroff v. Chestnut Lodge, Inc. (In press). Toward a New Standard of Care in Psychiatric Malpractice. *California Law Review.*

Pope, K. S., Simpson, N. H., & Weiner, M. F. (1978). Malpractice in outpatient psychotherapy. *American Journal of Psychotherapy, 32,* 593–602.

Robitscher, J. (1980). *The powers of psychiatry.* Boston: Houghton-Mifflin.

Roy v. Hartogs. (Sup. Ct. 1976). Mipc. 2nd 891, 381 N. Y. S. 2nd 587. Schutz, B. M. (1982).

Legal liability in psychotherapy. San Francisco: Jossey-Bass.

Shah, S. A. (1969). Privileged communications, confidentiality and privacy. *Professional Psychology, 1,* 56–59.

Silverstein, C. Homosexuality and the ethics of behavioral intervention. *Journal of Homosexuality, 2*(3), 213–219.

Slovenko, R. (1977). Group psychotherapy—privileged communication and confidentiality. *Journal of Psychiatry and Law, 5,* 405–466.

Stone, A. A. (1971). Suicide precipitated by psychotherapy: A clinical contribution. *American Journal of Psychotherapy, 18,* 18–26.

Stone, A. A. (1984). *Law, psychiatry and morality.* Washington, DC: American Psychiatric Association Press.

Szasz, T. S. (1963). Law, liberty, and psychiatry: An inquiry into the social uses of mental health practices. New York: Macmillan.

Tarasoff v. Regents of the University of California, 551 P 2nd 334 at 347 (Sup Ct. Cal. 1976).

Trilling, L. (1951). *The liberal imagination.* New York: Viking.

Walter, H. (1980). Malpractice liability in a patient's suicide. *American Journal of Psychotherapy, 34*(1), 89-98.

Zipkin v. Freeman, 436 S. W. 2nd 753 at 761 (Sup. Ct. Mo. 1969).

Chapter 9

Bermant, G., & Warwick, D. P. (1978). The ethics of social intervention, power, freedom, and accountability. In G. Bermant, H. Kelman, & D. P. Warwick, *The ethics of social intervention.* Washington, DC: Halsted Press.

Flanagan, S. G., & Liberman, R. P. (1982). Ethical issues in the practice of behavior therapy. In M. Rosenbaum (Ed.), *Ethics and values in psychotherapy* (pp. 207–236). New York: Free Press.

Gillis, J. S. (1974). Social influence therapy: The therapist as manipulator. *Psychology Today, 8,* 90–95.

Goldberg, C. (1977). *Therapeutic partnership: Ethical concerns in psychotherapy.* New York: Springer.

Grayson, H. (1982). Ethical issues in the training of psychotherapists. In M. Rosenbaum (Ed.), *Ethics and values in psychotherapy* (pp. 51–66). New York: Free Press.

Haley, J. (1977). Ethical issues in therapy. In J. Haley, *Problem-solving therapy.* San Francisco: Jossey-Bass.

Lane, J., & Cormick, G. (1978). *The ethics of intervention in community disputes.* In G. Bermant, H. Kelman, & D. P. Warwick, *The ethics of social intervention* (pp. 205–232). Washington, DC: Halsted Press.

Lebensohn, Z. M. (1977). Defensive psychiatry on how to treat the mentally ill without being a lawyer. In C. Goldberg (Ed.), *Therapeutic partnership: Ethical concerns in psychotherapy.* New York: Springer.

London, P. (1986). *The modes and morals of psychotherapy* (2nd ed.). Washington, DC: Hemisphere.

Michaels, R. (1981). Training in psychiatric ethics. In S. Bloch, & P. Chodoff (Eds.), *Psychiatric ethics* (pp. 295–305). New York: Oxford University Press.

Widiger, T. A., & Rorer, L. G. (1984). The responsible psychotherapist. *American Psychologist, 39*(5), 503–515.

Index